CAROLINE MATILDA,
QUEEN OF DENMARK

QUEEN CAROLINE MATILDA *(Cotes)*

HESTER W. CHAPMAN

Caroline Matilda

QUEEN OF DENMARK
1751–75

JONATHAN CAPE
THIRTY BEDFORD SQUARE LONDON

FIRST PUBLISHED 1971
© 1971 BY HESTER W. CHAPMAN

JONATHAN CAPE LTD,
30 BEDFORD SQUARE, LONDON WCI

ISBN 0 224 00504 9

PRINTED AND BOUND IN GREAT BRITAIN BY
RICHARD CLAY (THE CHAUCER PRESS) LTD, BUNGAY, SUFFOLK

Contents

PART III *CELLE*

List of Illustrations

Acknowledgments

The author's grateful thanks are due to Her Majesty Queen Elizabeth II for gracious permission to reproduce the portrait of Caroline Matilda as a child and that of Christian VII: to the Courtauld Institute for that of the Queen reproduced in the Frontispiece: to the National Portrait Gallery for those of Frederick Prince of Wales, of Augusta Princess-Dowager and of George III: to the Curator of the Museum of Fredericksberg for those of the Castle, of Caroline Matilda in uniform and of the Princess Louise: to the Curator of the Rosenborg Museum for the portraits of Frederick VI, Count Struensee in middle age and the print of Hirschholm: to the Tourist Bureau of Celle for the photographs of the Castle and of the Memorial to Caroline Matilda in the French Garden.

Especial thanks are given to Dr Iversen, Miss Rosamond Lehmann and Mr George Rylands for their invaluable criticisms and advice; and lastly to Dr Patrick Woodcock for expert suggestions in the matter of the lunacy of Christian VII.

TO SELINA HASTINGS

I had wealth and ease,
  Beauty, youth—
Since my lover gave me love,
  I gave these.

                Robert Browning

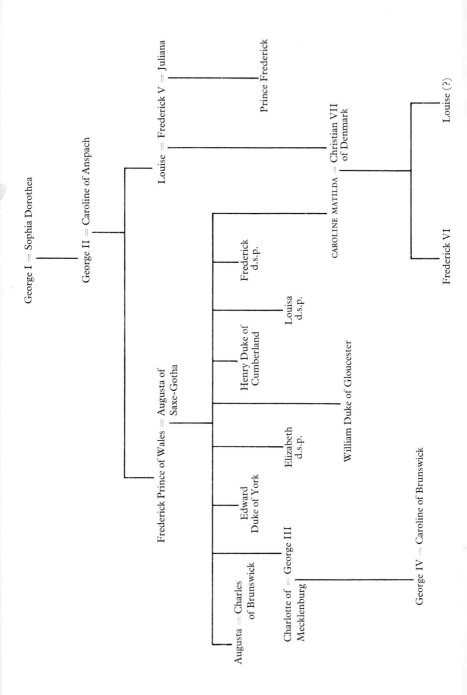

Foreword

In the French garden of the town of Celle, some twenty miles from Hanover, a marble monument dominates the scene. Undulating round its base, several figures, among which are those of Charity, Innocence and Grief, recall the exuberant symbolism of Roubillac and Nollekens—and thus rather obscure than set off the medallion of a young woman's head in profile. It is that of Caroline Matilda, wife of Christian VII, sister of George III and posthumous child of Frederick Louis, Prince of Wales.

The drama of which this princess was the heroine has inspired three plays, two novels, an opera and a film. It is now either briefly outlined or shunned altogether by historians, presumably because it had no connection with world affairs. For although Caroline Matilda's marriage, its failure and her disgrace became the talk of Europe, her career was politically isolated. The first stages of the Industrial Revolution, Clive's triumphs in India, the conquest of Canada, the Seven Years' War and the American War of Independence succeeded one another during her lifetime; yet none of these events even remotely affected her actions or her fate. Her story was then ignored by all but a few memoirists, perhaps because it appeared too incongruous to be acceptable. Indeed, that record of madness, treason and adultery is one more suited to the age of Webster and Tourneur than to that of powdered hair, hooped skirts and convoluted brocades. Now, such contrasts have a certain affiliation with anomalies we take for granted; and so this tragedy—violent and foreordained—seems to call for re-creation.

PART I
London

I

Antecedents

GEORGE I was fifty-four when he succeeded Queen Anne in 1714. Accompanied by his only son, the future George II, his daughter-in-law, Caroline of Anspach, and three grandchildren, he reached London on September 29th in a thick fog, thereafter settling down to rule a people he disliked, whose language he never attempted to learn. Indeed, why should he? He had been installed by the Whig party to represent the Protestant and anti-Jacobite cause, and was therefore received rather in a spirit of thankfulness than of enthusiasm by the majority of his subjects, with whom he never became popular. This did not concern him. Attended by German advisers, Turkish valets and two grotesque and elderly mistresses, he refused to be ruled by his Ministers, insisted on regular visits to Hanover and maintained a relentless hostility towards his heir and 'cette diablesse de Madame Caroline'. He disliked and mistrusted them both, perhaps because they were connected, in his mind, with the sinister and mysterious circumstances of his wife's adultery and his divorce from her in 1694.

George I never referred to that tragedy, about which there were many stories. His loveless marriage to his half-French, sixteen-year-old cousin, Sophia-Dorothea of Celle, had ended with the murder of her lover, Count Philip of Königsmarck, and her incarceration in the castle of Ahlden at the age of twenty-eight—where she remained until her death, thirty-three years later. He did not trouble to defend himself when it was said that he, his father the Elector Ernst-August and that prince's mistress had deliberately planned to get rid of Königsmarck, whose body was never found, and who had in fact been killed against their orders by one of the officers sent to arrest him.[1]

When it was rumoured that the Prince of Wales deeply resented his father's treatment of his mother, any question of their achieving a harmonious relationship was eliminated. The resultant enmity was carried on by the Prince for his heir, Frederick Louis, who was seven when his family were established in England, leaving him in Hanover in the care of a great-uncle and a group of courtiers and tutors.

The dislike, eventually amounting to hatred, of the Prince and Princess of Wales for their eldest son—they were devoted to their other children—began when Frederick Louis, a pretty and intelligent little boy, was four years old; it might well be described as pathological. Declaring war on him when he was in the nursery, they refused to let him join them, and made no attempt to keep in touch with his Governor. It was George I who sent over a tutor to teach him English, and received him during his first return to Hanover in 1716 (he made him Duke of Edinburgh, and also of Gloucester, a year later) although he found his behaviour most unsatisfactory. At the age of nine, Frederick Louis gambled, drank and swore, and had been hopelessly spoiled. Yet he was attractive and lively. Lady Mary Wortley Montagu, who saw him at this time, reported him as having 'all the accomplishments that it is possible to have at his age, with an air of sprightliness and understanding, and something so very engaging and easy in his behaviour that he needs not the advantage of his rank to appear charming'. After talking alone with the boy, she noted his 'quickness and politeness', and long remembered his neat figure and yellow hair.[2] In fact, Frederick Louis was already clever enough to see that he must please the English people. Only so would he be able to take his place at the Court of St James's; and for the next twelve years he prepared to achieve the position successfully.

That time of waiting resulted in a change for the better, for which Frederick's English tutors may have been responsible. The detrimental influences were removed, and he began to acquire an interest in the arts—in architecture, painting and music especially—which remained with him all his life. He became trilingual, speaking German to his servants and staff, and French to his intimates; his English, although accented, was fluent and grammatical. He wrote verse, not very successfully, in the last two languages, played several instruments and delighted in outdoor sports. He had an easy, natural way with him and got on well with nearly everyone; so his reputation made him an alarming figure from his parents' point of view.

Frederick's grandfather did not want him to come to England; he and his son and daughter-in-law were united only in that resolve and by their dislike of the kingdom in which they occupied opposite camps. The future George II, a stupid, hot-tempered man, adored and was ruled by his brilliant wife. As they grew to maturity, all their other children subscribed to their parents' opinion of Frederick, whom the younger ones had never seen.

When George I died in 1727, George II combined with Queen Caroline in resisting the new Prince of Wales's installation. A year went by before they were forced by their Ministers, of whom Sir Robert Walpole was to become the most influential, to let him leave Hanover. On December 7th, 1728, he arrived, having been separated from them for fourteen years.

They could not bring themselves to allow him a public welcome. He entered St James's Palace by a back way—and their worst fears were realized. The Prince, although not handsome, was elegant and graceful; his protuberant blue eyes and long nose resembled those of his father; his charm of manner recalled his mother's effect on her circle; and so his appeal to the public was—alas!—a certainty. As his parents' hostile attitude made him very uneasy and produced a nervous, almost sycophantic approach and a tendency to prevaricate, it was the work of a moment for George and Caroline to describe Frederick as a liar, a coward and a fool. So once more the royal entourage, and presently the kingdom, were divided. Those looking to the future—they did not anticipate that George II would reign for thirty-three years—gathered round Frederick Louis; the others, headed by his five sisters, Sir Robert Walpole, and that *mauvaise langue* of genius, Pope's 'Sporus', Lord Hervey, continued to malign the Prince, and to twist his too free chatter into treasonous utterances, while mocking his efforts to please the common people.

At twenty-one, Frederick was anxious to marry and settle down. The idea of Fretz, as they called him, with a family and a household of his own was quite odious, and the King would not consider it. He managed to put off his son's wedding for seven years, first by forbidding an alliance with the princess whom Frederick himself had chosen, and then by offering him the deformed and elderly daughter of the King of Denmark. In 1736 George II decided to settle for Princess Augusta of Saxe-Gotha, a tall, plain, intelligent girl of seventeen. She and Frederick were married forty-eight hours after their first meeting, and seemed to like one another well enough. During the next fifteen years they produced eight children—five boys, of whom the eldest was to become George III, and three girls.

Those years were more exasperating for the King and Queen than for the Prince of Wales. While they continued to abuse everything

English—cooking, manners, arts and sports—Frederick became an adept at cricket and tennis, patronized painters, poets and musicians and formed what evolved into an opposition centre. At his principal residences—Leicester House in the square of that name, Carlton House and the country palace of Kew—he entertained his protégés and the group described by Walpole as the Patriot Boys; so the English people, still disliking George II, naturally turned towards his heir, with the result that his parents' hatred and fear became a frenzied loathing, expressed with a violence that staggered even Hervey and Walpole. Their former, comparatively mild hostility ('Fretz is undutiful, childish and silly') rose to acclaim Hervey's comparison of him to Nero.[3] They encouraged the Princesses to snub Augusta, turned her and Frederick out of St James's, refused to speak to him at receptions, halved his allowance and, during the first months of his marriage, accused him of impotence; later, they described him as a crypto-Jacobite and a mental degenerate. His continued attempts at reconciliation were furiously rejected. When Walpole, alarmed by the resultant gossip, begged Their Majesties to relent, the Queen tried to do so, and failed. The Prince, his father announced, was a puppy, a mean-looking scoundrel, a poor-spirited beast, and the lowest stinking coward in the world. 'I wish he would drop down dead,' exclaimed his mother, 'I curse the hour of his birth!' Watching him walk across the courtyard of St James's Palace, she said to Hervey, 'There he goes—that wretch—that villain!—I wish the ground would open this moment, and sink the monster into the lowest hole in hell!'[4]

Frederick's rather superficial and insensitive temperament enabled him to ignore his parents' hatred, and to create a happy private life for himself, his wife and their children. An affectionate and careful father, he made his sons' training his especial concern. Augusta was strict; he was easy-going; both were conscientious, capable and comparatively enlightened. The King described the hobbies and interests they shared as fiddle-faddle nonsense.

The climax of George II's detestation was reached when the Prince, having helped to put out a fire, was greeted by the Londoners with shouts of 'Crown him! Crown him!' as he got into his coach. Then the King began to consider replacing him by his younger brother, William Duke of Cumberland, and thus inspired one of Lord Stanhope's most celebrated witticisms. 'It is true that he is Your Majesty's son,' he said, 'but the Son of God Himself was sacrificed for the good of mankind.' George II, an orthodox Christian, was shocked; but the idea—not of murder, but of some more seemly kind of disposal—remained in his mind.[5]

Lord Granville described the division between Frederick and his parents as part of the Hanoverian tradition, and prophesied its continuance into succeeding generations. Yet the maniacal enmity of George II and his wife for the Prince cannot reasonably be compared either to the attitude of George III towards the Regent or to that of Queen Victoria to the Prince of Wales. While taking the comparatively harmless forms of insult and deprivation, it rather resembled the murderous instincts of certain Russian Emperors. The King and Queen of England, while more civilized and less powerful than the Tsars, were equally passionate; they really desired Frederick's death and were enraged by his existence. Yet the object of all this hysteria was neither a strong character nor an ambitious one. The breach between him and his parents, sustained over a period of more than thirty years, affected his children in varying degrees, and especially the behaviour of the daughter he did not live to see. Meanwhile, the Queen's venom resembled that of a spiteful adolescent. She encouraged Princess Caroline to instruct Dunoyer, Frederick's dancing-master, to tell the Prince that he ought to be hanged. When Dunoyer did so, Frederick spat into the fire and remarked, 'Oh, you know Caroline's way—she is always like that.'[6] Princess Augusta shared her husband's detachment; her independence of mind was to have an undesirable effect on their youngest child.

In 1737 the Queen's last illness began. Frederick sent constantly to inquire, and begged her to receive him. Refusing, she replied that his concern was part of his usual hypocrisy, and George II exclaimed, 'I always hated the rascal, and now I hate him worse than ever. He wants to come and insult his poor dying mother—false, lying, cowardly, nauseous puppy!' When it was reported that the Prince had said, 'I am sure I am a good son—it cannot last long, I wish her out of her pain,' he was accused by his father of gloating over his mother's death, and, later, of having caused it. Presently, after agreeing to a formal reconciliation, the King, who had not spoken to Frederick for some four years, received him at a levee and managed to say, 'I hope the Princess is well?' after which their estrangement was resumed.[7]

By this time, the Prince and Princess had ceased to worry about the King's hostility, were leading contented and useful lives and had become very popular. They were seen at the opera, Ranelagh, the chocolate houses and in Bath, and were not much put out when

George II refused Frederick the regency during his next visit to Hanover. The Prince received another rebuff when he was denied a command during the Scotch rebellion of 1745, and accused of frivolity when he fell back on his favourite hobby, that of private theatricals, and appeared as Paris in a masque by Congreve. With the help of a professional actor, James Quin, he produced his children in Addison's *Cato*, for which he wrote a prologue; in the following year they put on Rowe's *Lady Jane Grey*. Then, assisted by Vertue, the Prince made a catalogue of his paintings and sculptures.[8]

In 1749 he was allowed to take the eleven-year-old Prince George to Hampton Court to receive the Garter. When the boy began his speech of thanks, George II cried out, 'No—no!' and struck him. The bewildered child burst into tears.[9]

So once more, Frederick and Augusta took refuge in amusements and visiting. His acquisition of a mistress did not trouble her; in fact, she had little or no cause for complaint, for she and her husband spent much time together, absorbed in the education of their children, in their collections, and the garden-planning in which they both delighted. The little Princess Louisa was delicate and slightly deformed; the two elder Princes were backward. These disappointments were philosophically accepted, as was the privately printed appearance of a squib in the form of a fairy-tale, entitled *Histoire du Prince Titi*. This reflected on the King's treatment of the Prince, and for a long time was thought to have been written by Frederick himself; the identity of the author was never revealed.[10]

In October 1750 Augusta conceived her ninth child, remaining, as always, in excellent health. In March of the following year Frederick caught a chill and became feverish. On the evening of the 20th he was sitting up in bed, attended by Dunoyer and Augusta. Suddenly, he called out, 'Je sens la mort!' and fell back, dead. All that night the Princess remained by his body. Next day, Prince George, on being told what had happened by his tutor, pressed his hands on his chest in silence. Then he gasped out, 'I feel—something—just *here*, just as I did when I saw those two workmen fall from the scaffold at Kew.'[11]

George II was at cards when the news was brought to him. 'Why, they told me he was better,' he said, and went on with the game. A few moments later he became very pale. Then he got up, whispered to his partner, '*Fretz ist tot*,' and left the room. Two days afterwards he visited Augusta, to whom he had sent a note of condolence.

The Princess knew that her husband had been driven into tacit rebellion—and into a good deal of silliness and extravagance—by his parents' behaviour. In deep grief, for they had loved one another, her concern now centred on George II's attitude towards his thirteen-year-old successor. At all costs the young Prince must not be looked on as a rival or an enemy by his grandfather. She therefore prepared to abase herself in order to achieve a better relationship with the irascible, unbalanced, lonely old man, whose Court, since the death of the Queen, had become dull, gloomy and soullessly formal. Realizing how highly he rated subservience and respect, she set out her apartments as for the reception of a mighty potentate; a canopied chair of state, draped in black, was placed against the wall. She and the two eldest boys, George and William, stood ready to receive him. The other children—Henry, Edward, Frederick, Augusta, Elizabeth and Louisa—remained in their rooms.[12]

The sight of those three mourning figures—and perhaps also of the tribute to his regality—touched the King. He raised Augusta from her knees, passed by the chair of state and leading her to a sofa, made her sit beside him. He could not pretend to personal grief (a few months later, he told a friend that he was glad of Frederick's death),[13] but he was sorry for his daughter-in-law and for her children. In that first, short talk he wept with the Princess and promised to be kind to her. Then he beckoned to the young Princes, and said, 'You must be brave boys, obedient to your mother, and deserve the fortunes to which you were born.'[14] A few days later, he made George Prince of Wales, and arranged that he should remain with his mother. (She had been afraid that he might be established in a separate household.) But he could not resist cutting down the ceremonies of Frederick's funeral—no member of the royal family attended it—and of his burial in Westminster Abbey, which took place on April 13th, in pouring rain.[15]

Frederick's family and friends continued to mourn him; but when it was known that his debts amounted to £160,000, public feeling rose against his memory. 'He has left a great many small children,' a workman engaged on repairs at Leicester House was heard to say. 'Ay, and what is worse, they belong to our parish,' his companion replied.[16] The famous Jacobite squib summed up the dislike of the English people for the dynasty. This was eventually overcome by the early popularity of George III.

> Here lies poor Fred,
> Who was alive and is dead;

Had it been his father,
I had much rather;
Had it been his brother,
Still better than another;
Had it been his sister,
No one would have missed her;
Had it been the whole generation,
Still better for the nation;
But since 'tis only Fred,
There's no more to be said.

After a short retirement, the Princess-Dowager resumed her duties. She maintained the routine her husband had worked out for his sons—they got up at seven, and were occupied with lessons and games till prayers and bedtime at half past nine—and assisted in the slightly less strenuous training of the Princesses. At six in the morning of July 11th, 1751, her pains began; two hours later, she gave birth to a daughter; five days after that, she was out and about as usual.[17]

It was then decided that the child should be christened Caroline, after her grandmother—that would please the King—and Matilda, which would connect her with the Angevin monarchy.

NOTES

1. H. W. Chapman, *Privileged Persons*, p. 162.
2. Lady Mary Wortley Montagu, *Letters*, p. 83.
3. Lord Hervey, *Memoirs*, p. 307.
4. Op. cit., pp. 671–7.
5. Op. cit., pp. 822 and 891.
6. Op. cit., p. 792.
7. Op. cit., pp. 849 and 891.
8. J. H. Jesse, *Memoirs of the Reign of George III*, vol. I, p. 15.
9. Horace Walpole, *Letters*, vol. II, p. 295.
10. J. H. Jesse, *Memoirs of the Court of England*, vol. III, p. 120.
11. Ibid.
12. P. Edwards, *Frederick Louis, Prince of Wales*, p. 105.
13. Jesse, *Memoirs of George III*, vol. III, p. 44.
14. Op. cit., p. 160.
15. Bubb Doddington, *Diary*, p. 105.
16. Walpole, op. cit., vol. III, p. 44.
17. Op. cit., p. 244.

II

Family Life

UNTIL CAROLINE MATILDA reached her fourteenth year, her life was so ideally arranged as to make it almost impossible for her to adapt her behaviour and way of thought to a less agreeable or more taxing existence. From the nursery to the presence-chamber—journeying, between outriders, from the capital to Kew—petted and indulged by five brothers and three sisters—she had no notion of what the ordinary world was like; nor could she have realized, until it was too late, that anyone about her—anyone who mattered—might be unjust, cruel or malicious.

The England of the 1750s and 1760s provided many delights for a Princess whose privileges were taken for granted, whose duties were non-existent and whose education was exactly suited to her temperament. Living in a pleasant microcosm, she never came in contact with the horrors of Hogarth's England—that of *Gin Lane*, *The Harlot's Progress* and *The Four Stages of Cruelty*: nor had she any knowledge of Dr Johnson's circle, nor any acquaintance with the thrilling narratives provided for her elders by Samuel Richardson. In the idyllic settings presented by Gainsborough, Reynolds and Van Loo—in the 'wild' gardens and 'natural' prospects evolved by fashionable landscapists—in rooms furnished by Chippendale and Ébénistes—feasting off Queen Anne silver and Chelsea porcelain—she was surrounded by beauty and elegance. As the youngest of a large family, she was spared the rigours of Court routine. And when she began to walk and speak, it became clear that she was the liveliest and most engaging of them all. She might well have become imperious and self-absorbed; but the Princess-Dowager's strict training, reinforced since widowhood, created in Caroline Matilda the instinct to please and to respect authority.

She had her favourites: the Prince of Wales and Princess Augusta. The sister fourteen years her senior provided a doting affection of which the Princess-Dowager was incapable; the younger children were nearly always ready to play with Matilda (she dropped the use of her first name before she reached her teens) and the entourage took up a sentimental attitude towards this posthumous child. They had no need to pity her, for she had most of the graces and many of the qualities of the heroine in a romance. Her red-faced, explosive grandfather, seldom seen, had no terrors for her; and she took naturally to the accomplishments—languages, music and dancing—required of an eighteenth-century *jeune fille à marier*. Most important—and, finally, most fatal—of all these advantages, she was free, within that enchanted circle of wealth and luxury; for her mother maintained the open-air, easy-going manner of life instituted by the late Prince. His friends called to sit and talk, and play cards, or to help the children with their gardens, or to applaud their acting and singing, as visitors to a private household. Indeed, Caroline Matilda's later behaviour shows that she looked on privacy and informality as her right. When she wanted something, she had only to ask for it; and her lot lay in so fair a ground that her demands were rarely, if ever, unreasonable. Hardship, anxiety and suffering were therefore unknown to this healthy, contented little girl. And she was intelligent and biddable enough to see that naughtiness was not worth her while.

Great events—she was six when Clive founded the Anglo-Indian Empire, and nine when Quebec fell—had no meaning for her, except as occasions for sitting up late, watching fireworks and being dressed in her newest finery. Foreign countries, great or small, were coloured patches on the globes in the schoolroom. The riots, the drunkenness, the filth and violence of the London mob were far-off shadows, glimpsed momentarily from a coach, between the Mall and Leicester Square. References to Court intrigue, palace revolutions and political crises were uncomprehended murmurs, forgotten as soon as heard.

Like her brothers and sisters, Caroline Matilda spoke French and English with equal facility, but did not read much in French. Her knowledge of English literature was more extensive, because she had to learn speeches, and sometimes whole scenes, from the plays of Shakespeare and Addison, and was often called upon to recite them. Later, she learnt Italian, but only had occasion to use that tongue in her singing lessons. The Princess-Dowager, who knew no English before her marriage, spoke it fluently, although with an accent. With the exception of Dunoyer and a few other attendants, the whole household was English, as were all Frederick's circle. Of these, two were especially intimate with his widow—Bubb Doddington, later

Lord Melcomb, and John Stuart, Marquess of Bute. Caroline Matilda became used to the presence of this oddly contrasting pair throughout her childhood.

Doddington, a grotesque eccentric, was enormously fat, and so short as to appear almost as broad as he was long. He dressed ostentatiously, and used much pomp and ceremony, but not during his visits to the Princess-Dowager. Although stiff and reserved, she disliked formality, and confided in Doddington, to whom she poured out her worries about the Prince of Wales. He was still very backward (he could not read till after his eleventh birthday) and was not, she believed, being properly taught; but as his tutors had been appointed by his grandfather, there was nothing to be done. On one point she was determined, and that was, to keep George from any frequentation of the nobility, whether Whig or Tory; his contemporaries in either party were dissipated, irreligious and mannerless.[1] She subscribed to Lord Chesterfield's view of their behaviour; in a famous passage from the *Letters*, his description of how *not* to conduct oneself shows that this careful mother may have been right to isolate her children from circles in which 'an awkward fellow' would let his sword get between his legs and trip him up as he entered a room. 'There,' the writer continues, 'he soon lets his hat fall down; and, taking it up again, throws down his cane; in recovering his cane, his hat falls down a second time ... If he drinks tea or coffee, he certainly scalds his mouth, and lets either the cup or the saucer fall, and spills the tea or the coffee in his breeches.' At dinner, this hypothetical oaf 'daubs himself with soup and grease ... coughs in his glass and besprinkles the company ... eats with his knife ... picks his teeth with his fork, and puts his spoon, which has been into his mouth twenty times, into the dishes again.' So it came about that the Prince of Wales's brothers and sisters were his only companions.[2]

In this arrangement his mother was supported by Bute, who became, it was rumoured, her lover, shortly after her husband's death, and whose constant attendance accustomed Caroline Matilda to the spectacle of an openly conducted intimacy. Bute was strikingly handsome, tall and graceful, with a classic profile and great charm of address. Having become acquainted with Frederick at a cricket match, he was now indispensable to the Princess-Dowager, calling on her every day. When he appeared, her stiffness vanished, and there was heard 'a mellowness in her German accent' as they talked, which was, Horace Walpole observed, 'often and long'. She was so moved by the

Marquess's looks, that her eyes sometimes filled with tears as she watched him. Meanwhile, the Prince of Wales also submitted to his spell, and the heir to the throne was said to be 'shut up' with his mother and her friend. This situation lasted until after Caroline Matilda's nursery days were over, and its effect on her later actions was extremely unfortunate. She was some six or seven years old, when Princess Augusta, who usually dined with her mother and Bute (the Princes dined with their tutors), reappeared for that meal in her sisters' apartments. The household was told that the Princess-Dowager had observed that her eldest daughter was putting on weight, and must eat more sparingly. Augusta, a bold, sharp-witted girl, knew very well that cheese-cakes upstairs were no more fattening than meat downstairs—and said so.[3]

The Princess-Dowager's strictness was therefore marked down as hypocritical, and she became very unpopular. This suited the King's jealous nature, but stirred up the Londoners, with the result that the elder Princes and Princesses became objects of ridicule. When George rode out in the Mall, he was hooted, and asked, 'Are you going to suck?' as he entered Carlton House.[4]

Caroline Matilda's prettiness, developing into beauty as she matured, ensured a very different reception. Her silvery-golden hair, large blue eyes and natural gaiety of manner set her apart from her sisters, who were plain. When Princess Elizabeth died in 1759, and Princess Louisa sank into invalidism, she gained importance in the household, but not beyond it. She did not fear her mother, who was dreaded by her sons. She would have been surprised if she had heard Prince William's reply to the Princess's sharp inquiry as to what he was thinking about, when she saw him looking melancholy. 'I am thinking', he said, 'that if ever I have a son, I will not make him as unhappy as you make me.'[5] Nor was Caroline Matilda afraid of her uncle, 'Butcher' Cumberland, who, drawing a sword to amuse one of his nephews, was horrified when the boy shrank away. She knew little or nothing of the Forty-five—of which the repercussions were to affect her whole life—for she was as ignorant of English history as of that of any other country.

In these early years, she and her youngest brother, Prince Frederick, were a precocious couple. At the age of nine—presumably in the absence of the Princess-Dowager—he was heard trying to explain to a lady what eunuchs were. 'I can't tell you the word,' he said, 'but I will show you how they make them'—and began to unbutton his breeches. He was walking in the Mall with the Prince of Wales when a famous woman of pleasure went by, whom he described as a Miss. 'Are not all girls misses?' said his brother. 'Oh, but a particular sort of miss—a Miss that sells oranges.' 'Is there any harm in selling oranges?' 'Oh, but they are not such oranges as you buy,' Frederick persisted, 'I believe they are a sort that my brother Edward buys.'[6]

At the age of twenty, Prince Edward had more freedom than George, who was romantic, serious and shy. With his grandfather, who received him ungraciously, the Prince of Wales appeared flustered and confused. 'He is fit for nothing but to read the Bible,' said the old King. Women alarmed him, as did the idea of a household of his own, which he had refused when he came of age. Tall, fair and handsome, he continued to model himself on Bute; his manners were now unexceptionable, and by the time he reached his twenty-third year, he was no longer awkward. A few months later—on October 26th, 1760 —George II was found dead in the privy at Kensington Palace, and in Carlton House it was felt that a golden age had begun.

Almost at once, and quite unexpectedly, the young King broke away from the influence of his mother and the Marquess. Unknown to them, he had fallen in love—desperately, and for the first time— with a highly unsuitable girl. Caroline Matilda was nine when this drama became common knowledge. She saw her favourite brother utterly subjugated and determined to marry after his own heart—just like the prince in a tale by Perrault or Madame d'Aulnoy.

NOTES

1. Doddington, *Diary*, pp. 178 and 244.
2. Chesterfield, *Letters*, p. 9.
3. Horace Walpole, *Memoirs and Portraits*, p. 545.
4. W. H. Wilkins, *A Queen of Tears*, vol. I, p. 23.
5. Walpole, *Letters*, vol. IV, p. 246.
6. Op. cit., p. 267.

III

Growing Up

LADY SARAH LENNOX, younger sister of the Duke of Richmond and great-granddaughter of Charles II and Louise de Kéroualle, was fifteen when George III succeeded. A high-spirited, alluring creature, with grey eyes and black hair, she had become a toast before the old King died, and may well have thought that she had only to stretch out her hand for whatever she wanted. When George III first saw her, she was in love with Lord Newbottle, who seemed to return her affection. He then decided that she was not a good enough match, and made this clear in a rather brutal fashion. Almost at the same moment, the young King announced that she was 'the fittest person to be a queen', and proceeded to court her.[1] Lady Sarah, unable to marry the man she loved, felt that she might as well become Queen of England, and encouraged the King's advances. Still he hung back, although he was passionately devoted to her; he knew that if he insisted on marrying a subject, as Edward IV and Henry VIII had done, he would have to face the furious disapproval of his mother.

In the Princess-Dowager's mind, Sarah Lennox's Stuart blood counted against her even more than her temperament, which was capricious and self-willed; there would be no ruling such a daughter-in-law; and, with Bute, she was planning a dynastic marriage for her son. While the King continued to pursue Lady Sarah, his mother told Bute to exercise his influence. He did so, and the result was a pathetic outburst from his pupil. Rather than sacrifice the Marquess's love and approval, he wrote, he would give up all thought of Lady Sarah 'though my heart should break'.[2] Yet still he could not keep his eyes off her when she appeared at Court; still he drew her aside for private talk. She then perceived that he either could not or would not marry her, and came to the conclusion that he wanted her to be his mistress.

George III's father, grandfather and great-grandfather had all publicly established their mistresses, and no great objection would have been made if he had followed their example. Such a relationship was never considered by him, then, or at any time during his long life. He submitted to Bute and the Princess-Dowager, and in the spring of 1761 negotiations began for an alliance with Princess Charlotte of Mecklenburg-Strelitz. She arrived in September, they were married on the 10th of that month and crowned a fortnight later.

The effect of the Lennox episode on Caroline Matilda was delayed. She remained a background figure, appearing at the coronation service in a white-and-silver gown with hanging sleeves, her hair drawn up to the top of her head, in the new fashion.[3] She took little or no part in the festivities in which the young Queen—'a sensible, cheerful, genteel' girl, with a pale face, wide mouth and flattened nose—appeared to please the public, her bridegroom and even the fastidious Walpole.[4] But the King's yielding to his Minister (Bute was now Groom of the Stole) seems to have created in Caroline Matilda the spirit of revolt. As she grew up, she began to dislike the Marquess—partly because Augusta had always done so—and to resent his domination of her mother and brother.

She was too young to stay up for the banquet which inaugurated the wedding night. Nervously, the new Queen sat on with her ladies till the small hours; then, attended by the Princess-Dowager and two German maids, she withdrew. Rejoining the family group, the latter asked Prince William to stay a little. 'What should I stay for?' he replied. 'If she cries out, I cannot help her'—and the party dispersed.[5]

Next day, the young couple received the homage of the Court. The disrespect, bordering on contempt, of the nobility for the royal house began to give way to praises of the King, who, announcing that he gloried in the name of Briton, was described by Walpole as graceful and amiable.[6] The Princess-Dowager, sure of Bute's hold over his master, withdrew into greater privacy. Her younger children were nearly always at Kew, absorbed in games, lessons, gardening and private theatricals. In this enclosed world Caroline Matilda became more than ever dependent on Augusta, and the people saw almost nothing of her. No comments were made on her upbringing—which was not suited to a girl destined for a public position—or on her development. In the fairy-tales, the youngest Princess is always the most beautiful and the least noticed. So it was with Caroline Matilda. And Kew Palace, with its exquisite gardens and romantic isolation, provided a perfect setting for this cloistered yet luxurious existence.

In May 1762 Bute became Prime Minister and received the Garter.

C

This drew attention to his relationship with the Princess-Dowager, and enraged the London mob, who shouted 'No Scotch favourite!' whenever they saw her drive out; and his enemies remembered Frederick saying that Bute was the kind of envoy best suited to a small German court, 'where there is nothing to do'. George III's brothers and sisters all took against the Marquess—and that Caroline Matilda shared their feelings is proved by her comments in later years. Bute was considered haughty, affected and obsessed by his own appearance. The Princess-Dowager ignored the abuse she received on his account. 'Poor, deluded people,' she remarked, 'I hope they will know better by and by.'[7] The effect of this indifference on Caroline Matilda could hardly have been worse. The fact that she herself pleased the crowds gave her the impression that this would always be so, no matter how she behaved.

Queen Charlotte resented her mother-in-law's supremacy, until her own power was established by the birth of a Prince of Wales, later George IV, in the summer of 1762. 'The prospect of your old neighbour at Rome [the Young Pretender]', Walpole wrote to Horace Mann, then minister in Florence, 'does not improve. The House of Hanover will have numbers in its own family sufficient to defend their crown.'[8]

This view was not shared by George III and his advisers. Memories of the Forty-five were still alarmingly vivid; and they set about arranging a marriage for Princess Augusta which would strengthen the Protestant cause. Prince Charles of Brunswick-Wolfenbüttel was selected, and the contract drawn up in January 1764.

On arrival, this 'slim, martial, agreeably weather-worn' young man was received by the King and Queen before he waited on the Princess-Dowager. He had not been sent a portrait of his bride; but they seemed pleased with one another, and both declared that they would not otherwise have consented to the union.[9] They were married privately at Leicester House, and spent the night there, leaving for Germany three days later. Caroline Matilda stood at her mother's right hand during the ceremony, thus taking precedence over Princess Louisa.[10] This indicated a rise in her status which she may not have understood. She and Augusta parted in tears. She was then informed that her own marriage was next on the list, and that she must prepare herself to leave England within two years.

At the age of thirteen, two years seems a long way off; and she was not told what plans were being made for her. Yet a shadow had fallen

over her life, which went on as before, except that more attention was
paid to deportment and fashion. In this respect she was fortunate; for
the new dresses were well suited to an unformed figure, and the
toppling coiffures being produced in Paris had not yet crossed the
Channel. The wide, flattened hoops of the 'fifties had diminished, and
the billowing oblong of the skirt was emphasized by a narrow, V-
shaped waist-line. Iron corsets had been replaced by structures of
whalebone or cane, and the low-cut bodices had frilled sleeves to the
elbows. Hair was drawn away from the face, simply dressed and
powdered only on state occasions. Pale colours—lavender, eau-de-nil,
pearl grey and robin's-egg blue—prevailed. The general effect was one
of evanescent fragility, and might have been especially designed to
show off Caroline Matilda's beauty. The enamelled, staring cosmetics
used by older women were not enforced in her case; her clear colouring
and platinum-blonde hair were enhanced by silk flowers and strings of
pearls.

She did not know that she had replaced her sister Louisa, whose
hand Frederick V of Denmark had desired for his son, the future
Christian VII. His envoy, Count Bothmar, noting Louisa's frailty,
came to the conclusion that she was unlikely to produce healthy
children; he therefore suggested to Mr Titley, his opposite number in
Copenhagen, that Caroline Matilda should be considered. George III
did not at first take to the idea; Matilda could not be married till after
her fifteenth birthday, and even then, surely she would be too young
to be sent into a strange country. Bothmar, entranced by her health
and beauty, insisted, and his King was persuaded to wait; meanwhile,
these plans were kept secret from the Catholic and pro-Jacobite Powers.
George III did not want to part with his little sister; but the alliance
was too valuable to be refused (he himself was now involved in a
political crisis) and the Princess-Dowager considered that her youngest
daughter was perfectly fitted to be a queen. So the question of Caroline
Matilda's dowry was raised, and an Anglo-Danish treaty set in hand.

Some perfunctory inquiries were then made about the prospective
bridegroom. To these, Titley replied, 'The amiable character of the
Prince of Denmark is universally acknowledged here, so that, the
union appearing perfectly suitable and equally desirable on both sides,
I hope soon to have an opportunity of congratulating you ... upon its
being unalterably settled and fixed.'[11]

It is just possible that the English envoy, who had been established
in Copenhagen since 1728, did not know that Prince Christian, then

aged sixteen, was a drunkard, and that he had shown signs of mental derangement; but as King Frederick had always treated Titley, who was constantly at Court, as a friend, this seems unlikely.

NOTES

1. E. R. Curtis, *Lady Sarah Lennox*, p. 39.
2. *Letters of George III*, pp. 38–9.
3. Wilkins, *A Queen of Tears*, vol. I, p. 39.
4. Walpole, *Letters*, vol. V, p. 103.
5. Op. cit., p. 108.
6. Op. cit., vol. IV, p. 455.
7. Jesse, *Memoirs of the Court of England*, vol. III, p. 163.
8. Walpole, op. cit., vol. IV, p. 232.
9. Op. cit., vol. V, p. 434.
10. Wilkins, op. cit., vol. I, p. 44.
11. Op. cit., vol. I, p. 47.

IV

The Last of England

DURING THE seventeenth and eighteenth centuries certain writers added to their earnings by the production of biographies and letters of well-known persons which were almost entirely fictitious. The *doyenne* of this group was Madame d'Aulnoy—now remembered chiefly for her fairy-stories—whose *Mémoires de la Cour d'Angleterre* have little or no basis in fact; she invented the conversations and adventures of celebrities she herself had known, thus creating an imaginary world peopled by the circle of Charles II, which is still sometimes accepted as genuine. Similarly, the liaison between Caroline Matilda's great-grandmother, Princess Sophia-Dorothea of Celle, and Count Philip of Königsmarck was described, with suitable additions, in a contemporary novel entitled *The Roman Octavia*, which was thereafter used as factual by several historians. In the same manner, a life of Caroline Matilda, called *Memoirs of an Unfortunate Queen, interspersed with Letters written by Herself to Several of her Illustrious Relatives and Friends*, and published in 1776, was the work of an anonymous hack writer.

That most, if not all, of the letters in this production were faked, is proved by the fact that George III destroyed his sister's correspondence shortly after her death, as did her other relatives. But no censorship, of this or any other kind, could then diminish the appeal of Caroline Matilda's notoriety. The invented letters were still accepted as genuine; and because a few which she really had written survived and were interpolated, it became difficult to separate the true from the false.

When, at the age of thirteen, Caroline Matilda commiserates with Princess Augusta for being 'obliged to live in exile for the sake of a husband', and declares that 'what may be expected in a Court is only to diversify *ennui*', suspicions arise; but when she goes on, 'Pray let me know how you like your ridottos and operas,' they sink, if only because such an inquiry, while of no great interest, is to be expected. Again, it seems unlikely, to say the least, that Caroline Matilda ever wrote to an unknown girl friend, 'I ... have become quite proficient in my knowledge of exotics,' or that she misses her companion's 'approbation of my horticultural embellishments'.

Caroline Matilda and her sisters had no companions but each other and their ladies; their mother saw to that; therefore, when she informs another anonymous friend that, in the case of royal marriages, 'failure of love will summon pride against a divorce', mistrust becomes disbelief. Apart from the fact that all her letters were supervised, when not actually dictated, she could never have thought on these lines. Her isolation, even from her older relatives, is shown by her having been forbidden by her mother to accompany her unmarried aunt, the Princess Amelia, to Bath. So it came about that she never left London, except for visits to Windsor and Kew, until she began her journey to Denmark. She saw nothing of rural or provincial England; she knew no one outside the family circle until she sat for her wedding portrait to Sir Joshua Reynolds. She now faced parting from everyone she knew and loved within a comparatively short time. Terror and despair brought on floods of tears. The great artist did his best: but the task was beyond him. He produced a portrait of someone who might be twenty-five or thirty years old.[1]

When the Princess Amelia tried to console her niece for the disappointment about Bath by observing that she would soon be making longer and more interesting journeys, the tears began again. 'I know what you mean,' said Matilda, 'but surely it would be happier for me to stay where I am than to go so far for a Prince I have never seen.'[2] She did not want to be a queen; her ladies saw her become sadder every day. She was now learning German—her only preparation for her new life; there was no question of her having lessons in Danish.

On January 10th, 1765, the announcement of the betrothal was made in both countries, and the plenipotentiaries began to discuss terms. Frederick V told Titley that he was delighted with the Princess's portrait, which now hung in his son's dressing-room; there, according to the envoy, the Prince 'surveyed it over and over again, with great attention and inexpressible pleasure'.[3] George III then formally required Parliament's approval of the union, 'as soon as the respective ages of the Prince Royal of Denmark and Princess Caroline Matilda will permit', and was told that this further strengthening of the anti-French and Protestant cause was 'most pleasing' to the nation. Five days later, he gave a ball at St James's, opened by Matilda and Prince Edward, who danced a minuet together. It was observed that the Princess's figure had developed; the only criticism made was that her under-lip protruded a little; in all else, her appearance had become that of a fashionable beauty—large eyes, a round plump face, a chin which would now be thought receding, and outlines of voluptuous exuberance. The impression given is that she looked sulky but appealing.

During the next six months she continued to receive congratulations with forced smiles; she took no interest in her trousseau, and was constantly in tears. The Princess-Dowager then lectured her on the duties of royal personages, recalling her own wedding to a bridegroom she had met for the first time barely forty-eight hours before the ceremony. Caroline Matilda, who celebrated her fifteenth birthday in July of this year, began to cheer up a little, returning to Kew, where she spent more time than usual in gardening. She took up local charities, visited her mother's tenants and seemed comparatively resigned.

On January 13th, 1766, Frederick V died, and Christian, now in his seventeenth year, became King of Denmark. A dowry of a hundred thousand pounds was settled on Caroline Matilda, her proxy wedding put forward to October 1st, and her departure fixed for the following day. The King arranged for the ceremony to take place in Carlton House at seven o'clock in the evening, and appointed Prince Edward to represent the bridegroom. 'It is not to be doubted', declared the *Annual Register*, 'that the amiable Princess whom His Danish Majesty is about to espouse will contribute greatly to ... those good dispositions ... which exist between our Court and nation and those of Denmark.' Titley described the new King as 'regular and sober ... compassionate and good ... well seasoned with the principles of virtue and religion. He is impatient for ... his marriage.'[4]

Caroline Matilda's behaviour now began to show the hopeless ineptitude of her upbringing. Having had but slight experience of grief and frustration, she was unable to conceal her misery; nor could she attempt to conduct herself as became her station. At fifteen, these efforts were beyond her. Although she did not plead with her brother for the remission or postponement of her sentence, she wept—both publicly and privately. No doubt there were many who pitied her; but it occurred to no one that her attitude might militate against the success of the marriage. George III and his advisers probably assumed that, after a period of homesickness she would settle down to becoming a contented wife and mother, as her own mother had. Meanwhile, she was warned that the Queen-Consorts of Denmark were not allowed to establish a single attendant from abroad in their entourage. When she reached the frontier she would have to part with all her ladies, and thenceforth be surrounded by strangers, with whom she might have little or nothing—perhaps not even language—in common. To become the bride of a Dutch or German prince would have been less alarming; for Danish customs bore no resemblance to those of other Protestant kingdoms; and she had never been taught how to adapt herself to any existence but the one she had always known, that of a private gentlewoman in a family setting.

Parting from the eighteen-year-old Princess Louisa was Caroline Matilda's greatest grief; she may have guessed that they were unlikely to see one another again, for Louisa, who died two years later, was gradually succumbing to a tuberculous infection. The sisters had become much closer since Augusta's marriage, and the death of Prince Frederick William in 1765. These losses had not affected the Princess-Dowager's ambitions for her youngest child; but now, as the wedding-day drew nearer and Matilda's depression increased, that resolute lady began to feel concern—what if she were placing Matilda in a position for which she was unsuited? As one propitiating the fates, she had a ring engraved with a posy—'May it bring thee happiness'—which she put on the girl's finger just before the ceremony. This was performed by the Archbishop of Canterbury, and attended by the whole Court and a number of foreign Ministers. After the banquet which followed Caroline Matilda knelt to receive George III's farewell blessing, and then retired to her own rooms—for a few hours only; she had to be ready to leave at half past six the next morning.

Pale and exhausted, almost beyond weeping, she stepped into her coach to find the streets through which it passed lined with soldiers. As she drove along, her brother Gloucester at her side, the tears burst forth once more, and the bodice of her pink dress was stained. The women in the crowd, many of whom had waited all night to see her go, began to cry too: and their children, dimly aware that something very sad had happened, were sobbing and wailing as the coach, with its outriders and escort of life-guards, rolled on towards Mile End, and thence to Lord Abercorn's house at Witham, where the Queen was to dine and sleep before leaving for Harwich.

Here the royal yacht awaited her. By this time, although she could not manage to smile, she had stopped crying. 'On the whole,' according to the *Public Advertiser*, 'she carried on an air of serenity and majesty, which exceedingly moved everyone who beheld her.'5 Sailing was delayed by storms, and she spent the night at the house of the Customs Officer. Next morning she said goodbye to her brother and went on board; but the yacht remained in the Roads all that day, standing out to sea as twilight fell. Matilda came on deck and stood leaning over the rail to watch the shore lights, until they faded into the darkness. Then, with her principal attendant, Lady Mary Boothby, she went below.

For those who had seen her drive out of London, it was as if she had been condemned to death; her grief became common talk, and people began to say that she had been harshly used. 'The poor Queen of Denmark', wrote one lady to another, 'is gone out alone into the wide world, not a creature she knows to attend her any further than Altona ... It is ... dying out of one bad world into another just like it ... How bitterly she cried ... !'[6]

Storms prolonged the crossing for six days and nights; the yacht did not put in at Rotterdam till October 11th. Six hundred miles lay between that port and Copenhagen. Matilda and her entourage were transferred from her brother's vessel to that of the Stadtholder, which carried them to Utrecht. She then proceeded overland to the English colony of Hanover, sleeping at Osnabrück in the very same room— perhaps in the same bed—where her great-grandfather, George I, had died. She travelled on through Germany, stopping at Lingen, Bremen and Hamburg, and thence sailing down the Elbe to Altona, the frontier city.

During these weeks a complete metamorphosis took place. The Queen of Denmark was seen to be radiant, gracious and smiling. Her response to the cheering crowds, the salutes of cannon, the splendid cavalry escorts and the courtesies of the local grandees was all that could be wished. At last, she began to look forward to her new status and to enjoy its privileges. The praises of her beauty, the serenades, the speeches, the banquets and balls of which she was the central figure had a miraculous effect; with the volatility natural to her age, and to one hitherto kept in the background, she seems to have felt that being a queen was quite delightful. The over-disciplined little schoolgirl was now a great lady. People crowded to see her; flowers strewed her path; she looked prettier every day.

At Altona she was greeted by the Stadtholder of Schleswig-Holstein. She entered the city at dusk, over a bridge covered with vermilion cloth; on either side stood richly dressed burghers and young girls carrying flowers. Passing under a brilliantly illuminated arch, she was ushered into the town hall, where the Mayor welcomed her on behalf of the kingdom. 'Our fidelity', he told her, 'is surpassed by none, although in every part ... Your Majesty will receive from your faithful subjects transports of joy.'

Matilda's reply was well phrased and competently delivered. Next day, escorted by a troop of Danish cuirassiers, she made ready to leave Altona. It was now time for her to say farewell to Lady Mary Boothby and her English suite. She gave Lady Mary a diamond watch and an order for a thousand crowns.

Then, suddenly, homesickness, dread of the unknown—perhaps also of a husband—overwhelmed her. To the dismay of her Danish attendants, particularly of Madame de Plessen, her Mistress of the Robes, the Queen burst out sobbing—and would not be comforted.

NOTES

1. R. Northcote, *Memoirs of Sir Joshua Reynolds*, vol. I, p. 60.
2. Wilkins, *A Queen of Tears*, vol. I, p. 50.
3. Op. cit., vol. I, p. 67.
4. Op. cit., vol. I, p. 81.
5. *Public Advertiser*, October 5th, 1766.
6. N. Carter, *Letters*, vol. III, p. 64.

PART II
Copenhagen

I

The Court of Christian VII

THE LAW which had the greatest—and most fatal—effect on Caroline Matilda's career in Denmark was the Lex Regia evolved and established by the ministers of Frederick III in November 1665. It decreed that the realms of Iceland, Schleswig-Holstein, Norway and Denmark were the King's private property, that he was subject to God alone and that all public acts must be decided by him, sealed with his seal and signed by his hand. His absolutism was therefore complete; neither Charles V, Louis XIV, Catherine the Great nor any English monarch ever achieved this supremacy, which endured, with certain lapses, until and long after the accession of the sixteen-year-old Christian VII in 1766.

Christian's father, Frederick V, had had the sense not to abuse his powers, and his reign benefited chiefly the upper classes. The peasants were bound to their respective landlords, and many suffered accordingly. Yet because they were, as a rule, fairly well housed (although not adequately fed), they made no attempt to rebel, submitting to impressment in the army and navy. These arrangements did not produce a very high standard of prosperity. When Frederick V succeeded in 1746, he inherited a kingdom allied with Russia and France; he further strengthened his position by marrying Louisa, the daughter of George II, Caroline Matilda's aunt. So the new Queen was her husband's first cousin.

Frederick V, who died of drink, might have overcome his alcoholism if his English wife, to whom he was devoted, had not herself died after eight years of marriage. She bore her husband five daughters; their only son, Christian, was three when he lost his mother. Six months later, Frederick married Juliana Maria of Brunswick-Wolfenbüttel, who bore him one child, another Frederick. Custom required that Christian should be placed in a separate household; and so his stepmother, who was quite ready to take his mother's place and, in these early years, inclined to be sorry for him, had nothing to do with his upbringing. Nor had his grandmother, Sophia Magdalena, another German princess, who survived his father by several years.

Describing himself as the first servant of the nation, Frederick had been extremely popular, in spite of—indeed, perhaps because of—his insobriety, his extravagance and his public debaucheries. Night after night, he and his courtiers issued from the brothels and taverns of Copenhagen, collapsing in the gutter, to be picked up and driven back to the palace of Christiansborg by their coachmen. Between attacks of delirium tremens, the King organized his Court on what he liked to think of as a Franco-cosmopolitan basis. Versailles, which he had never visited, was his model; neglecting the rest of his kingdom, he spent large sums on turning Copenhagen into what he visualized as a rival centre of European culture; he became a patron of the arts and sciences, sending for painters, sculptors, mathematicians and philosophers from Germany and France, in order to sustain his reputation as the Maecenas of the North. He had charm, intelligence and energy—but not much heart, nor any inclination to curb the habits which killed him in his forty-seventh year.

Described by his subjects as Frederick the Good, he was much regretted, partly because of his lenient administration of the Lex Regia, which had originally been instituted in order to curb the power of the nobles and the upper clergy, their treatment of those they ruled having caused much distress. In his careless way, Frederick had been the father of his people; he had never subscribed to the rigid Lutheranism which took hold of Denmark in the early sixteenth century; indeed, he had set an example of unrestrained self-indulgence and complete disregard for the conventions. His attitude towards capital punishment was in advance of his age; the Danes were condemned to death for murder and high treason only; torture was rarely used; adulterers and fornicators were fined and given short terms of imprisonment. So it was that, in the capital at least, those who could afford it rioted and drank to excess without fear of the law. When Caroline Matilda became Queen of Denmark, Copenhagen had the reputation of a gay city; certainly, it was gayer, in one sense, than Carlton House or Kew Palace; but there was a coarseness, a lack of discrimination and elegance in its citizens' rather naive self-identification with what they thought of as the French tradition; and this attitude was linked with various social snobberies which reached a point of absurdity in Court and Government circles. To achieve places and honours became a passion. When Christian VII succeeded, there were three grades of officialdom: Councillors, State Councillors and—most important of all—Chamber Councillors. They were headed by no less than two hundred Chamberlains, whose duties were nominal. This farcical hierarchy produced corruptions and abuses ignored by Frederick V, while bestowing unlimited powers on those responsible for the education of his heir.

Before the bar of history Christian VII appears a pitiable figure, who never, as we say now, had a chance. This sensitive, quick-witted, motherless child was subjected to a regime of calculated and sadistic brutality, with the result that by the time he reached his teens he had become a degraded and ludicrous exhibitionist, hopelessly self-indulgent and a schizoid personality, incapable of any but the most trivial relationships.

The man responsible for this murderous assault on the character of a child who was physically robust and far from stupid, was Ditlev Reventlow, a country nobleman; he took charge when Christian was six. His 'hardening' treatment was based on a system of alternately flogging, threatening, mocking and terrifying his pupil. He would beat him until, falling on the ground, Christian was seen to foam at the mouth in an apparently epileptic convulsion. (These seizures became intermittent thereafter.) When overcome by exhaustion at church or during his lessons, he was kept awake by pinches and kicks, and whipped for the slightest fault of memory. His tutor, a Lutheran pastor, subscribed to these methods; between them, he and Reventlow might have turned Christian into a hopeless invalid, if a certain toughness in the boy's character had not produced the defences of slyness, cruelty, overwhelming conceit and sexual promiscuity. This development seems to have prevented him, for a time, from succumbing to the insanity which later became permanent. Such was the bridegroom whom Mr Titley presently described to George III as sober, compassionate and good, with a sound understanding and well seasoned with the principles of virtue.

Shortly after the Prince's eleventh birthday the Danish tutor retired, and his place was taken by Reverdil, an intelligent, kindly and experienced Swiss, whose system was in direct opposition to that of his predecessor. It was too late. In any case, Reventlow remained in control.

Superficially, Christian improved. He learnt how to please; his address became graceful, sometimes even charming; he danced and dressed well, and was not outwardly uncouth. Yet he remained egocentric, uncertain of himself, violent, capricious and cold-hearted. Towards women he used a hollow and rather silly gallantry; in fact, he preferred men's company, specifically that of subservient and half-educated persons. For some years, his favourite companions were two pages, Sperling and Kirchoff, who indulged his appetite for excitement with obscene ingenuity. As Christian grew up, he shrank from his destiny. Resembling his bride in this respect, he dreaded kingship, responsibility—and, above all, a wife. Despising Court ladies and unable to appreciate such *salonnières* as Copenhagen could produce, he determined to follow the fashion by acquiring a mistress; he took care not to do so until after marriage, in order to demonstrate his scorn for the conventions.

Shortly before his accession, Christian had undergone a 'test' in theology; he had no interest in this or any other intellectual pursuit, Reverdil's tuition having had but a superficial effect on his development. Yet because it was essential that he appear scholarly and pious, his confirmation was celebrated by a 'declaration' which he learnt by heart and recited before the Bishop of Zeeland, while Reventlow stood ready to prompt him. He did not falter, and was acclaimed as a phenomenon of religious learning.

Christian had received no training for his duties as a ruler: he knew nothing of European politics, economics, or of the countries allied to his own. When he presided over State Councils he made no attempt to listen, very soon ceased to attend, and left piles of official papers and letters unopened. Reverdil, observing this neglect with dismay, was not in a position to protest. Reventlow, whom Christian still feared and sometimes obeyed, forced him to tackle his correspondence; but the effect of his bullying was momentary. Titley then reported to King George that His Danish Majesty was beginning to understand State matters, and that 'his application is equal to his capacity'.[1]

So it happened that before his seventeenth birthday Christian became aware that deceit was taken for granted by those on whom he was supposed to rely; he can hardly be blamed for abjuring even the semblance of responsibility. He returned to his real interests—drinking, amateur theatricals and practical jokes. He excelled at the last, delighting in the terrified shrieks of his Aunt Charlotte when he sprang out from under a table, disguised as a Negro and howling like a wolf. He dropped slices of pastry from an upper window on the head of a visiting bishop, sprinkled sugar on his grandmother's hair, hurled a cup of tea in the face of a Court lady at a reception, and, with Kirchoff

CHRISTIAN VII *(Dance)*

AUGUSTA PRINCESS-DOWAGER *(Philips)*

CAROLINE MATILDA
AS A CHILD *(Liotard)*

and Sperling, brutally attacked the watchmen during his nightly sorties into the city. At this point, Titley described him as 'equitable and firm ... with a not uncultivated understanding'. Reverdil records that the only books he read were 'daring' French novels, and that he cared for none of the arts; nor did he like sport, nor any kind of game, however frivolous.[2]

Reverdil's hopes for Christian's improvement were encouraged by Bernstorff, the Prime Minister, who managed to oust Reventlow shortly before Caroline Matilda's departure from England. Sycophantic and disingenuous, Bernstorff was nevertheless a more desirable influence than his rival, in that he gave Christian self-confidence by representing his marriage in a romantic light. By the time Caroline Matilda crossed the frontier, Christian had begun to see himself as a gallant and chivalric figure; and his people's love of pageantry created a general longing to see his bride. A picture of triumphant and amorous youth—of a boy and girl who would wear their crowns with grace and gaiety—captured the imaginations of both the King and his subjects. As Caroline Matilda approached the ancient cathedral city of Roskilde, where their meeting was to be publicly celebrated, Christian became increasingly impatient. When he heard of her arrival there at seven o'clock on the morning of November 2nd, he covered the twenty miles that separated them in record time.

Meanwhile, Caroline Matilda's spirits had rallied once more. She was rather nervous; but the acclaim of her new subjects had banished homesickness; and in Madame de Plessen she found the support, the almost maternal care she needed. The character of this elderly widow closely resembled that of the Princess-Dowager; she was formal, strict, learned and dominating. As soon as the young Queen ceased to be frightened of her Mistress of the Robes, she began to rely on her, and to accept all her judgments, however arbitrary or out of date. Instinctively, she placed herself under Madame de Plessen's authority, and consulted her in everything relating to protocol, etiquette and general behaviour. During their three days' journey from Altona to Roskilde that masterful lady made herself indispensable, if only because her mistress had no knowledge of national customs, and no training as a public figure.

Caroline Matilda's time of waiting for the King's arrival was therefore not unduly taxing. She knew that she was pretty, admired and more than welcome. So, surely, she must find favour in the eyes of the young man with whom she was to spend the rest of her life.

D

There is no record of her having seen his portrait—which in any case, would have been designed to flatter. In all the stories, youthful kings are not only handsome, but attractive; and Christian's reputation was that of a lively and elegant leader of fashion, admired by women and imitated by his courtiers. Also, Titley had assured Matilda's relatives that he was abstemious, dignified, reliable and already half in love with her.

She may even have felt a certain pleasurable excitement as she heard the clatter of his coach, the clash of arms and the sound of footsteps running up the marble staircase of the Bishop's palace. The trumpets blared. The doors were flung open. And the cousins faced each other.

NOTES

1. P. Nors, *The Court of Christian VII*,   2.   Ibid.
   pp. 21–30.

II

Married Life

As SOON as she recovered from the shock of this confrontation, it must have seemed to Matilda that she was looking at one of her brothers, or at a portrait of her father as a boy. For the resemblance between Christian and his Hanoverian cousins was remarkable. Not only was he flaxen-haired, blue-eyed, and with identical colouring; his profile—he had a narrow, backward-sloping forehead, a receding chin and a long nose—exactly reproduced theirs. The difference between his appearance and that of her stalwart, solidly built family lay in his proportions. He was minute; although she was not tall, his head barely reached her shoulder; and his slight figure was that of a child.

There was another difference, which she may not have observed till later on—his look of slyness, combined, when he became irritated, with one of malicious disdain. Assuming an amiability he could never feel, his courtesy appeared curiously false. An Englishman mould have described him as a Frenchified dwarf; a Frenchman as a ridiculous *petit maître*.

Christian himself was agreeably surprised, indeed enraptured, by his bride's looks; for her portrait, painted when she was at her worst, had given no indication of her colouring, nor of her grace, nor of a certain innocent—and now hopeful—sweetness of expression. In one of her favourite pink gowns, with a wreath of white roses, a pearl necklace and a diamond stomacher, she was exquisite: the perfect companion for a fastidious *coureur de femmes*. Delighted with what he seems to have visualized as his personal choice, Christian ignored etiquette, advancing to kiss her hand and then her cheek with eager gallantry. She was not halfway through her curtsey when he raised her; his welcome drowned her carefully rehearsed homage.

The attendant Ministers then came forward, bowed and retreated in dazed relief. The courtiers interchanged glances of congratulation at this happy-ever-after climax to an alliance for which some of

Christian's intimates had prophesied disaster. The English princess had triumphed; now, nothing could go wrong.

This first presentation should have been followed by Christian conducting Matilda to her coach; then they were to have proceeded, separately, through the city to the palace of Fredericksberg, where she was to hold court until the wedding-day. Christian would not countenance such a tiresome formality. He handed Matilda into the huge, gilded equipage—it was drawn by six white horses and preceded by a glittering escort of cavalry—and took his place beside her. They were cheered all the way to Fredericksberg, which they reached at noon. Here the Dowager Queens and Prince Frederick, the heir-presumptive, waited to greet them.

Within a very short time, Matilda's pleasure in her success and in Christian's admiration had further enhanced her appeal, not only to the general public, but to those two formidable ladies, of whom Juliana Maria, Prince Frederick's mother, had been dreaded by her as potentially hostile. For this marriage, which was almost certain eventually to produce an heir, meant that her son would lose all chance of the succession; and she had reason to believe that her Frederick would make a better king than his half-brother. Fortunately for Matilda, Queen Juliana was at this time fairly well disposed; she had long resigned herself to Christian's founding a family; it was only necessary that his bride should be pleasing and dutiful. After an hour or so, she was reassured on both points; and her approval was shared by Christian's grandmother, who informed Titley that she was 'extremely satisfied and charmed with the person and conversation of the new Queen'. George III's representatives then hurried to report— and for once, neither lied nor even exaggerated—that his sister 'has everywhere been received ... with the greatest demonstrations of joy. She seems to gain universal applause and affection.'[1] Their relief no doubt equalled that of Reverdil, who had been rather anxious. 'The Queen', he says, 'captured all hearts, from the moment of her arrival,' adding that this conquest was based on a combination of genuine feeling on the part of the people, and of real goodness on hers.[2] Matilda's popularity might have endured until her death. It was her husband—with one other—who partially destroyed it.

She now appeared more radiant than ever: and indeed, she had reason to be. Not only was she praised and acclaimed by her new family and people; she was mistress of one of the most beautiful palaces in Europe. Fredericksberg, reflected in the translucent waters of the lake, with its castellated towers, splendid interiors and intricate baroque outlines, must have been a revelation to one used to the sober cosiness of Kew and Carlton House. It might have been especially designed to set off the treasures—silver and ivory furniture, Flemish tapestries and the famous Copenhagen porcelain—which now surrounded her. As soon as she arrived there she held court and, with Christian and the Dowager Queens, dined in public. The King then returned to Copenhagen, and Matilda remained in Fredericksberg for the next six days, holding receptions and preparing for her public entry into the capital on November 8th.

In a gown of silver tissue trimmed with ermine, escorted by scarlet-cloaked guards and mounted lackeys in cloth of gold, 'the English rose', as they called her, drove through decorated streets, under triumphal arches and past groups of allegorical figures to the palace of Christiansborg in the centre of the city. Here she was received by Prince Frederick, who conducted her to the banqueting-hall, where Christian was waiting; once more, in the company of some eight hundred guests, they dined in public; he pledged her in a goblet of crystal and gold which is still to be seen. She then retired to rest and change her dress for the wedding ceremony in the palace chapel. By nine o'clock that evening the alliance was irrevocably sealed; she and her diminutive cousin were husband and wife. All that night, the citizens of Copenhagen feasted and sang in the brilliantly lit streets.

Two days later, the King and Queen opened a State ball by dancing a minuet together—and then Matilda made her first mistake. Instead of summoning the *doyen* of the diplomatic corps, a Spanish grandee, for the next dance, she took the floor with Gunning, her brother's envoy. This trivial gaucherie was followed by an awkward and disagreeable scene, for which she was not responsible.

Towards midnight, Christian gave orders for a country dance—the *Kehraus*—which he desired his sister and her husband, Prince and Princess Charles of Hesse, to lead. They were followed by himself and Matilda and the whole Court—several hundred couples—who proceeded to dance through all the ground-floor rooms of the palace. By this time Christian was, of course, drunk, but amiable, if slightly belligerent; and Matilda was still enjoying her triumph.

They danced on without hindrance or mishap until they reached Matilda's apartments, to find Madame de Plessen on guard, disgusted by the general rowdiness and this open defiance of propriety. Standing before the great double doors, she waved them back, and dared them to enter. The Hesses paused. Christian shouted, 'Don't listen to that old woman's nonsense!' and dragging his wife along with him, thrust her Mistress of the Robes aside, thereafter staggering through the bed-chamber and a series of galleries and ante-rooms until they regained the starting-place.

The talk caused by this incident was so prolonged as eventually to reach England, horrifying George III. He got the impression that Matilda had embarked on a round of dissipations, thereby injuring her good name and that of her country. He decided not to remonstrate with her himself, desiring General Conway, his Secretary of State, to protest to Gunning, who would then warn his sister. 'Her Majesty' (Conway wrote) 'is entering upon the most important period of her life, and, at a tender age, is launched, as it were alone, into a strange and wide ocean, where it might require the utmost care and prudence to steer with that nice conduct which may at once conciliate the affections of her Court and people, and support the dignity of that high station to which Providence has called her.'[3]

This letter seems to have had some effect on Matilda's behaviour; nevertheless, she could not publicly disobey her husband when he forced her into flouting the conventions. Then, as the parades and festivities came to an end, Christian began to suffer from reaction and to look about for further amusement. Within a few days of the *Kehraus* scandal—for it was no less—he came to the conclusion that his new manner of life did not suit him. And besides, he told Reverdil, who implored him to remember who and what he was, 'a person of royal blood seems to me—when one is in bed with her—rather worthy of respect than of love'. According to Christian's standards, an uxurious husband was a figure of fun, and married life a wearisome and in-elegant business. And something was said about Louis XV and the Parc aux Cerfs.[4]

While the Anglo-Danish envoys continued to report on the marriage with sycophantic optimism, Ogier, the French Ambassador, having no need to do so, wrote to his master, 'The Princess has made little impression on the King's heart; and had she been even more charming, she would have met with the same fate. For how can she please a man who quite seriously believes that it does not look well for a husband to love his wife?'[5]

This aspect of the marriage could not long remain concealed; nor did Christian desire that it should; for he was bent on demonstrating what he thought of as his sophisticated, cosmopolitan attitude towards his wife. Three days after the wedding, he advised one of his intimates never to marry; that any pleasure could result from such a state was a bourgeois illusion, unworthy of a man of fashion. He confirmed this view by avoiding Matilda's apartments, and renewed the bachelor evenings which were followed by semi-incognito expeditions to the brothels and taverns of the city. Appalled, his Ministers asked for an audience, and pointed out that this neglect would merely suggest that His Majesty was not so much fashionable as impotent. Christian had not thought of that; although Matilda's appeal to his senses had faded, he decided—after a short interval—to sustain a semblance of gallantry, and visited her regularly, with the result that her first effect on his vision of himself as a Don Juan was partially re-created. Yet he could not keep it up; and he may have been afraid that the group of ineffably silly young men with whom he took his pleasures would laugh at him. So his behaviour towards the bewildered girl alternated between artificial amorousness and bored indifference.

Matilda, totally unprepared for this series of poses, was in despair. She did not know what to do, how to behave. And the shock of realizing that she was not, as she had thought, a success, paralysed such adaptability as she possessed. If she had joined her husband in his orgies—not that he suggested her doing so—she would have been censured by the Dowager Queens, of whom she was very much in awe, and reproved by her brother's envoys; when she conducted herself as became her station, he simply deserted her. The one atmosphere he could not tolerate was that of domesticity; and that was the only atmosphere in which she moved with ease. When one of his Ministers drew Christian's attention to the Queen's downcast looks, he replied, 'What does it matter? It is not my fault. She has the spleen, I suppose.' The younger courtiers then began to treat her without respect, and Gunning gave up all hope of her influencing Anglo-Danish relations, while Conway urged him to 'apprise Her Majesty who are the best friends of her native country'.[6]

At fifteen, without training, without friends, in a strange land, among people whose standards she could not understand and was beginning to dislike, she sank into deep depression. Drooping and pale, she sat silent at meals, and went through the motions of a public figure as if wound up to do so, making no attempt to hide her feelings. The only companion who seemed to care about her, not as a queen, but as an individual, was Madame de Plessen. Matilda turned to her for advice, as she would have turned towards her mother; for the resemblance between the German princess and the Danish aristocrat was a reminder of all she had left behind.

Madame de Plessen was ready with a whole programme, a carefully evolved technique. Matilda listened, was naively impressed, and agreed to co-operate. A great lady, a native, an older person, must know what to do for the best, quite apart from the fact that no one else had sympathized with or troubled to counsel her. She followed Madame de Plessen's instructions to the letter—and the result was disastrous. A number of contemporary and other historians have denounced Matilda for her silliness and lack of tact; those who expect innocent and sheltered girls to behave like women of the world are quite right to condemn her.

Her mentor's notions about courtship and marriage were not only medieval, but literary rather than historical. Madame de Plessen based her precepts on the *amour courtois* ideas of the twelfth-century Provençal troubadours. It is unlikely that she ever studied their works, even in translation; she was dedicated to their traditions.

Ignoring the rule that wives, of whatever rank, must obey their husbands, Madame de Plessen maintained that subordination to feminine caprice was the only way to ensure the devotion of the male. In the early days of marriage, a wife must keep her husband on tenterhooks of suspense, refusing her favours and withdrawing from his advances until he became desperate with desire. Uncertain of her moods, he would then be her slave, like those fictional lovers of great ladies celebrated by Chrétien de Troyes and Guillaume de Lorris. Only so could a satisfactory—and dignified—union be achieved, and the husband, thus bound to the wife, would continue to reverence and adore her. Madame de Plessen then issued her instructions for the practical side of the procedure.

Chess, rather than cards, was the official amusement of the Danish Court. At stated times, the King and Queen and the Queen Dowagers sat down to play; when the evening gaiety became uproarious and heavy drinking began, the ladies retired to their rooms, where they might continue their games before getting ready for bed.

Sometimes, Christian would send a messenger to ask whether Matilda had been undressed and was waiting for him to join her. This shocked Madame de Plessen, who finally persuaded her pupil to reply that she was in the middle of a game of chess, and would not be going to bed until it was finished. With unusual amiability, Christian waited till midnight, and then appeared to find the game nearly at an end.

As soon as it was over, Matilda, glancing at Madame de Plessen, said, 'I must have my revenge'—and received an encouraging smile, upon which Christian left the room, banging the door. He then avoided Matilda for a fortnight.[7]

On another occasion, he entered her dressing-room without warning, and drawing aside her neckerchief, began kissing her shoulders. Madame de Plessen protested, and Matilda followed her lead by complaining that he had crumpled her dress. Not unreasonably, the young man, enraged, tore the neckerchief to shreds, threw them underfoot and marched out of the room. He then complained to her secretary, Nielsen, of his wife's coldness, adding that Madame de Plessen was to blame. Nielsen, trying to heal the breach, begged the Mistress of the Robes not to interfere. She replied, 'His Majesty's conduct towards the Queen was of the kind only tolerated in brothels.'[8]

Naturally, Matilda should have broken away from this absurd and mischievous jurisdiction; she might have done so, if Madame de Plessen had not been supported by the Queen Dowagers; and she herself was incapable of pretence or coquetry. Christian, the first man who had made love to her—the only man with whom she had ever been alone—had touched neither her heart nor her senses. His insolence and neglect, following within a few days of the wedding, had so wounded her as to make response impossible. She had never been taught that it was her duty—part of her profession—to win him over; and she could not forget the sneers and insults which had preceded his latest advances. Unskilled and dazed, she blundered along behind him, no doubt wondering why Madame de Plessen's plans were ineffective. Then came a temporary change for the better; it might have become permanent, if it had not been brought about by artificial means.

The only tastes shared by Matilda and Christian were for fancy balls and private theatricals. He inaugurated these by a series of masquerades; in costumes copied from those of the Commedia dell' Arte, he, Matilda and their younger courtiers would dance two or three times a week till the small hours, to the horror of Madame de Plessen and the Dowager Queens. Then the King, who had some talent as an actor, built a private theatre in the palace of Christiansborg, on which he spent a great deal of money. He sent for a company of professional players from Paris, and, with them, himself appeared in several productions, notably in Voltaire's *Zaïre*. Matilda did not go so far as to act with him; but this kind of entertainment was one she had been used to at home. She enjoyed its renewal, and may even have admired Christian's performance. Whether, as is reported, he really distinguished himself, is uncertain; he believed that he did, and became absorbed in his new hobby.

The resultant expense was much resented by the majority of his subjects, who had to pay for productions they were not allowed to see; and they began to say that the new Queen was responsible for this selfish and undignified innovation. The older courtiers and their wives joined in the people's censure. Christian's intimates at once declared war on his critics, who were headed by Madame de Plessen. The King then decided personally to humiliate his principal enemy.

He commanded an expedition to Charlottenlund, a park some three miles from Copenhagen, in which the whole Court was to share. When they came out of the palace, Christian passed by his wife, and, approaching Madame de Plessen, asked her to grant him the honour of her company; he had long wished, he said, to drive her in his sleigh. Madame de Plessen, recognizing, as she thought, the offer of an olive branch, accepted, and was driven off at tremendous speed. As they approached the snow-drifts surrounding the city, Christian, shortening his reins, slewed his horses' heads to one side and, leaping out as the sleigh overturned, threw Madame de Plessen into a ditch; then, as if attempting to rescue her, he rolled her over and over, pulling up her dress, plastering her face with snow and tearing off her petticoats, while his gang of hooligans, who had been looking forward to this exploit, stood round in ecstasies of laughter. Finally, the King extricated himself and sent for a coach, in which his victim returned to the palace. Matilda seems to have arrived shortly afterwards.[9]

Once more, she was blamed for a prank in which she had not shared. It could not have happened, people said, without her knowledge and approval. Madame de Plessen remained undaunted. This was open war; and she put up a series of barriers, based on outmoded etiquette, between the King and Queen. Her determination, and the force of her personality were fatally effective. Christian resorted again to his bachelor habits; and again Matilda was deserted. In despair, Gunning informed Conway, 'All access to either the King or Queen ... is rendered so difficult that ... I can never expect to approach either of Their Majesties but in public ... The French Minister encourages ... intrigues against us ... the principal people about Her Majesty being our inveterate enemies.'[10]

NOTES

1. Wilkins, *A Queen of Tears*, vol. I, p. 97.
2. Prince Charles of Hesse, *Mémoires*, p. 73.
3. Wilkins, op. cit., vol. I, p. 107.
4. Hesse, op. cit., p. 74.
5. C. F. L. Wraxall, *Life and Times of Caroline Matilda*, vol. I, p. 87.
6. Wilkins, op. cit., vol. I, p. 111.
7. Hesse, op. cit., p. 41.
8. Ibid.
9. Nors, *The Court of Christian VII*, p. 62.
10. Wilkins, op. cit., vol. I, p. 112.

III

Conflict

THAT A game of chess and a torn scarf could form part of the basis of European relations was taken for granted by the potentates of the eighteenth century. Denmark was one of England's most valuable allies; and the prospects of Caroline Matilda's success or failure as its Queen were eagerly debated by the rival powers of France and Russia. The French wanted her to fail and thus weaken England's connection with Denmark; the Russians needed her success, as forming part of their co-operation with England against the French. The Danish Court was therefore divided into opposing camps, one headed by Madame de Plessen's group on behalf of Louis XV, the other by Bernstorff for Catherine the Great. French hopes rested on Matilda's failure to influence her husband; if they became completely estranged, then Louis XV would bring about a pro-French and anti-Russo-British policy. The fact that the Lex Regia gave Christian VII absolute power made the issue entirely personal; whoever dominated him—and he was bound to be dominated—would become dictator of Denmark. If Matilda achieved this position, her orders from George III would ensure English control; if she did not, her brother would be diplomatically defeated by the Catholic and pro-Jacobite kingdoms.

During the winter of 1766-7 Matilda became aware of what was expected of her; but she was helpless, partly because Queen Juliana and her party were allied with Madame de Plessen and the pro-French contingent, who at this time were more influential—in spite of Christian's dislike of the Mistress of the Robes—than their rivals. The correspondence between Conway and Gunning shows that England was losing to France, and that Christian might, at any moment, become subjugated by persons he did like, who would be in the pay of Louis XV.

He was now in the hands of two favourites—the Counts of Holck and of Brandt, wild young men of fashion, who, although bribable, were inefficient and untrustworthy; it was doubtful whether they would be of any use to either party, for their habits unfitted them for political intrigue. Their having declared war on Madame de Plessen and her group of elderly courtiers delighted Christian: but that was all; as tools, they were valueless, for their interests were entirely frivolous. They were now encouraging Christian to think of himself as a great actor, and to believe that no other aspect of his position need be considered.

As public resentment of the expenses incurred by the King's private theatricals rose to anger—enhanced by the sermons of Pastor Münter, the people's favourite preacher—Christian decided to placate them by increasing his audiences. He admitted a number of his subjects to the Christiansborg theatre; then, with his French players, he appeared on the stage of the opera-house of Copenhagen. When this display lost its novelty, he, with Brandt, Holck and their group of toss-pots, began a series of raids on the city brothels. Part of the fun lay in his maintaining his incognito; and on one occasion he had to jump out of the window in order to avoid the watch. He was too drunk to escape those waiting outside the building; and they set upon him. When he shouted, 'Stand back! Do you not know your King?' they laughed, refused to believe him and gave him such a thrashing that he had to be carried back to the palace in a state that necessitated his staying in bed for several days.

Again Matilda was blamed; why could she not keep her husband in order? 'The Queen', Gunning reported, 'is under the greatest uneasiness, lest this should be imputed to her having any inclination for a diversion of this kind ... The uncommon degree of prudence and discretion she is endowed with must ensure a large share of happiness; but ... I cannot flatter myself that this will bear any proportion to what Her Majesty ... deserves.'[1]

Matilda was no paragon; and the discretion of fifteen-year-old girls is seldom outstanding. Nevertheless, she deserved a better fate than that of marriage to a youth who was not only vicious, but becoming so eccentric as to alarm his Ministers. Yet they had no more hold over him than she had. The unauthorized story of Matilda gazing tearfully at the message engraved on the ring given her by the Princess-Dowager —'May it bring thee happiness'—originates from this time. She knew herself a failure; and Conrad Holck, who was sometimes able to rouse Christian from his fits of ennui, took care to impress on her that she had become an object of contempt, if not of dislike, in her husband's eyes. Matilda made no secret of her hatred of the Count, who told his circle that this was because he had refused to make love to her.[2] Meanwhile, Christian's moods so varied that every now and then his former pleasure in her company seemed to revive.

Holck may have been responsible for the rumour that Matilda, becoming pregnant in April 1767, was the mistress of another courtier, who was the father of her son. This story is recorded by a contemporary writer, Dorothea Biehl, who heard it from Nielsen; it can neither be swallowed whole nor absolutely discounted. The fact remains that the future Frederick VI was then and always accepted as Christian's legitimate heir, and grew up to look exactly like him.

In April 1767 Christian fell ill, and Matilda, seeing a chance of reconciliation, helped to nurse him, with the result that they got on very much better until and after their coronation, which was celebrated on May 1st. In a suit of gold brocade, red-heeled shoes and an ermine cloak, Christian crowned himself and his wife before they left the throne-room for the chapel. There they sat on a dais under a canopy supported by figures of angels. His throne was of ivory set with amethysts, hers of silver; beneath the dais lay three silver lions. After a sermon and the anointing, a procession formed and moved into the banqueting-hall, where the choir sang, 'While Christian and Matilda live, there shall be nothing but joy.'

The King and Queen then came out on to the balcony to watch the people drink wine from the fountain in the intervals of devouring portions of an ox roasted whole and stuffed with mutton, pork, geese, ducks and chickens. The huge creature, lying on a car, was wheeled forward by eighteen laurel-wreathed sailors in red and white uniforms, whose leader threw largesse to the crowd. Christian and Matilda looked on for a long time, and seemed to be on excellent terms.

Two months later, Matilda celebrated her sixteenth birthday. Christian forbade all feasting, public or private, and spent the evening with Holck, Brandt, a young Englishman and the Russian envoy. They then organized an expedition to smash lamps and windows, and beat up the watch. As a memento of his triumph over that body, the King captured a watchman's club, which he hung in his bedroom.[3]

This and similar exploits created general havoc; for it became the fashion to imitate Christian's night raids; and very soon the gangs of marauding youths so increased that the city guardians could no longer deal with their attacks. Nor could anyone control the King himself; the only persons able to influence him were those who instigated and fostered the drunkenness and violence caused by the virus of boredom.

At last, Reverdil evolved another and less dangerous diversion. Christian's tortured vanity and his need to dramatize himself might, he thought, find relief in appearing as the embodiment of regal power, graciously receiving homage. Such a presentation could not now be achieved in Copenhagen; but elsewhere, in the remoter parts of his kingdom, whose inhabitants had never seen him, the mystique of monarchy still prevailed. If he toured the country for a month or two, his behaviour in the capital would fade from the public memory, and he would respond, if only for a time, to the adulation of his people. So arrangements were set in hand for him to visit Schleswig and Holstein.

Christian was eager to go; but his pleasure in the prospect of appearing to new audiences was damped by two demonstrations of hostility, one from his Aunt Charlotte, and the other from Prince Charles of Hesse. The Princess, who was very rich, had just died; and it had always been assumed that her entire fortune would come to her nephew. But his practical jokes had antagonized her; and her millions went to various charities. This set-back was followed by the discovery that Prince Charles was championing Matilda; as the King's brother-in-law, he could afford to speak out on her behalf—and did so. His attacks struck at Christian's shaky self-esteem, and he became more than ever enraged with his wife, who had counted on visiting the duchies with him. When he refused to take her, and announced that he would be accompanied by Holck, her rage burst forth, and a series of scenes ensued. Reverdil—with Reventlow, who had just returned to Court—intervened, and eventually Christian gave in to the point of rejecting Holck; but he would not take Matilda, and set off with Reverdil, whose hopes of a successful tour were but partially realized.

In Holstein, Christian was acclaimed, 'as a god', according to his former tutor, and this caused him to declare that he would cancel the ancient laws which bound the peasants to the properties of their respective landlords.[4] When he returned to Copenhagen, this scheme was abandoned in favour of another appearance in Zaïre. Meanwhile, Reverdil observed a marked deterioration in the King's mentality; he had become 'feeble and distracted', and was firm only in his enmity towards his wife. He would not answer her letters; he could not forgive what he saw as her victory over Holck. Reverdil argued and pleaded; finally, he himself wrote letters to the Queen, which Christian copied and signed.[5]

These efforts were successful. Matilda answered affectionately and at length. But in the long run, the deception added to her difficulties, for she was led to believe that Christian's attitude had changed, and that their estrangement was over. This helped her to support the grief caused by the death of her favourite brother, Edward of York. Madame de Plessen broke the news to her, and Christian was at last persuaded to write to her himself, thus further encouraging her to think that their relations had improved, and that when he returned they would be happy together. Meanwhile, although he insulted and shocked the Holstein nobles, Christian sustained his hold over the common people.

When the King reached Ascheberg, a village in the extreme north of Holstein, one of his suite made friends with a young German doctor, whom he presented to his master. His name was Johann Friedrich Struensee. He so impressed Christian—and Reverdil—that he was asked to join the royal party. Travelling with him, he continued to please, not only the King, but his whole entourage. When they reached Traventhal, it was suggested that he should return with them to Copenhagen, where he might be given a minor post on the fringe of the Court circle. Struensee, who seemed to be at a loose end, accepted. He was at this time some thirty years old.

NOTES

1. Wilkins, *A Queen of Tears*, vol. I,
   p. 119.
2. Nors, *Court of Christian VII*, p. 65.
3. Wilkins, op. cit., vol. I, p. 130.
4. P. Reverdil, *Mémoires de la Cour de Copenhagen*, p. 80.
5. Ibid.

GEORGE III *(Ramsay)*

FREDERICK PRINCE OF WALES *(Mercier)*

THE CASTLE OF FREDERICKSBERG

COUNT JOHN FRED. STRUENSEE.

DR STRUENSEE

IV

Dr Struensee

JOHANN STRUENSEE, the youngest of four brothers, was born at
Halle in 1737. His father, Adam Struensee, a Lutheran pastor, came
from a sea-going family (hence the name, originally Strouvensee, a
stormy sea) and his mother was the daughter of one of Frederick V's
physicians. All the boys were clever, Johann exceptionally so.

They began their education at the local grammar school, which
Johann left soon after his fourteenth birthday for the University of
Halle. Here, rebelling against parental orthodoxy—and no doubt
against the long discourses and dreary services of the Lutheran faith—
Struensee became a free-thinker. He later declared his belief in a First
Cause, but denied all possibility of a future life. At nineteen he received
his degree in medicine, but was too young and inexperienced to
practise, and so had to remain at home, dependent on and in revolt
against his parents, and full of schemes for a brilliant future—which
seemed unlikely to materialize—while his father continued to deplore
his ambition, love of pleasure and intellectual pride.

In 1757 Pastor Struensee was offered the incumbency of Altona,
and there the young man got his first chance. His talents were soon
discovered; he became town physician and, later, country physician
to the districts of Pinneburg and Rantzau. When the father moved to
Holstein, the son remained in Altona, where he bought a house,
entertained a circle of friends, and with one of them started a magazine
entitled the *Monthly Journal of Instruction and Amusement*. As a writer,
he showed little talent; but his medical qualifications were far in
advance of his age; his interest in and understanding of what are now
called psychoses showed him to be very unusual; and his favourite
authors—Voltaire, Rousseau and Helvétius—gave him a revolutionary
and inventive habit of mind. At this time, he advertised his originality
by demonstrations of the eccentric and the bizarre (two skeletons,
carrying candelabra, stood on either side of his bed) and was known
as a witty and delightful host and a first-rate doctor. Tall, elegant and

E

handsome, he was especially attractive to women ('They are my best friends,' he used to say) and through them became the favoured guest of the local aristocracy. Among these, Count Carl Rantzau, a middle-aged owner of large estates and great wealth, was his chief patron. Rantzau, a rather disreputable character, had political ambitions; he and Struensee made a pact that whoever first achieved a Court post should help the other. Another friend was Baron Sohlenthal, the step-father of Count Brandt; and Struensee's most important patient was Madame Berkentin, who later became Mistress of the Robes to Queen Juliana. Yet none of these potentially useful acquaintances heeded the young doctor's hints about pushing his fortunes. When he came out into the open and said, 'Get me to Copenhagen, and I will carry all before me,' they made no move.

Struensee, now heavily in debt, had decided to start a new career in Spain, just at the moment of Christian's arrival in Ascheberg, where he himself was on holiday. Rantzau and Madame Berkentin recommended him to the King, who made him his 'travelling', and therefore temporary, physician. So it was that he reached Copenhagen, where Holck, hearing of his skill, praised him to Christian, who soon found that he could not do without this sympathetic and intuitive attendant. Struensee could not only talk on any subject—French novels and plays, new forms of amusement—but provided remedies for the after-effects of debauchery and for the nervous symptoms to which Christian so often succumbed.

He took care to behave as became his position—something between an upper servant and a below-the-salt professional—and was so charmingly modest that no one objected to his influence over his new master, whom he saw every day. He was at the same time discreet, subservient and amusing. Aware that his post was impermanent, he set about making himself indispensable, while furthering his career unobtrusively and without any apparent inclination to climb. Everyone liked him—except Matilda. Because he was the protégé of Holck and Brandt, she mistrusted his influence, and would have nothing to do with him.[1]

She had been looking forward to Christian's return, and set off to meet him on the outskirts of Copenhagen in high spirits. He received her coldly, but was persuaded by Reverdil to get into her coach, and appearances, at least, were kept up during the first weeks of reunion. Then he tried to force Holck upon her as master of her household. With tears of rage, she refused, and Christian revenged himself by setting up a famous courtesan as his public mistress. This girl, formerly a dancer, known as Gaiter-Catherine (her stepfather was a tailor) had been kept by an English diplomat for some years, and was now on the market again. She was beautiful, high-spirited and always ready to join in any riotous venture Christian might suggest. Shortly after his return from the duchies, he sent for her to a Court ball, danced with her the whole evening and paraded her at supper. Matilda, whose pregnancy prevented her being present, was told of this demonstration the next morning, with the result that she and Christian were again estranged until the birth of the heir on January 28th, 1768.[2]

A few days later, the baby's condition began to cause great anxiety, and Christian, who had planned a series of festivities for the christening, was told that his son must be baptized privately and at once. So the ceremony took place in Matilda's bedchamber, in the presence of the chief Ministers and Councillors. Sponsored by Queen Juliana, whose hopes for her own son were now destroyed, the Prince was called Frederick. He remained delicate, and much coddled, for the next three years.

Matilda's enjoyment of her triumph was marred by Madame de Plessen's obsession with etiquette. She insisted that the child should be placed in charge of a series of Court ladies, chosen by herself, in order of rank. Although the resultant changes of routine were nearly fatal, the little Prince's hold on life was sustained. The Mistress of the Robes then arranged that Matilda should hold a reception, propped up in her state bed, while the baby lay in a cradle beside her. The whole Court filed slowly past them, and formal congratulations and thanks were interchanged. After some hours of this ordeal, Matilda collapsed; the Prince appeared to be dying.[3]

Christian now resolved to dismiss Madame de Plessen, but was persuaded not to do so until his wife and son had recovered. He did not tell Matilda what was being planned, for he had begun to shrink from her furious protests. For some time the gentle sweetness of her disposition had been soured by resentment and injured pride. Also, her hold over the people, the support of Madame de Plessen and the Hesses, and the loyalty of Reverdil had brought out her latent strength of character. She made it clear to Christian that, however he might behave, she was not going to be browbeaten. So he ran away to Fredericksberg, whence he wrote ordering Madame de Plessen to retire from Court, without saying goodbye to the Queen. She had been gone some hours when Bernstorff told her mistress what had happened. Bursting into tears, Matilda exclaimed, 'I will never forgive the King for this!' and refused to listen to the Minister's explanations and attempts to console her.[4]

Madame de Plessen's dismissal was followed by that of several other ladies, and her post was given to the detested Holck's sister, Madame von der Lühe. The new chief lady-in-waiting was Fräulein von Eyben, whom the pro-Russian contingent employed as a spy. Meanwhile, the junior Russian envoy, Saldern, who described Madame de Plessen as Matilda's flea-catcher (this post actually existed at the Court of Catherine the Great) reported, 'My great torment is the Queen ... The King and I laugh [about her] together.'[5]

When Christian returned to Copenhagen Matilda told him that he ought to be ashamed of himself. 'The whole city', she added, 'says that you are governed by Saldern.' Christian took refuge with Gaiter-Catherine and in plans for another performance of *Zaïre*. At Reverdil's suggestion, Matilda agreed to make one more effort at reconciliation: with the ex-tutor, she entered her box, to find herself faced by Gaiter-Catherine, glittering with jewels and surrounded by the King's group of hooligans. Matilda left the theatre, and Reverdil, seeking out Holck, said, 'A man can be neither a good subject nor a good servant, who does not weep to see such a creature defy the Queen, and the King make himself—to the peril of the state—the *greluchon* [puppet] of a foreign minister.' Holck turned away. Next morning, Christian sent a note to Reverdil, desiring him to leave Copenhagen within twenty-four hours, and that faithful servant departed to his own country.[6]

Gaiter-Catherine then induced the King to give her the title of Baroness and buy her a palace. There he spent the nights, often returning to Christiansborg dead drunk and on foot, in the early hours of the morning, to be hissed—and, on one occasion, stoned—by the people. That same evening, he and his mistress would be seen walking about, arm in arm, she dressed as a man, generally in naval uniform. Finally, her palace was stormed by the citizens, and the police told Bernstorff that a revolution was imminent.[7]

The Minister resolved to alarm Christian to the point of dismissing Catherine. This was easily done. Terrified, shaking with nerves, Christian signed the order. Catherine was deported to Hamburg, where the municipal authorities imprisoned her. She remained in a house of correction for the next three years.

Christian was in despair. Weeping, he declared that he had lost the only woman he had ever loved—and his mental disturbance increased.

Hearing that the confession of a criminal was to be extracted by torture, he insisted on attending the procedure. A few days later, he spoke gloatingly of the victim's agonies, and had a rack made, on which he stretched himself, while Holck whipped him till the blood ran.[8] Appalled, the Court physicians declared themselves helpless; and Struensee's position as travelling doctor barred him from their consultations. Calmly, he awaited his next chance. It was nearer—much nearer—than he could possibly have imagined.

By this time Matilda was completely isolated. She may not have realized that her hatred of Saldern and her loyalty to Madame de Plessen had placed her—theoretically—in the anti-Russian, pro-French group. In any case, her ignorance of politics, inability to intrigue and dislike of all Christian's favourites made her powerless; and her having produced an heir to the throne had now added Queen Juliana to the number of her enemies. From the moment of the Prince's birth that lady's jealousy centred on the younger woman, whom she regarded as a rival and despised as a failure.

In fact, even those few who pitied Matilda felt that she was partly to blame for the estrangement from Christian; they either would not or could not grasp that he was nearing the state now described as that of diminished responsibility. He might do anything—and that would result in a revolution in the capital which would bring on civil war. Action must be taken; and the only way to restore good relations between King and people was to send him abroad—'for his studies' seemed to be the best euphemism—first to England, and then to France, for some months. The thought of such a scheme delighted Christian; he merely stipulated that he should go incognito—and without the Queen.

Matilda was aghast. She implored Christian to let her be with him, if only during his stay in England. It was her last chance to see Louisa, who had but a few weeks to live; she longed for her mother, and may have counted on pouring out her troubles to George III; while rejoining William and Henry would have been a wonderful happiness. Christian was adamant. If she forced herself upon him, then he would not go. Bernstorff tried to appease her by a promise of the regency. Aware that this offer was meaningless—for Juliana had already claimed the position—Matilda renewed her prayers; and was ignored.

In the first week of May 1768 news came of Louisa's death; a few days later, Christian, with Struensee, Bernstorff and a large suite began his journey via Schleswig, Hamburg, Frankfort and Brussels, and so reached Calais. There he boarded George III's yacht, which put in at Dover on August 9th. Meanwhile, Matilda had retired, with her son, to Fredericksberg. All her care was for the baby; he slept in her room; she spent the whole day with him; and gradually she settled down into a domesticity that resembled the peaceful contentment of Kew and Carlton House. She visited the cottages surrounding the palace, helped those in need—and then, as they came to her with their troubles, decided to do without an interpreter and learn Danish. She seldom visited the capital; when she did, she received a clamorous welcome. The elder Queen-Dowager, Sophia Magdalena, was friendly and sympathetic; Madame von der Lühe turned out to be quite unlike her brother; she and Matilda became pleasantly intimate; and in Christian's absence there were no scenes and no humiliations. So an unexpected happiness was achieved, increasing as summer turned to autumn and winter began, while the Prince Royal seemed to be getting a little stronger. 'He is greatly grown', Gunning reported, 'since his removal to the country. The resemblance between His Highness and the King's family is striking.'[9]

NOTES

1. Wilkins, *A Queen of Tears*, vol. I, pp. 193–9; C. Wittich, *Struensee*, pp. 45–50; Count Falkensjold, *Mémoires des Comtes de Struensee et Brandt*, pp. 20–32; Reverdil, *Mémoires*, p. 80.
2. Reverdil, op. cit., p. 102.
3. Wilkins, op. cit., vol. I, p. 139.
4. Op. cit., p. 143.
5. Ibid.
6. Ibid.
7. Op. cit., p. 146.
8. Reverdil, op. cit., p. 129.
9. Wilkins, op. cit., vol. I, p. 180.

V

The Danish Invasion

GEORGE III's reception of his brother-in-law was so cold as to border on discourtesy. He seems to have felt that, having sent the royal yacht to meet him, he need do no more than instal him and his suite of a hundred persons in St James's Palace, while he himself, with the Queen, retired to Richmond, where he proposed to remain during the greater part of Christian's visit. That he and his Court were still in mourning for the Princess Louisa was the official reason given for this withdrawal; in fact, while unable personally to bar his doors to an important ally, the English king had been so enraged by the reports of Christian's treatment of Matilda, that he decided to see as little of him as possible; and the thought of having to spend vast sums on entertaining his Danish guests for what looked like a long stay appalled him. Christian's reputation as a debauchee was a further cause of dislike on the part of his strait-laced cousin, who determined to cut down his hospitality to a minimum.

This attitude did not trouble Christian in the least; indeed, he hardly took it in. Travelling incognito as the Count of Traventhal, he had come to enjoy himself and be admired, achieving both aims immediately. From the moment of his arrival he set himself to please—and succeeded. The citizens of Copenhagen would have found it difficult to identify this gallant, high-spirited young man with the morose and insolent alcoholic whose extravagances they had had to endure—and to pay for—and who had brought their country to shame in the eyes of Europe.

This outward metamorphosis was caused by Christian's joy in escaping from Denmark, from kingship—and from his wife. Now, at last, he could behave as a carefree, although gracious, bachelor, whom the English people crowded to see, and, seeing, acclaimed vociferously and at length. He was so informal—so gay—so generous—so elegant; and his toy-like proportions were quite endearing, to women especially. He was rather wild, of course: and unpredictable. But these characteristics contrasted agreeably with the stiff correctness of their own King and Queen, their rare appearances and economical habits.

So Christian's progress from Dover to London was a series of triumphs; and with each burst of applause his spirits rose, as did his standards of behaviour. No one, hearing him laugh and chatter and pay compliments, could have guessed that he had ever succumbed to mental disturbance, or that this resurgence was temporary, an interval between bouts of hideous depression and frenzied lust. Meanwhile, some of those who saw him in more intimate circumstances than the general public did, regarded him as a harmless freak. Horace Walpole, contemptuously amused at the fuss made of the 'Northern Scamp', told a friend that His Danish Majesty was 'as diminutive as if he came out of a fairy-tale,' and 'as well as one expects a King in a puppet-show to be ... He ... struts in the circle like a cock-sparrow ... This great King is a very little one; not ugly nor ill-made ... The mob adore him ... for he flings money to them out of his windows.' Later, Walpole described Christian as 'an insipid boy' and 'a very silly lad ... He has neither done nor said anything worth repeating.'[1]

After a brief reception at Buckingham Palace, which Queen Charlotte refused to attend, the Danish party settled in at St James's, described by Holck as 'not fit for a *Christian* to live in', regardless of the fact that George III had spent three thousand pounds on doing up his brother-in-law's apartments, was allowing him eighty-four pounds a day for expenses and had lent him Henry VII's gold plate. These attentions were wasted on Christian, who was interested only in public appearances and the entertainments provided by the aristocracy and the City fathers. Every day he emerged from St James's to find crowds waiting to cheer him, and was delighted when a young woman burst through the lines, lifted him up in her arms, and having embraced him, declared that she had kissed the prettiest fellow in the world.[2] He then arranged to dine in public four times a week, but could not escape visiting his mother-in-law, who cross-examined him about Matilda's health and spirits, and begged him to let Madame de Plessen resume her duties. Christian replied that if that lady returned to Court, he and his wife would have to live in separate palaces. As the Princess-Dowager renewed her inquiries about her daughter, he did not trouble to answer, but, turning to Holck, said in a stage aside, 'Cette chère Maman m'embête terriblement.' When he next called upon Augusta, she and her ladies were telling fortunes by the cards. 'Which card am I in your pasteboard Court?' he asked. 'Lady Hertford', said the Princess-Dowager, 'calls you the King of Diamonds.' 'And what do you call Holck?' Christian pursued. 'The King of Hearts.' 'And pray, dear Mamma, what do you call my Lord Bute—the Knave of Hearts?' Christian inquired. The Princess-Dowager, red with anger, picked up the cards in silence, while her ladies interchanged glances of dismay. Christian knew as well as they did that Bute had lost the premiership and fled abroad in disgrace.[3]

Christian then called on his and Matilda's Aunt Amelia, who bluntly inquired why he had turned against her favourite niece. 'Why? Because she is so fair,' said Christian airily, and departed to the theatre, where Vanbrugh's *The Provok'd Wife* was being performed. 'There', Walpole told Sir Horace Mann, 'he clapped whenever there was a sentence against matrimony—a very civil proceeding, when his wife is an English princess!'[4]

Masquerades, City banquets and public receptions preceded Christian's tour of England, which included visits to York, Cambridge, Oxford, Liverpool and Manchester. When he returned to London, he and Holck, disguised as sailors, resumed their habit of nightly expeditions to the brothels. After attending a banquet given by the Lord Mayor, they visited the Marshalsea, where Christian paid the debts of several prisoners, and then strolled about the streets, throwing gold and silver coins to the people.

By this time, George III was beginning to feel that Christian had stayed long enough, and asked him to what he described as a *'farewell function'* at Richmond. Christian took the hint, and prepared to leave for Paris, after holding a last reception at St James's. One of the guests was Garrick, to whom he talked for two hours, and presented with a diamond-studded snuff-box. Having distributed £3,000 among the palace staff, £500 to the Lutheran mission and £2,000, in gold, to the crowds, who, not surprisingly, ran after his coach far beyond the capital, he left in a blaze of popularity, all agog for further triumphs at the Court of Louis XV.[5]

He reached France in the second week of October 1768, and stayed at Versailles and in Fontainebleau for two and a half months, entertaining and being entertained at such a rate, that he broke down and had to go to bed for several days. Louis's courtiers then observed that he had succumbed to what they called distraction. He would receive them with a flood of meaningless talk, and answer their remarks at random. He was always attended by Bernstorff, who would give him a warning glance when his conversation became particularly wild. A little later,

Christian developed a horror of women's society, and sought the company of handsome young men. This change of taste kept him out of the brothels, but displeased his hosts. Finally, after a dinner to which he asked, among other intellectual celebrities, d'Alembert, Diderot and Helvétius, he announced that he must return to his own country. In fact, he was bored, a state of mind described by Bernstorff as 'craving for home life and serious occupations'.[6]

This optimism was justified, in a different sense, by the welcome of Christian's people, who received him as if he had never offended them. At Roskilde he found Matilda equally radiant, and seemed delighted to see her. On January 14th, 1769, they made their public entry into the capital, which had been brilliantly illuminated. With the Dowager Queens, they then held a reception at Christiansborg.

So it appeared that Bernstorff's cure had succeeded, although at fearful expense to the nation. The opinion of Struensee, who had remained in the background during most of his master's eight months' tour, was not recorded; perhaps not even required. Intermittently employed, he waited for the next phase.

Matilda had consistently ignored the opportunity created by Christian's absence. At the last moment, Queen Juliana was refused the regency, and the Government came under the jurisdiction of three ministers—Thott, Moltke and Rosenkrantz. It did not occur to the seventeen-year-old Queen, whose nature was still that of a strictly brought-up adolescent, either to ally herself with these men, or to use her popularity with the people in order to gain political power. Absorbed in her child and in country pursuits, she stayed at Fredericksberg from May 1768 until January 1769, instead of establishing herself in the capital and thus impressing her personality on the citizens by regular public appearances. She remained what she had been ever since her arrival in Denmark—a symbol of monarchy, acclaimed for her beauty and her charities. Her strength of purpose was then, and continued to be, applied to private interests. Now she knew how a queen should behave; she was admired and beloved; but to employ these triumphs for ambitious reasons was beyond one who had been dominated by a strong-minded mother for the first fifteen years of her life.

It may be that Matilda's inability to achieve a satisfactory relationship with her husband, and her fear of the Dowager Queens had deprived her of initiative; or that her sufferings had so exhausted her that complete privacy—the privacy in which she had been brought up—

was her only need. She must have dreaded Christian's return; but, incalculable as ever, he rejoined her in the role of an attentive—indeed, an almost devoted—husband; and for a reason that explained, if she had only been able to grasp it, the endemic unreliability of his character. He had been rapturously happy in England, much more so than in France. Matilda was English—and therefore admirable. He rejoiced in her company, because he associated it with that of Garrick, of Lady Hertford, of the London mob and the courtiers of George III. He now decided to ask her brother Gloucester for a long visit. Meanwhile, he set himself to appear, with her, as the gracious and dutiful ruler of his people.

This improvement did not last; but Matilda seems to have assumed that it would, for she met Christian more than halfway, arranging entertainments and parties for him every evening. The only flaws in this new situation were his continued attachment to Holck and his dependence on Struensee, whom he made his permanent surgeon-in-ordinary. Matilda detested them both; but Christian's change of mood made up for their prevalence; and his pleasure in her success ('The English send us not queens, but angels' became a catch-phrase) was unshadowed by jealousy. Their courtiers began to say that the King had fallen in love with his wife; his masquerades and nightly sorties were abandoned; he and Matilda dined together, sometimes in public, every afternoon; and Gunning reported, 'The society of the Queen seems alone to constitute his happiness. Her Majesty will now ... obtain that just and proper degree of influence which her ... qualities entitle her to, and which she should have much earlier enjoyed.'[7]

The Duke of Gloucester arrived in time for the celebrations of his sister's eighteenth birthday in July 1769, and their magnificence atoned for the neglect of the past two years; he himself was not a success. Silent, clumsy and plain, he was interested only in food and drink; his manners were gross; his looks caricatured the Hanoverian type: his mentality was sub-normal, his appetite gargantuan—and so his departure came as a relief. When Christian asked Holck what he thought of the Duke, the Count replied, 'He reminds me of an English ox'—and the King at once repeated this not very amusing remark to Matilda, who was incensed. So the split between husband and wife was renewed, and then widened by Holck, who now set himself to estrange them for good. At all costs, Matilda's hold over Christian must be destroyed, and his own domination secured.

This was not difficult; for already, the King was wearying of regular habits and seemly behaviour. Holck, now married to an heiress, was given the Blaagaard palace; his power over Christian became such that they communicated three or four times a day, and the messengers carrying Christian's letters had to ride so fast that their horses sometimes dropped dead. Then, suddenly, the King ceased to appear in public. His melancholia predominated, yielding only to bouts of delusion. He became too weak to move and spent his days in bed, weeping and muttering to himself. His physicians were powerless to help him.

At last Brandt, the ally of both Holck and Struensee, suggested that the latter should try his hand at a cure, and, rather to the surprise of all three, Christian submitted himself to the German doctor's authority. Struensee's remedies, gently and tactfully proposed, were apparently effective, and the King seemed to progress. Struensee knew that this improvement was transitory; naturally, he did not say so.

Then Matilda became gravely ill. Her symptoms were not described, either by Gunning or by the Danish faculty. The nature of her disease —or diseases—is still in dispute.

NOTES

1. Walpole, *Letters*, vol. VII, pp. 212, 215, 219; Walpole, *Memoirs and Portraits*, pp. 229–30.
2. Wilkins, *A Queen of Tears*, vol. I, p. 169.
3. Op. cit., p. 157.
4. Walpole, *Letters*, vol. VII, p. 229.
5. Nors, *Court of Christian VII*, p. 89.
6. Op. cit., p. 92.
7. Wilkins, op. cit., vol. I, p. 184.

VI

Struensee's Progress

CHRISTIAN'S ENGLISH hosts had been much impressed by the handsome young doctor who accompanied him everywhere, and whose graceful manners and brilliant conversation were in marked contrast to those of the King's other companions. Struensee received honorary degrees from the Universities of Oxford and Cambridge, and was entertained by many of the great London hostesses. He then took riding lessons at Astley's, and spent large sums on dress. It was said that he had become the lover of a wealthy lady, and that she had given him her miniature, which he wore next his heart for the rest of his life; but a serious attachment seems unlikely. Struensee had no intention of committing himself abroad; his plans were based on the opportunities awaiting him in Denmark, and he never, at this time, relaxed his discretion.

His reserve, and his refusal to discuss his relations with Christian, irritated his parents, whom he visited on his way back to Copenhagen. When his father accused him of arrogance, he did not trouble to defend himself. With his brother Karl August, he was more outspoken, describing a dream in which he had been talking to a beautiful woman —whose name he withheld, so exalted was her rank—in the gallery of Fontainebleau. 'Everything', he concluded, 'is possible.'[1]

Struensee had already advised Christian, who was in perpetual alarm about his health, to drink less and take more exercise. He now renewed his persuasions, with the result that his patient followed the hunt in his carriage, which he drove himself, Matilda at his side. One day, his horses grew restive; he could not control them, and the carriage overturned; both he and the Queen were thrown into a ditch. Neither was hurt; but Christian refused to drive himself again. This mishap rejoiced those who were beginning to resent Struensee's progress. He set about re-establishing it by other means.

He knew that Christian's mental health would soon break down altogether; and he had observed Matilda's popularity with the people,

as also her neglect of her opportunities. He came to the conclusion that
if she did not exert herself, Christian's power would eventually fall
either to Holck or to Bernstorff. Yet it was impossible to influence, or
even to approach the Queen with a view to forming a party headed
by himself and her, because she refused to speak to him. Struensee
therefore abandoned his scheme of an alliance with Matilda, and
applied himself to distracting Christian. Shortly before the Queen fell
ill, Struensee became the lover of a married woman, the beautiful
Madame Birzette von Gabel, whom he introduced to the King, on the
understanding that she should promote his interests. Christian and
Madame von Gabel became intimate; just as Struensee's position
seemed secure, she died in childbirth.

Matilda, infuriated by Struensee's pimping for her husband, described him to her entourage as a low and contemptible blackguard. It
was at this point that she became ill—some said of a venereal infection
passed on to her by Christian. 'A perfect re-establishment', Gunning
reported, 'may be attended with some difficulty, unless Her Majesty
can be persuaded to pay unusual attention to herself,' adding that
Matilda had not only refused the prescriptions of the Court doctors,
but would not let them examine her. She longed for death. Nothing,
not even the thought of her son, could prevail against her determination to leave a world in which she had suffered so much misery and
shame.[2]

This suicidal attitude gave rise to a great deal of gossip, of which
Matilda herself was unaware. One of her ladies, Madame von Gramm,
said that she had taken lovers during Christian's absence, one being
Monsieur La Tour, a Parisian actor, and that Mademoiselle von Eyben
was in the habit of introducing attractive young men to the Queen for
the same purpose; she hinted that Matilda had been infected by one
of them, and not by her husband. But as Matilda's illness remained
undiagnosed—she herself thought it was dropsy, now a generic and
therefore meaningless term—these stories may be partially discounted.
Gunning's guarded accounts of her state ('Some very unfavourable
symptoms ... [It is] highly necessary to obviate worse symptoms') give
the impression that he wanted to conceal what was wrong from
George III, whom he begged to reason with Matilda. Gunning may
have believed Mademoiselle von Eyben's reports of her mistress, but
was not necessarily right in doing so. And the extraordinary, indeed
phenomenal, rapidity of the Queen's recovery seems to indicate a very
different kind of malady; for in the eighteenth century, cures for

venereal infection took many months, sometimes even years, to succeed, when they succeeded at all. Gunning thought that George III should write to his brother-in-law urging him to use 'affectionate expostulations' with Matilda, and pointing out 'the very great import-ance of her life'.[3] But was Christian in a state to do this? (His epileptic fits had recurred.) And what effect would his pleading have on the wife who had begun to loathe him? The envoy could only wait upon events. And then a miracle—two, in fact—took place.

Matilda's illness began in October 1769. During the next few weeks her health became a cause of greater anxiety than Christian's; for Struensee had managed to frighten him into leading a quieter life; and with his improvement the King's attitude towards his wife changed once more. Also, George III's letters begging him to reason with her were having effect. He was so terrified of illness and death, his own or another's, that he set himself to do everything he could towards her recovery. As she continued to ignore his suggestions, he asked Struen-see's advice. Matilda ought to consult him—but how could she be induced to do so?

Unmoved by the Queen's hatred, Struensee said that Christian should persist. Matilda took no notice. Then George III wrote to her. He knew nothing, except by hearsay, of Struensee's skill; but he seems to have told his sister that it was her duty to obey her husband in order to resume her position as mother, wife and queen. After some further resistance, Matilda began to yield, partly because Christian—no doubt at Struensee's suggestion—said that he was very sorry he had treated her so badly. He promised to reform, if only she would grant him this one favour, and consult the man in whom he had absolute faith.

Oddly enough, Christian was sincere. He had begun to be fond of, even to depend on, the wife he had insulted and despised. So Matilda, once more persuaded of his change of heart, agreed—and Struensee was summoned to her bedside. Her distrust of him had not diminished: he was being forced upon her; but her sense of duty, and the hope that by consulting him, and thus meeting Christian halfway, she might save her marriage, helped her to make the effort. Their first interview took place in the middle of December, some eight weeks after her decision to end her life.

The circumstances in which Struensee was ordered to prescribe for Matilda could hardly have been more unfavourable. Yet his obsessive belief in his great destiny made it quite easy for him to disregard her

mistrust of him, as a man and as a physician. He had always known—
or rather, felt—not only that he would succeed, but that he would
eventually achieve power and fame. He therefore approached Matilda
with deep respect and perfect self-confidence. He was not in the least
intimidated by her rank or by her hostility. He knew that he would
prevail, as he had with so many 'difficult' and unhappy young women,
whom he had charmed out of despair. And then he knew all her
circumstances. His months of attendance on Christian had provided
him with the whole background, and part of the basis, of her case. He
and the Queen appear to have remained alone together for about two
hours ...

Matilda, usually so ready with her confidences, did not make a
single comment on Struensee. She sent for him the next day—and the
next—and the next. Thereafter, he saw her every morning, and again
in the afternoon; often, he visited her two or three times within twenty-
four hours.

Christian was jubilant—he had proved his case. He told Matilda
that the more often she consulted this wonderful man, the better it
would be for them both. Every now and then, having made inquiries,
he would send Struensee to her before she had asked for him. And
so he was able to proclaim his triumph—and Struensee's—to all the
Courts of Europe. He was right, when everyone else had been wrong.
For in less than a fortnight Matilda's health was completely restored.

Struensee's methods were the exact opposite of those of the Court
physicians, whose approach to royalty was pompous and sycophantic;
a whole series of compliments had to be paid and acknowledged before
any discussion of symptoms began. In Matilda's case, a very few
inquiries, quietly and simply put, sufficed to show Struensee that she
believed herself stricken with dropsy, and was prepared, indeed,
desired, to die. He seems to have examined her in such a manner that
she felt neither self-conscious nor distressed. He then told her what he
had probably known all along, that she was not dropsical, and that her
illness could be cured with comparative ease.

In their first interviews he continued to instruct her about herself.
Ennui—or the spleen, as it was then called, or in modern medical
terms, acute depression—had brought her very low; this was a disease
that could only be dealt with by altering her manner of life. By making
it clear that he had diagnosed her state, he eliminated the first barrier
almost before she realized how intimate they had become. At a later
point, he told her, in the same matter-of-fact manner, that distress of

mind, combined with a sedentary life, had temporarily deprived her of resistance. He neither used technical terms, nor looked mysterious; nor did he assume omniscience, nor did he belittle her unhappiness. 'Your Majesty does not require medicine so much as exercise, fresh air and distraction,' he said. 'Ennui is caused by the monotony of etiquette.'

Matilda seems to have pointed out that the observance of ceremony was unavoidable in her position, to which Struensee replied that those duties should be confined to certain times, and not allowed to occupy all her waking hours. Having let this sink in, he then suggested that she should take up riding, a pursuit never practised by Danish ladies. If Her Majesty introduced it, she would start a new fashion, besides restoring her own health.

As Matilda had never ridden in her life, she decided to take lessons, and in a very few days found that she had a natural aptitude for the exercise; she became a skilled and fearless horsewoman, and the result was not only beneficial but extremely becoming. She had put on too much weight (hence her belief that she had dropsy, presumably), but now regained her figure. 'Your Majesty', Struensee told her, 'must set the example.' Already his tone had become authoritative. 'They may be scandalized at first, but fashion and custom will make them regard the matter more favourably.' Amused and curious—and perhaps tempted by the notion of causing a mild scandal—Matilda found the general disapproval yielding, first to her expeditions on horseback within the confines of the royal parks and gardens, and then to those in the streets and squares of the capital. Not only did the younger women copy her, but she was praised by the press. ('At last, Matilda, you have taught Danish women to use their legs.') She also formed the habit of walking about Copenhagen with her ladies, and thus greatly increasing her popularity.[4]

Her sickness, so quickly overcome, would now almost certainly be described as a nervous breakdown, long overdue. Her excellent physique combined with her youthful optimism to respond to Struensee's treatment, just as he had known they would; but this was only the first stage of a long-term plan. His ultimate aim was her reconciliation with her husband; thus, directing them both, he would dispose of all his rivals.

Struensee's *festina lente* methods were also those of a physician who, having inaugurated a certain treatment, leaves his patients to look after themselves on the lines he has indicated. He was far too intelligent to

F

touch on the difficulties of Matilda's situation in an officiously sympathetic manner until she herself raised the subject. As soon as her health
was restored, she began to feel the need of improving her circumstances in other ways, and Struensee, observing this change of mood,
anticipated its expression by advising her to be more social. A queen
should not live in retirement, and thus become ignored.

This opening was irresistible. Matilda replied with an account of
the attacks made by Holck and his group on her relationship, such as
it was, with her husband. 'Although I have not ventured to raise this
question until now,' Struensee said, 'I had observed with surprise and
indignation the lack of deference paid to Your Majesty in your own
Court.' He went on, 'The desire of my heart is to serve Your Majesty.
If you would listen to me, I could help you in this as I have in the
matter of your health.'

A short while ago, Matilda might have received this speech as a
piece of impertinence. She now desired Struensee to proceed. He began
by telling her that the King's days of sanity were numbered. Unless he
became dangerous, and had to be confined, he would still, officially,
retain his authority, which would then fall to the person most likely
to influence him. Why should this be Holck—or even Bernstorff?
Surely the position was Her Majesty's. But she could only achieve it
by re-establishing herself in the King's affections.

Neither a diplomat nor a schemer, Matilda rebelled against this plan.
Also, it seemed to her that Struensee's attitude was extremely suspect.
She remembered that everyone else on whom Christian had become
dependent had succeeded in estranging her from him. She now
detested her husband—why should Struensee want to bring them
together?

'The King', that gentleman replied, 'will have to be ruled by
someone. And it would be more to my interest that he should be ruled
by Your Majesty than by another.' He added that Christian genuinely
desired a reconciliation: but he needed encouragement. As Matilda
remained suspicious, Struensee described his own hopes. He had been
so favoured by Christian as to rise from nothing to an excellent
position, in which he wished to remain. Holck and Bernstorff would
throw him out of it as soon as the King's mind gave way, and one
of the two would then become supreme, thus further relegating and
humiliating the Queen. Whichever favourite governed Christian
would eventually be ousted by a rival, and the fate of such persons was
not one Struensee wished to share. He wanted to work for both the

King and Queen; and Matilda could bring about this arrangement by dominating a husband who needed her rule. Christian was unfit to reign; the sceptre lay ready to her hand. But if she continued to hesitate, Holck, or at best, Bernstorff, would seize it—and then ... Matilda remained doubtful and uneasy. Struensee said no more, and seems to have been dismissed with the promise that she would think over his suggestions. It is worth considering what effect they would have had if he had not been handsome, distinguished and exceptionally charming.

At this time, Struensee wore his own hair, unpowdered; it was light brown and very thick. His eyes were blue; his profile was aquiline. His tall figure stood out in any gathering, and his quiet elegance was the expensive substitute for simplicity. While his appearance drew all eyes, his address never disappointed; he listened or conversed in the manner of a man well aware of the force of his own personality. In fact, Matilda had never met anyone like him.

There remained one difficulty which she did not think even he could solve—Christian's artificial and sneering gallantry of manner whenever he addressed her. She could not penetrate that barrier. It antagonized her more effectively than any other form of hostility, and was far more chilling than violence or abuse. During her next talk with Struensee she described her horror of this approach. No doubt he had already observed it; he may have thought that if she could bring herself to be friendly, Christian would discard that particular weapon. Whether he did or not, the situation gradually eased itself between December 1769 and January 1770, partly through Christian's increasing amenability. The Queen's response, faint at first, became quite natural —artificiality was beyond her—and she tolerated when she could not ignore, her husband's caprices. It was at about this time that Struensee told her, 'Your Majesty requires a confidant—and the best kind is one whom the King trusts. The misfortune of persons of Your Majesty's rank is that of having no equals, and being surrounded by inferiors and sycophants.'[5]

Then, suddenly, disaster fell on Copenhagen. Smallpox swept over the city and its environs. Twelve hundred children died. To Matilda's frantic appeals, Struensee replied that the Prince of Denmark must be vaccinated—and the entire faculty sprang to arms. Such a notion was fantastic—impossible—murderous. At last, the upstart quack had revealed himself for what he was: the embodiment of evil.

NOTES

1. Wilkins, *A Queen of Tears*, vol. I, p. 202.
2. Op. cit., p. 192; Nors, *Court of Christian VII*, p. 216.
3. Wilkins, op. cit., vol. I, p. 192.
4. C. F. L. Wraxall, *Life and Times*, vol. I, p. 218; Reverdil, *Mémoires*, p. 149; Falkensjold, *Mémoires*, p. 26.
5. Reverdil, op. cit., pp. 150–51; Wilkins, op. cit., vol. I, pp. 211 ff.

VII

Achievement

'WE HAVE no liberty of choice between good and evil,' declared Struensee's favourite author, whose *De l'Esprit* was publicly burnt in Paris. He continued, 'Self-interest, founded on the love of pleasure and fear of pain, is the spring of judgement, action, affection.'

Struensee's enemies generally quoted this and similar cynicisms as inspiring all his actions; and because few if any of them had seriously studied Helvetius's theories, they did not connect the German doctor's achievements with one of the philosopher's more important messages — 'True happiness is only to be found in making the interest of one that of all.'

In his way, Struensee was rather an idealist than a buccaneer. Reverdil, who was allowed to return to Denmark later on, soon became aware of this, and admired him accordingly. He thought him ruthless, rash and far too self-confident, especially in his approach to the Queen, whom he dominated from the moment that he persuaded her to let him vaccinate her son. Yet Reverdil perceived a streak of genius in Struensee, although he deplored his disregard of the conventions. This brilliant innovator now inclined to carry out his schemes without waiting upon events; and the ease of his success encouraged him to believe that he would always be able to do so.

At first, Matilda was so unwilling to let the Prince be vaccinated that Struensee's reassurances had no effect until he pointed out that delay might be fatal. Ignoring the protests of the Court physicians, she then consented, and they retired to Fredericksberg with the two-year-old heir, whom Matilda nursed under Struensee's direction. Thus they spent some ten days in isolation; the Prince took the infection without mishap; as his mother and Struensee spent the nights watching over and comforting him, the courtiers began to say that they were lovers. It was not so. At this time, Matilda was concerned only for her boy's progress; she gave no thought to her reputation. Her early upbringing had combined with Christian's behaviour to make her heedless of gossip. Just as she had once been aware that her mother was spending hours alone with Bute, so Matilda took it for granted that Struensee would be in and out of her son's sick-room by night and by day.

The result was justified by the Prince's rapid recovery—a fearful set-back for Struensee's rivals. He had forced through what they thought of as a very dangerous process with the utmost coolness; if he did feel anxiety, no one suspected it, Matilda least of all. Now her faith in him was unassailable—and that of her husband firmer than ever. Neither could do without him: he had become their sheet anchor; their alliance depended rather on him than on one another.

So Christian and Matilda began to reach an understanding, partly because it was becoming easier for her to ignore his vagaries. As his powers failed, he ceased to trouble her, or those responsible for his kingdom. The brothels knew him no more; and thus Holck's hold over him loosened. He did not even want to appear in public; when he had to do so, he seemed unaware of his surroundings. He clung to Struensee—and also to his wife. They had become his guardians; it was as if he felt safer with them than with anyone else.

Christian was therefore indifferent as to whether Holck went or stayed; while Struensee, whose ally he had once been, owed the Count nothing, quite apart from the fact that Holck's function as Christian's procurer and go-between had come to an end. But Matilda, who considered that her hopes of happiness in marriage had been destroyed by Holck's malice, was determined to get rid of him, and desired Struensee to bring this about. Struensee pointed out that the Count was negligible; his fangs were drawn. At last Holck, seeing his power slipping away, appealed to Bernstorff to use his influence against their common enemy before it was too late. Bernstorff dismissed his warnings. A middle-class professional could not possibly harm either the Prime Minister of Denmark or a nobleman of Holck's standing. Struensee had been, and would no doubt continue to be, very useful; his powers were limited to his medical capacity. A few weeks later, Matilda suggested that he should be given the posts of Christian's reader and private secretary, which entailed his being made a Councillor as well. Bernstorff maintained that this promotion, being merely Struensee's reward for services rendered to the Prince of Denmark, was of no significance.

When Holck retired, defeated, the Russian Ambassador, Filosofov, entered the lists. He had formerly had great influence with Christian;

now, assuming that this was still the case, he warned the King against Struensee, after persuading Gunning to do the same. Christian appeared not to heed either diplomat, and made no comment. A little later, he reported his talks with them to Matilda and Struensee, so that the doctor, already aware of Filosofov's enmity (they had once courted the same lady), prepared himself for an attack.

It came during an interval at the opera. The Russian was in the habit of spitting, as were most of his compatriots, but in such a manner as not ostensibly to offend. He now deliberately bespattered the German's coat, in the presence of several courtiers.

Struensee realized that this provocation could not be met by a challenge; the difference between his rank and Filosofov's made that impossible. He therefore behaved as if the assault was accidental, wiped his coat and walked away. A few moments later, he was sent for to the royal box, to be followed by the furious Russian, who spat on him again. Struensee then challenged him. 'In my country,' said Filosofov, 'Ambassadors do not fight with physicians—they thrash them.'

It was obvious to the spectators that Filosofov, an elderly man, would have some difficulty in defeating Struensee in this manner. And that the representative of Catherine the Great should set his valets on the favourite attendant of his mistress's principal ally was out of the question. The quarrel was hushed up, through Bernstorff, whom Filosofov warned in vain. 'If you do not get rid of Struensee,' he said, 'he will get rid of you'—and was ignored.[1]

After this triumph, Struensee, who now had the entrée to Christian's private apartments, and dined with him and Matilda several times a week, was unobtrusively powerful. With the friendship of Brandt and the tolerance of Bernstorff, he had a strong backing, quite apart from the favour of the King and Queen. He was given suites of rooms in the palaces of Christiansborg and Fredericksberg, a large salary and equal standing with the Danish aristocracy; so it seemed to Bernstorff that he had reached his peak. While not entirely approving, the Prime Minister made no attempt to reduce Struensee's powers; it did not occur to him that the young man's ambitions and schemes were those of a politician and a revolutionary. (Bernstorff had never studied Helvétius.) Nor did he take in the full extent of Matilda's dependence on Struensee—nor the uses to which he might put it.

Towards the end of the eighteenth century and throughout the nineteenth, Struensee was described as a cold-blooded intriguer, an *arriviste* without ideals, faith or honour. His care for the less privileged classes of the nation he had made his own, his qualities as a reformer, his dislike of cruelty and tyranny, were dismissed as part of a cleverly worked out pose, designed to impress those he wished to dominate. That he presently used both Christian and Matilda to achieve political supremacy was condemned in the strongest terms; that they and their people benefited, if only for a time, by his manipulation of that supremacy was either forgotten or passed over as accidental.

A closer consideration of Struensee's character, while complicating the issue, reveals a mass of contradictions. He was calculating and impetuous, perceptive and heedless, self-contained and outspoken. His values were rather those of a thinker than of a materialist; and his attitude towards the medieval *mores* of the Danish administration was constructively critical. He had no desire to amass great wealth and live in idleness—he was a worker. His standards exactly matched his plan of work—to dress shabbily and go unattended would have weakened his authority and diminished his prestige—which he intended to carry out through a partnership with Matilda. When she fell in love with him, he so responded as to give her the greatest happiness she had ever known. Obtaining the minimum, in a worldly sense, for himself—he intended to live like any other courtier or Minister—he delighted in her company as much for its own sake as for the benefits it brought him. Her indignation at Filosofov's insults, Holck's jealousy and her ladies' attacks ('I am enraged with this scoundrel,' exclaimed Madame von Gramm, 'I wish I could give him a hundred cuts and send him back to where he came from') was not made use of by Struensee, who looked on revenge as uncivilized and petty. He accepted the Queen's devotion gratefully; his advance was courteous and gentle. Chivalrous in his approach—consciously so, no doubt—he served his probation as physician, adviser and friend before taking the final step.

This process reached its climax in May 1770, just before Matilda's nineteenth birthday. In the preceding weeks, she had spent whole days with Struensee, walking, riding, driving, playing cards—and listening while he read aloud. He read well; but then he did everything well. 'I owe him a great debt for all he has done for me,' she told her ladies, adding innocently, 'He always takes my part. And he has so much sense and goodness.'[2]

One evening, Struensee was reading to Matilda in her boudoir; they were alone, sitting on a sofa. He paused, broke off, looked down at her; then the book was laid aside.[3] Reverdil, to whom he later described this scene, was strangely moved, although disapproving. A queen and a foreign doctor! It was wrong—deplorable—*lèse-majesté*. Yet neither of the lovers appeared furtive or ashamed; they continued to go about together, openly, as usual; and the King accompanied them. He looked ill and worn, but was perfectly contented, as long as he could be with his wife and their friend; he fretted only when they left him to himself. He also was happier than at any time in his life, for now no one forced him to do what he did not like; and he had retired into a world of his own.

For some time, it had been common knowledge that he was a husband in name only, and that he could no longer perform such monarchical duties as he had troubled to undertake in his days of comparative normality. Yet although he had become a cypher, he was still, from time to time, paraded, and the majority of his subjects did not know that signing the papers Bernstorff put before him was all he could accomplish. From a distance—driving out, between Struensee and Matilda, opening a ball, seated on his throne at a reception—he appeared much as he always had; and Bernstorff took care to shield him from any contacts which might betray his real state. But Christian did not like Bernstorff; he was afraid of the man he dimly visualized as representing duty and responsibility, while Struensee and Matilda were his protectors and friends.

Matilda's happiness in Struensee's company was enhanced by the fact that she was beginning to exercise the authority and occupy the position hitherto denied her. She was sorry for her husband, and invariably kind to him; he had become a dull, semi-invalid child, who must be cared for and indulged according to the precepts laid down by her lover. So they were all three happy together; for Christian neither understood nor interrupted her talks with Struensee, who delighted in training her in her new duties; he ignored the resentment and jealousy thereby created. As long as the Lex Regia remained in force, and Bernstorff, as Prime Minister, refused to curb Struensee's growing domination, the doctor was impregnable.

Very soon, Struensee began to treat Matilda as an equal; and she welcomed and encouraged this advance. There must be no barriers between her and the man whose love was her whole life. For she believed, and not unreasonably, in his devotion. She had given him all he most needed and desired; through her, he saw his great destiny being fulfilled; she was beautiful, ardent, eager to learn. They were perfectly matched. So it was that, as Reverdil observed, 'This princess hardly took her eyes off him, insisted on his presence at all gatherings, and allowed him, publicly, to take liberties which would have ruined the reputation of any ordinary woman, such as riding in her coach and walking alone with her in the gardens and woods. Had he but been of the nobility! But Struensee, physician, reader ... and thus of the second rank, was not yet a high Court official.'[4]

Some years after Matilda's death, her defenders laid the whole responsibility for the affair on Struensee's machinations; they maintained that for many weeks the Queen had tried to resist temptation. The proof of this struggle lay (they said) in her having written, with the point of a diamond, on the window of her room, 'O keep me innocent, make others great!'[5] It seems unlikely, to say the least, that this inscription, which was destroyed in the fire of 1859, could have come from Matilda's hand. Her love for the man to whom she owed all her happiness was as innocent, in her own eyes, as if they had been husband and wife. She gloried in it; and was rather mistaken than sinful in her refusal to conceal their connection. What she could not or would not grasp was its danger for them both; and this blindness was inevitable in the case of a young woman whose forebears—Sophia-Dorothea of Celle, George I, George II and her own parents—had all had extra-marital relations. Even her strait-laced brother had made no secret of his passion for Sarah Lennox, before being forced into marriage with a plain, dull wife—a marriage that ended in the tragedy of porphyrian disease. Matilda was no exception; and her recklessness resulted from a disastrous upbringing.

Few of her contemporaries censured her; of those who did, Queen Juliana was the leader. Matilda's ladies described Mademoiselle von Eyben as her go-between ('She is the only one capable of ruining this child!' exclaimed Madame von Gramm), but mistakenly. No go-between was needed once Matilda had given herself up to the raptures of first love. Meanwhile, she did her best to please Christian. Remembering his preference for seeing women in male dress, she had herself measured for several sets of small-clothes, military overcoats, gold-laced vests and top-boots. Christian was charmed, and insisted on her wearing them—with plumed beaver hat, spurs and lace ruffles—whenever she rode out, astride, attended by Struensee. Matilda herself so delighted in this flouting of convention that she often wore male dress both indoors and out. It did not really suit her exuberant, ultra-feminine outlines; but as her husband praised it, and Struensee had advised her to indulge his whims, she was more often seen in the buckskin breeches and scarlet coat of a cavalier than in the tight-laced gowns of ceremony.

Her ladies exclaimed in horror. 'If only', cried Madame von Gramm, 'she were well made, I could understand her walking about in that costume; but just think of her hips, her—quarters!'[6]

Worse was to follow. In the last week of May 1770 Queen Sophia Magdalena died, was embalmed and lay in state in the palace of Christiansborg. Matilda came to see the body dressed in her military riding-habit and leaning on Struensee's arm. This gesture was inspired by Christian who, unable to bring himself to look upon death, sent his wife, thus unsuitably attired and escorted by her lover, in his place. There was, of course, an outcry—and so Bernstorff employed his former tactic of distracting public attention from the scandal by arranging for Christian and Matilda to visit Holstein. But he had to let them take Struensee with them. The King utterly refused to be parted from him; and they all set off together.

NOTES

1. Wilkins, *A Queen of Tears*, vol. I, p. 206.
2. Op. cit., p. 224.
3. Reverdil, *Mémoires*, p. 152.
4. Op. cit., p. 153.
5. Wilkins, op. cit., vol. I, p. 218.
6. Nors, *Court of Christian VII*, p. 118.

VIII

Triumph

MATILDA COULD not prevent Holck accompanying the Court to
Holstein: but his doing so did not benefit him, for he was ignored by
Christian, who, attended by pages of Struensee's choice, was always
with his wife. Meanwhile, the Ministers left in charge of the Government received orders from the King—in fact, from Struensee—that
they must take no action, diplomatic or other, without his written
permission. Thus, all approaches from Catherine the Great were to be
rejected until Christian's return, when Struensee intended to inaugur-
ate his anti-Russian policy.

Bernstorff heard nothing of this arrangement until the royal party
reached the castle of Gottorp in Schleswig, the residence of Prince
Charles of Hesse, who was Viceroy of both duchies. It had never
occurred to him that Struensee was at last in a position to compose and
then make Christian subscribe to orders of national import, although
he had long known that his master would sign any papers put before
him. Now, realizing that he had been superseded, Bernstorff still
discounted the extent of Struensee's power, as also the possibility of his
bringing about a split with Russia. As Prime Minister of Denmark, and
therefore, through Matilda, England's ally, he was sure of his own
supremacy. It then dawned on him that the Queen had ceased to
represent her brother's interests, and was determined to break the
alliance with the Empress whose envoy had insulted her lover. Bernstorff became very uneasy; but even now he could not believe that he
might be the next victim, or that Christian would rather be guided
by Struensee than by himself.

Prince Charles's horror at the change in his brother-in-law lessened
after a day or two. At this time, travel and different surroundings
nearly always brought Christian back to a semblance of normality;
he enjoyed his visit, and appeared to be on excellent terms with his
wife. The Prince was, however, disgusted by the spectacle of their

joint dependence on Struensee, whom he disliked at sight—a dislike
not shared by the Princess.

Struensee, aware that Prince Charles would do his best to estrange
himself and Matilda, had made her promise that she would spend the
minimum of time alone with him; but it was difficult for her to keep
her word. After an hour's tête-á-tête, Matilda, taking Charles's arm,
said, 'Now, escort me to Princess Louise's apartments—but do not
take me through the ante-chamber'—where she assumed that Struensee would be waiting. 'We almost ran along the corridor', the Prince
continues, 'to the side door of the staircase, and then we saw some of
the suite coming downstairs. The Queen saw Struensee among them,
and said hastily, "I must go back, do not keep me." "I cannot very well
leave Your Majesty alone in the passage—"' Charles began; but Matilda
cried, 'No—no! Go to the Princess!' and ran down the corridor. 'I
was astonished,' he continues, 'but obeyed her orders. She was always
ill at ease with me when Struensee was present. At table, he invariably
seated himself opposite her.'

After dinner—'which was dull'—the Prince recalls, they sat down
to cards. 'And then', he goes on, 'I hardly like to describe Struensee's
behaviour to the Queen, or repeat the remarks he dared address to
her, openly, while he leant his arm on the table, close to her. "Well,
why do you not play?"—"Cannot you hear?" and so forth. I was
grieved to my heart,' he adds, not realizing that Matilda liked to have
Struensee's advice over trivialities. Prince Charles thought that she
was afraid of him—'She trembled, like a caught bird, when he spoke
to her'—thus failing to grasp that her agitation was partly caused by
her dread of the Hesses' disapproval of her lover. This possibility did
not trouble Struensee himself at first.[1]

A week or two later, his attitude changed. Matilda was very fond
of the Hesses, because they had tried, although without success, to
protect her from Christian's insults in the early days of her marriage;
and now it seemed to Struensee that there was a danger of the Prince's
influence weakening his own. He therefore suggested to Christian—no
doubt on grounds of health—that the Court party should leave Gottorp for the castle of Traventhal, a much smaller establishment, in
Holstein; but Matilda's falling ill delayed their departure. Struensee
then sent for Brandt, whom Holck had ousted from favour a year ago.
'Vous avez l'air de voir un spectre—avez-vous peur?' said Brandt,
delighted at Holck's dismay. 'Ce n'est pas les spectres que je crains,
mais les revenants,' Holck replied—reasonably enough; for as soon as

they reached Traventhal, he, his wife, his sister and Mademoiselle von Eyben were all desired to return to Copenhagen; the reason given was that there would not be enough room for them and their attendants in the castle.[2] Now, of all Struensee's competitors, only Bernstorff remained.

The inhabitants of the duchies, who had been eagerly awaiting their first sight of Matilda, were shocked and disappointed when, at Christian's desire, she not only appeared in male dress, but insisted on privacy. She, Christian and their diminished Court seldom showed themselves, thus creating rumours of secret orgies and general dissipation. Count Rantzau, whom Struensee, according to his promise, sent for and installed, was cynically amused. 'When I was a wild young man,' he said, 'everybody else was respectable. Now that age has sobered me, everybody seems to have gone crazy.' To Bernstorff he described the King's new circle as a pack of scoundrels, and the Prime Minister began to look on him as an ally. Rantzau then decided that he was going to join with Struensee in bringing about Bernstorff's downfall.[3]

He therefore helped to ostracize him, so that, within a very short time, Bernstorff could not even approach the King, let alone talk to him privately. He was made to dine apart, and, somehow, found himself separated from Christian and Matilda when they drove out or sat down to cards. In this way, Struensee hoped to engineer Bernstorff's resignation; but the old man refused to yield. Meanwhile, Rantzau was highly favoured. Matilda gave him a diamond snuff-box— Christian had bought it in London for a thousand guineas, but made no objection to her taking it away—and presented colours to the Count's regiment, of which she became honorary colonel. At his request, she stood to the Court painter, Als, for her portrait in uniform. Smiling, she looks out from the canvas in triumph, well aware that this particular costume is very becoming.

The whole party then left Traventhal to be entertained by Rantzau at his castle of Ascheberg; and here Bernstorff taxed Struensee with Matilda's change of attitude towards himself. Was she working against him? The doctor replied non-committally, but made it clear that Christian—in other words, Struensee himself—had no intention of letting Denmark join Russia in her war against Turkey. In great alarm, Bernstorff informed George III's representatives of this betrayal, and of the scandal caused by his sister's relations with Struensee. (Frederick the Great's comments had been particularly acid.) After conferring with his mother and the Duke of Gloucester, George III arranged for them to visit Princess Augusta and her husband in Brunswick, summoning Matilda and Christian to meet them on their way back to Copenhagen, so that the Princess-Dowager might remonstrate with her youngest child, point out her disloyalty and effect Struensee's dismissal.

Unwillingly, Matilda agreed to the Brunswick meeting, and in the last week of May she and Christian, accompanied by Struensee and their suite, returned to Traventhal, on the understanding that from there they would set off to stay with Princess Augusta. They remained at Traventhal for a month, in the hope that the Princess-Dowager would change her mind, when news came of her arrival at her son-in-law's principality, where a magnificent reception for the King and Queen of Denmark was in preparation. The days went by—and there was no sign of the visitors. Then Matilda sent her Grand Marshal with a regretful message. She was ill—too ill to travel so far; most unfortunately, her visit must be cancelled. Her doctor, whom she did not name, had said that such a long journey could not be risked in her state of health; the nature of her illness was not described.

The Princess-Dowager, who had been informed that Matilda was in the habit of getting up at five to hunt and going to bed at midnight, replied that in that case they had better meet at Lüneburg, a much shorter distance from Copenhagen. Advised by Struensee, Matilda decided to give in, and she and Christian met the Princess-Dowager in the last week of June 1770. They were attended by Struensee—and afterwards Christian confided in Reverdil. He had been very pleased, and still was, he said, at his wife's intimacy with Struensee, who supplied a felt want, that of the *cicisbeo*, an essential in all sophisticated circles. He rejoiced in this fashionable convenience, while being left to amuse himself in his own way. He presently lapsed into what would now be described as another episode of complete withdrawal into his own world, rousing himself, a few evenings later, to tease his favourite dog, Gourmand, who replied with barks and growls. 'Can you bark?' said the King. 'Well then, you can be a Councillor,' proposed the creature's health and voted him a salary.[4]

Meanwhile, the Princess-Dowager's journey to Brunswick had begun inauspiciously. Some said that she had set off to meet Bute, and so she was hissed as she left Carlton House and insulted at Canterbury. Others believed that the behaviour of her sons, the Dukes of Gloucester and Cumberland, was driving her out of England—for Cumberland had been cited as co-respondent in the Grosvenor divorce case, and Gloucester was supposed to be the lover of Lady Waldegrave, Horace Walpole's niece, whom in fact he had secretly married. On her arrival, it became clear that there was no love lost between the Princess-Dowager and Princess Augusta; the younger lady was very unhappy, and now blamed her mother for the disaster of her marriage. Of her six children, two were insane and another had been blind from birth. (The youngest, Caroline, was to be even more unfortunate, for she married the Prince Regent.) Finally, at Lüneburg, this over-ambitious parent had to face the consequences of the alliance forced upon Caroline Matilda—a husband almost completely withdrawn, and an all-powerful lover who, although ignored, presided over their first conversation. Not only so: the gentle little Princess of less than four years ago was now a cold and haughty young woman, who indicated that, as Queen of Denmark, she would be neither advised nor reproved.

Finding it impossible to eliminate Struensee, the Princess-Dowager, who knew that he had no English, addressed Matilda in that tongue, only to be told that she had forgotten it, and could not understand a word. The browbeaten lady, accepting this rebuff, continued in German, more guardedly, with a general statement on the duties of a queen. Matilda listened unmoved and, replying that it was too late in the evening for further discussion, left the room.

The Princess-Dowager was not so easily put down; early next morning, she summoned Matilda to her bedroom—the whole party had been established in a house in the main street of the town—and asked her if she really intended to dismiss her husband's Prime Minister, adding that this would be disastrous to the Anglo-Danish cause. 'Pray, Madam,' Matilda replied, 'allow me to govern my kingdom as I please.'

The older woman then launched into a diatribe about the favours shown to Struensee—a doctor, an insolent nobody—and threatened her daughter with public disgrace. Matilda replied with a mocking reference to Lord Bute.

The ensuing silence was broken by the entrance of Christian, who presently, as instructed, mumbled something about his mother-in-law and Gloucester visiting them in Copenhagen. She angrily refused, and the young couple left, reappearing in the afternoon for a formal farewell. A few days later, George III's envoy, Mr Woodford, reported to his master on 'the agitation visible in Mr Struensee upon his arrival at Lüneburg, and the joy that could be seen in his countenance as the

CAROLINE MATILDA
IN UNIFORM *(Als)*

THE CASTLE OF HIRSCHHOLM *(from a print in the Rosenborg Museum)*

STRUENSEE AS DICTATOR

moment of departure approached'. He added that the Princess-Dowager left in great distress, while Matilda was perfectly serene. Mother and daughter never met again.

'An extraordinary Princess,' was Horace Walpole's summing up of Matilda's behaviour. 'She showed a lofty spirit—but singular manners.' Walpole refused to believe in the reports of Christian's insanity; he was somewhat eccentric, perhaps—but no more.[5]

Returning to Copenhagen in time for the annual archery festival, Christian and Matilda were received as warmly as if they had never offended, and crowned their triumph by taking part in the competition. The King left his carriage, only to shoot and miss; Matilda, who arrived riding astride in male dress, hit the popinjay, to the delight of her younger subjects. (The older folk thought that she should have appeared beside her husband, in the carriage.) Everyone was struck by the contrast between her Amazonian radiance and his huddled posture and vacant expression. So her people became accustomed to seeing the Queen represent the monarchy, while Christian spent most of his time in the palace, teasing his dogs and playing with his pages. 'She is the better man of the two,' was soon a catch-phrase.[6]

After a series of these contrasting appearances, Christian and Matilda moved into the newly acquired and most beautiful of all their palaces —Hirschholm, formerly the property of Queen Sophia Magdalena— destroyed some thirty years later. Set on an island in the middle of a lake, beyond which lay the gardens, and beyond them the forest, it was so splendidly furnished as almost to rival Versailles. The old Queen had built it half a century before her death, adding to its wonders every year. Its magnificence did not preclude privacy, and so made a perfect setting for the idyll upon which Matilda now entered with her lover.

Christian was not neglected; he always accompanied them on their drives, following in the carriage when they left it to walk, arm in arm, along the bridle paths. Nor were they idle. Struensee's hours of work were very long, comprising interviews and discussions with the staff of secretaries and envoys that was still, nominally, the King's. Towards the end of the day Christian signed whatever documents were presented to him; he had no other duties, and was nearly always treated with courtesy and consideration; so he too led an ideal life, for he and Matilda seldom quarrelled—until a return to his former malice brought him back to what he had once been. On the last of these occasions, he told her that Madame von Gahler, the wife of a general,

G

was Struensee's mistress, and offered to prove it by 'discovering' him in that lady's arms.

In an agony of suspicion, Matilda—none knew Struensee's powers better than she—was foolish enough to consent. She and her husband stole into the suite occupied by the Gahlers, only to find them sleeping peacefully together.[7] Thereafter, no more mischief was made. On his achievement of power and the final elimination of Bernstorff, whom Christian dismissed in September 1770, Struensee remained entirely devoted to Matilda, and to the accomplishment of his reforms.

He, Rantzau and Brandt, who now formed a triumvirate, settled large pensions on those dismissed from office—Bernstorff received six thousand rix-dollars and retained his seat on the Council—while keeping their own Court within the Court in all the royal residences. Appearances were sustained at Hirschholm, described by Rantzau as 'cette nouvelle Cythère', by Matilda and Christian dining with their attendants in one banqueting-hall, while Struensee, unless asked to join them, sat at the head of the table in the exquisite Chamber of the Rose, of which the walls were decorated with designs in silver, mother-of-pearl and rock crystal; the ceilings and doors had been painted by Italian artists.

Matilda was always in the highest spirits; she had developed a vein of wit (she was an excellent mimic), dressed more elaborately than ever before, and charmed a circle which, unless Struensee was present, might have become rather dull; for Christian, staring, dazzled, at his wife, hardly spoke, politics were not discussed, and the other ladies' range of conversation was limited. The Queen's happiness enabled her to carry all before her; she revelled in the exercise of her profession, and was adored by her subjects. Her popularity masked Struensee's authority within the kingdom; beyond it, the representatives of Russia and England manoeuvred in vain. Gloucester came to stay, attempted to change the situation and returned, defeated. George III's letter to his sister desiring her to restore Bernstorff and dismiss Struensee arrived after the ex-Minister had retired to his country estate. Gunning was denied audience, and Rantzau had been instructed by Struensee to open discussions for a rapprochement with the French Ambassador. 'Their Danish Majesties', Gunning reported, 'are inaccessible to everyone but Mr Rantzau and the Favourite.' To George III's indignant protests Matilda coolly replied that in future all communications on policy must be made to her through her Ministers, who would answer according to her—or rather, Struensee's—instructions.

At about this time, Struensee outlined his plans for the reform of the Government to Brandt, who found them admirable, but doubted his being able to carry them out easily or with speed. Struensee did not trust Rantzau, violently anti-Russian though he was. (He had been dismissed from the Imperial Court by Catherine's orders.) Struensee relied principally on Brandt and on General Gahler, whom Gunning described as 'smooth, designing and self-interested'.[8]

After consulting Christian in such a manner as to give the impression that he was about to carry out his master's commands, Struensee began his civil revolution by tackling the problem of the national debt. This, the King was told, would be followed by arrangements for the freedom of the press and General Gahler's appointment as Chief of the War Department. Christian seemed to understand—and signed the necessary orders.

NOTES

1. Hesse, *Mémoires*, pp. 50–51.
2. Nors, *Court of Christian VII*, p. 125.
3. Reverdil, *Mémoires*, p. 156.
4. Op. cit., p. 154; C. F. L. Wraxall, *Life and Times*, vol. I, p. 240.
5. Walpole, *Memoirs*, vol. IV, pp. 161–3; Jesse, *Memoirs of the Reign of George III*, vol. I, p. 423; Reverdil, op. cit., p. 159; Falkensjold, *Mémoires*, p. 44; Wilkins, op. cit., vol. I, p. 250.
6. Wilkins, op. cit., vol. I, p. 252.
7. Nors, op. cit., p. 125.
8. Reverdil, op. cit., p. 163; Wilkins, op. cit., vol. I, p. 259.

IX

The Dictator

THE PURPOSE of Struensee's dictatorship was that of general reform.
Born and educated abroad, he observed the condition of Denmark
rather as he would have diagnosed the state of some sick person for
whom he had been called in to prescribe. He was not so much interested
in making his adopted country more powerful as in curing her ills and
fitting her to take her place in the modern world; and so he determined
to put her potentialities to the fullest possible use with the greatest
possible speed, through the Lex Regia. His schemes eventually entailed
the passing of several thousand laws; at least twenty years were needed
for their implementation; his personal government extended over less
than two; even so, some of his reorganization became effective and
permanent.

The trouble was that Struensee's ideal kingdom belonged rather to
the twentieth than to the eighteenth century. The improvements he
now put in hand were so far in advance of his time as to be incompre-
hensible and, in the end, odious, to the majority; the resultant cur-
tailing of the upper classes' privileges gave them the impression
that the German intruder was deliberately planning the destruction of
their order. In fact, he intended to restrict their power while using it
according to the precepts of Helvétius, and thus benefiting both them
and those they oppressed.

Struensee simplified and speeded up his administration by dominating the Council of State. Under Christian's hand and seal the ministers
were ordered to submit all decisions to him before putting them into
practice; the King—i.e. Struensee—would presently pass them or not,
as seemed best to himself. So the Council could only advise; the Lex
Regia eliminated any resistance. They were then told that they would
no longer be given audiences; all communications must be made in
writing; discussion and argument were thus abolished.

Christian was still, officially, fulfilling his function as absolute ruler of
Denmark; his people, seeing him appear in state from time to time,

looked on him as such; but those in Government circles, realizing that Matilda, under Struensee's direction, had taken over his authority, knew that nothing could be effected without her leave. 'Her power', Gunning reported, 'is unlimited,' adding that she had again refused him audience and desired her Chamberlain to tell him, 'You will be informed when Her Majesty has any orders for you. At present, she has none.'[1]

Having relegated the English alliance, Struensee set about clarifying his attitude towards Russia. Unlike Matilda, he was no longer interested in humiliating Filosofov, whom he could now afford to disregard; but he had determined to free Denmark from the jurisdiction of Catherine the Great. His appointment of Rantzau as second Head of the War Department enraged the Empress, who, having dismissed the Count from her own Court, assumed that he was permanently disgraced. Feeling herself personally insulted by his promotion, she ordered Filosofov to protest against it on her behalf, which he did with great violence and rudeness. Matilda replied by informing him, through her Chamberlain, that he would no longer be received. Filosofov then asked to be recalled, and just before his departure requested a private audience with Christian, which was refused. 'Your Excellency may take leave of His Majesty at an ordinary reception,' he was told—and left without taking any leave at all.[2]

Struensee, who had no intention of going to war with Russia, then made Christian's excuses for this rebuff to the Empress, on the grounds that, having discontinued private audiences, he could not make an exception in favour of Filosofov. Instead of addressing Catherine as 'Madame my Sister', his letter began 'Madame' and ended, as from himself, with 'I have the honour to be, Madame, Your Imperial Majesty's very humble and obedient servant', so as to make it clear that direct contact with Christian was at an end.[3] Struensee was censured and mocked for his ignorance of etiquette; it occurred to no one that this breach of custom was intentional, designed to show the Empress with whom she had to deal. Catherine refused to accept the apology, and demanded Bernstorff's reinstallation; receiving no reply, she threatened to bombard Copenhagen.

Struensee remained unmoved. He knew that although the Empress had ships and armaments, she lacked trained sailors; he therefore fitted out three ships of the line and two frigates, and gave orders for the building of several other vessels. Catherine, still involved in her

Turkish war, dared not invade, and confined herself to abusing Matilda and her *cicisbeo* in the coarsest terms. 'Give them enough rope and they will hang themselves,' she concluded. Struensee, having nothing to fear from England or Russia, continued his approaches to France—and went on with his internal reforms.

Although these were not so successful as his foreign policy, he was undaunted by the attacks made on his relations with Matilda from the press he himself had freed. The journalists, inspired and paid by his enemies, began with criticisms of his and the Queen's disregard of the conventions; this censure, increasing in severity, reached its climax in obscene squibs and cartoons, which enthralled the public and detracted from Matilda's popularity. But as a comparatively small number of these productions reached the provinces, and fewer still found their way to the remote districts of the kingdom, the harm they did was localized and temporary. Then, the excitement caused by decrees which affected the lives and fortunes of all the Danish people obliterated every other consideration.

For the Council of State Struensee substituted a Council of Conferences, headed by himself as Master of Requests. This was an advisory body of experts, whose members were his nominees; they supplied him with all the information he needed, while submitting to his decisions. The abolition of the former Council, which had been recruited from the aristocracy, delighted the merchants and the working classes, while infuriating the nobles, who began to organize a movement against Struensee's employees. He defended them by issuing a decree on behalf of those who were owed money by unscrupulous debtors; it was announced that these persons would be seized and imprisoned until they had satisfied their creditors, with the result that 90 per cent of the nobles fled from the capital to their country estates. A third decree forbade the resumption of their Court posts unless they could satisfy the King as to their qualifications. In future, His Majesty would make all such appointments on the grounds of efficiency and merit alone; thus the greater number of Struensee's enemies remained exiled and powerless. Their custom of paying their servants by giving them Government posts was made illegal; and so the administration of the kingdom was taken out of the hands of incompetents, and the number of departments greatly reduced. This was followed by the abolition of such caste privileges as the monopoly of torch-lit carriages by the upper classes. Everyone now had the right to drive out attended by servants carrying torches; and the medieval gloom of Copenhagen gave way to lighted streets, numbered houses and clean pavements.

The police were then forbidden to enter private dwellings without a warrant, and anyone who wished to work on Sundays and feast-days could do so without being imprisoned or fined. The compulsory service of labourers was limited to certain days and hours; and the salt tax, which fell most heavily on the poor, was abolished, together with the export of corn during hard winters, so that the price of flour was halved. This affected, although not too severely, the incomes of those landowners who had been in the habit of selling their grain abroad while their tenants starved.

Matilda then founded a children's hospital, with accommodation for six hundred patients, which was financed by a tax on saddle and carriage horses. Finally, Struensee turned his attention to the Church, and what he, in Christian's name, described as the improvement of morals. 'These cannot', that virtuous monarch was supposed to declare, 'be brought about by police regulations, which are an encroachment on human liberty ... Immoral conduct must be left to the conscience to condemn ... Constraint only generates hypocrisy.' Another decree announced that illegitimate children would no longer be ostracized or denied civil rights, and that their mothers were not to be punished. Thus, child-murder and exposure of unwanted infants became obsolete, and a Foundling Hospital was established under Matilda's patronage, together with a crèche attached to the Lying-In Hospital. To these was added a hospital for the treatment of venereal disease. The clergy then moved into the attack. But Struensee and his Council were ready for them.

Sunday after Sunday, the Lutheran pastors inveighed against this fearful encouragement of vice and the premium set on immorality. The fate of Sodom and Gomorrah was cited with grim regularity, and the increasingly nervous congregations were adjured to hold fast to the good old ways of their fathers. Pamphlets foretelling the doom of Denmark were circulated, peasants threatened with ruin, and soldiers and sailors told to make ready for invasion from rulers who would take advantage of their country's disintegration; but as the benefits of the new laws made themselves felt—as the corpses of unwanted babies no longer met the gaze of the passer-by—as street accidents diminished —as the humble and neglected were given rest and leisure—the diatribes gradually faded away. When the use of the pillory for adulterers was forbidden, the inevitable outcry did not last. And some of those who had begun by disapproving had to admit that no great harm—perhaps no harm at all—had resulted from the freedom bestowed by these startling decrees.

Then Struensee, determined to increase prosperity at the cost of tradition, went too far, too soon. He abolished the enormous number of feast-days, originating from pre-Lutheran times, replacing them with regular public holidays, such as are now held in most European countries, so that everyone shut their shops or left their fields at carefully spaced out intervals.

Once more, the clergy fell upon the Council. This elimination of ancient custom would not only offend the Deity but encourage dissipation. Drunkenness and crime were bound to increase through this capricious restriction. When the new holidays came round, the taverns and brothels would be overcrowded, and violence and rioting would outstrip the efforts of the police.

Struensee replied by throwing open a number of royal parks and gardens, first in the capital and then in the provinces. The castle of Rosenborg, a hunting-box built in the previous century just outside Copenhagen, was fitted up as a place to dance, eat, drink, and play games. Families were no longer separated in their times of leisure. Parents and children went together to Rosenborg, to listen to music, to stroll about the gardens and meet their friends. There were fireworks, shooting galleries, sheltered alleys for lovers and seats under the trees for the old and weary.

So the clergy were silenced. Only the nobles, fulminating helplessly on their estates, remained unreconciled and enraged. They could not be expected to see that the security of their order was being ensured by the improved conditions of those they had crushed and terrorized. That they themselves could still be of use, and therefore honoured, prosperous and respected, was beyond their comprehension. And knowing, as they did, that it was not the feeble creature on the throne, but his adulterous wife and her foreign paramour who were responsible for what they saw as a malicious attack on their hereditary status, they swore to reverse all his evil laws, and drag him and his besotted mistress to destruction. So they looked for leaders—and found them in Queen Juliana and her son. Their and her ultimate aim was to replace Christian by his half-brother. The former heir-presumptive was only fourteen; but his mother could rule for him till he came of age; and the claims of the Prince of Denmark would be disposed of on grounds of health.

Undeterred, Struensee proceeded with his innovations on a cultural level. Sending for his brother, Karl August, he put him in charge of an Academy of Arts and Sciences which was open to anyone qualified to teach or to study, regardless of rank. Those who could not afford the fees were subsidized by the State. Prizes were offered, professors from abroad invited to lecture and expeditions to other continents planned. Such an institution was bound to run at a loss: but Struensee and his advisers, determined that it should go on, scraped up the necessary funds here and there. This extravagance disappointed and bewildered many of those who had supported his earlier decrees; and indeed, he would have been wiser to wait before forcing it on the country. Yet it was as if he dared not delay—as if he felt the hand of Time upon his shoulder, and heard a voice whispering, 'It is later than you think.'

So strong was this feeling, that suddenly, in the plenitude of power and success, he said to Matilda that he was thinking of leaving Denmark. 'I can do no more,' he said. 'Let me go'—and knelt, taking her hand. Appalled, she exclaimed, 'Stay—or you will make me do something fatal.' This scene seems to have taken place in the autumn of 1770, when she must have known that she was carrying his child—how could she let him go? Afterwards, too late, she remembered that moment of foreboding.[4]

Realizing, as she did not, the dangers surrounding them both, Struensee doubled her guard, and began planning the move of the Court to Fredericksberg. Then he turned to a reorganization of the armed forces, where privilege still prevailed over ability. Here, he was moving in a territory for which his talents were utterly unsuited. He was not, and never could be, a man of war. Within a week, he was faced with a mutiny, and the total collapse of the regime.

NOTES

1. Wilkins, *A Queen of Tears*, vol. I, p. 264; Nors, *Court of Christian VII*, p. 138.
2. Reverdil, *Mémoires*, p. 172.
3. Ibid.
4. Falkensjold, *Mémoires*, p. 96.

X

The Edge of Disaster

THE OFFICERS of the Household Cavalry had already been deprived, some of their privileges, and others of their commissions by Struensee's abolition of the honorary posts which went with their hereditary places at Court. This branch of the army was now dispersed, and the other ranks were informed that they were at liberty to join the infantry, or to return to civil life, whichever they preferred.

It was an arbitrary and tactless move, especially as concerned the privates and non-commissioned officers, for they took great pride in their honours, their splendid uniforms and their proximity to the sovereign, and were admired and envied by the civil population. They therefore joined the nobles in threatening to disobey Struensee's order. He was driving back to the palace when he met them marching to protest—two squadrons of armed and furious men, whom he faced alone.

He told them that their grievances would be attended to—so persuasively, that they returned to barracks—and after consultation with Rantzau and General Gahler, decided to rescind the decree, as far as the lower ranks were concerned. He then announced that a new corps of picked men, called the Flying Bodyguard, would be formed, adding that those officers who failed to qualify for a commission were to learn a trade. This last suggestion appalled all classes; it seemed to presage anarchy, and even alarmed Matilda, whose support of her lover began to waver. She begged him to give in, and he did so to the extent of restoring the privileges of the non-commissioned Household Cavalry under their new name. So mutiny was avoided by what the public looked on as the intimidation of Struensee.

He then proceeded with reforms which further infuriated the clergy. Church-going ceased to be obligatory, and the people were told that they might subscribe to whatever faith they preferred—or to none at all, if they were free-thinkers. Struensee then issued decrees making everyone equal before the law; he dismissed corrupt judges and centralized legal administration, thus diminishing the incomes of a number of advocates. He reduced the enormous allowances of diplomats, set up a bureau of tourism, overhauled the admiralty and revised the taxation, pension and title systems.

Throughout Europe, Struensee became known as 'the champion reformer of the world', and in Denmark would have achieved the reputation of a great statesman, if he had not made an error of incredible folly. Hurrying to issue his proclamations, he allowed them to appear in German (he himself had never learnt Danish) and so was marked down as an interfering foreigner; even those whose lives had been changed for the better by his rule, spoke of him as 'the German scoundrel', partly because they suspected him—wrongly—of ill-treating the King. Also, his openly conducted intimacy with the Queen displeased the majority. On this point, it occurred to no one that ever since his accession Christian had been allowed to steal the horse, while Struensee must not now look over the hedge. In the meantime, Matilda's recklessness publicized her adultery. The Danes bitterly resented the resultant scandal; for this they blamed Struensee rather than the Queen, who was still very popular. It was believed that he had drugged the King into acquiescence in order to seduce his wife.

The complete subjugation of the King now became apparent to his people; whereas, if Struensee had had his proclamations printed in Danish, some semblance of the royal authority would have been maintained. The alternative—that of acknowledging that Christian was incapable of rule—was impossible, partly because he was not yet violent; he could still sign any documents presented to him, and had periods of sanity, during which he appeared at receptions or drove out with the Queen. When anyone did manage to approach him with some request, his invariable reply, 'Ask Struensee,' did not give the impression of lunacy. So it was assumed that Struensee had seized his master's power in a brutal and insolent manner, with Matilda's co-operation.

The fact that Christian was perfectly satisfied with his position, and that the administration of the kingdom had improved beyond all recognition, had no effect on the bitter fury of the more articulate and prosperous classes; and very soon their hatred of the dictator and his advisers became general. Like the Israelites who, once delivered from the Egyptians, began to grumble at the inconveniences of Moses's regime, the citizens of Copenhagen pettishly objected to various details, one being the numbering of their houses; this, they said, reduced their status to a dead level, and amounted to a serious deprivation. Another grievance was the Court's use of Hirschholm, which had become the focus, so it was thought, of dissipations that they were not allowed to share. The fact that Rosenborg and the park of Fredericksberg were now public pleasure-grounds had raised their standard—why should they be barred from Hirschholm simply because the Queen had handed it over to her lover and his advisers? Fearful tales began to circulate, enhanced by news of race-meetings and steeplechases on Sundays— which they hastened to attend—when the King presented the prizes. Then Count Brandt added to the scandal by preaching a mock sermon in the chapel. Neither the Queen nor Christian nor Struensee attended this entertainment (they may not even have known about it), but that was passed over, and great play was made in Queen Juliana's circle about the impiety; it was another example, the clergy declared, of the general licence encouraged by Matilda, whose ladies now rode astride, dressed in men's clothes and had abandoned etiquette for informality. The indecencies of Christian's former conduct were forgotten, and he was regarded as a martyr to his wife's self-indulgence and Struensee's ambition.

This campaign resulted in the Queen-Dowager's and her son's ostracism by Christian and Matilda. They were told that the Prince must no longer use the riding-school of Christiansborg, which was reserved for the Queen-Consort, and were invited to Court on formal occasions only. The elder Queen's palace of Fredensborg—which had an equally large riding-school—therefore became the centre of opposition to Struensee's rule. Meanwhile, the landlords and the clergy combined in frightening their tenants into hostility against his Government, which gained strength through panic. They were warned that all these seeming benefits would end in ruin for themselves and the vengeance of the Almighty—and so succumbed once more to terrors which had overshadowed them for generations.

Matilda now became alarmed for her son, who, in his third year, was still very delicate and rapidly becoming unmanageable. She shrank from the thought of his heredity, and saw no way of halting what seemed to be the first symptoms of degeneracy.

Struensee at once took charge. There was nothing amiss, physically or mentally, he said, with the little Prince. His routine must be changed, and he himself would see to the details. He began by dismissing all those servants who had indulged and enfeebled the child by carrying him about instead of letting him walk and run; his tendency to a weak chest was eliminated by his being sent out of doors in all weathers. As he grew stronger, which he did quite soon, his boned garments were replaced by loose suits of silk or linen. A diet of boiled rice, bread, milk and vegetables was substituted for spiced meats, ale and pastries. He was bathed in cold water twice a day, and a single attendant took over from the horde of valets who had run to carry out his orders. So that he should not be lonely, an orphan boy of his own age, known as Little Karl, was established as his companion, with whom he played and squabbled as with an equal. He was taught to pick himself up if he fell, and to find his toys for himself when he lost them. Finally, his meals were no longer set before him, nor was he waited on; food was hidden in the garden, and he had to search for it. He and Little Karl enjoyed this game, which became one of rivalry and competition, until, one winter's day, the Prince was found lying on the ground, half-dead with cold, having been missing for several hours. It was then decided to allow him soup and meat, and—as he had developed chilblains—to warm his rooms and put him in shoes and stockings during cold weather.

Naturally it was said that the heir to the throne was being cruelly used, and treated like an animal. The fact that he had ceased to whine and pout, and seemed quite happy eating out of a wooden bowl and drinking from a pottery mug, merely showed, Struensee's enemies declared, that he was being deliberately degraded; also, all standards of princely behaviour were destroyed by his having to apologize to Little Karl when he himself was found to have taken the offensive. He adored his mother, who spent a great deal of time with him—far too much, it was thought—and who punished him herself when he was naughty.

Gunning reported on this Rousseauesque treatment with sarcastic disgust. 'The philosopher of Geneva', he told George III, 'would hail the dawn of more enlightened days could he behold (as he might here) the scene of a monarch left to crawl ... upon his hands and knees ... and condemned to lose his meals, most philosophically concealed, unless he could discover them by the sagacity of his nose. Such are the maxims which obtain in the royal nursery of Denmark.'[1]

Struensee and the Queen persisted. A valet who picked up the child when he fell, was sent away; when Little Karl said, 'I am as much a Prince as you,' and his friend retorted, 'Yes, but not a Crown Prince,' they fought without interference, and when Frederick won, he was made to apologize for boasting. His lesson hours were shortened, and he was given a garden of his own, in which he worked with a miniature rake and spade; he was inclined to overwater his plants—this was not forbidden—and the Queen would sometimes work with him, to the horror of those who saw both mother and son sinking to a peasant's level.

Matilda did not live to see her boy grow up into a robust, intelligent, hard-working young man, and one of the best and most popular kings who ever ruled in Denmark. Nor did anyone admit, either then or later, that this was her lover's doing.

The rehabilitation of the heir destroyed Queen Juliana's hopes for her own son. Her hatred of Struensee, who had twice come to the Prince of Denmark's rescue, and may have saved his life, became more virulent than ever; she would have gone to any lengths in order to degrade him; but although she had potential supporters in every class, it was difficult to co-ordinate them. As long as Christian retained the smallest measure of sanity, Struensee was protected by the Lex Regia and his relations with Matilda. So Juliana began to work out a scheme for a *coup d'état*; for this to succeed she had to find an ally from within Struensee's circle—someone who, through spite or ambition, would provide evidence of high treason, apart from Struensee's 'seduction', as it would be called, of the Queen. In the first weeks of 1771 she discovered that Count Rantzau deeply resented having been given second place in the command of the army, and she set to work to recruit him. She had not much to offer; if Rantzau had not been a natural traitor, he would have ignored her overtures; he now began to consider changing sides.

The Queen-Dowager's schemes were frustrated by the activities of double agents, among whom Mademoiselle von Eyben, now restored to Matilda's service, was one of the most dangerous, for she seems to have worked either for or against her mistress rather as a hobby than for gain. She warned Matilda that she and Struensee were in grave danger, and begged her to exercise discretion. Struensee co-operated by arranging for Christian to appear more frequently, and it was announced that he and Matilda would hold Court once a week in Copenhagen. On such occasions, it was impossible for him to be seen for more than a few minutes at a time; Matilda would then take his place. He might sustain a semblance of normality for a whole evening, but could not be relied on to do so.

As her pregnancy was not yet apparent, Matilda continued to sit for her portrait—in blue satin trimmed with sable, in pink muslin, in lilac

silk and in sprigged brocade. The effect of these toilettes was sometimes marred by the Danish fashion of fastening a small, stiff bouquet
of artificial flowers on one side of the bodice, thus breaking the line;
and sometimes a pointed muslin cap combined with a tight ruff of
taffeta roses to disguise both her hair and her *décolletage*. She looked her
best in what must have been a favourite portrait, often reproduced,
which shows her in white draperies, with a classical circlet. In all these
presentations she looks melancholy, or proud, or both; no doubt she
found sitting a dreary business. When not with Struensee, she was
happiest with her son; she commissioned several sketches of him
gardening, some of which were sent to George III, and others to the
envoys of the allies Struensee was cultivating in his stand against
Catherine of Russia.

Of these, the Crown Prince of Sweden was one of the most important, and the preparations for his first visit to Copenhagen were very
elaborate. Balls, banquets, operas and levees were organized by
Struensee in smooth succession—but these efforts were coldly received
by the future Gustavus III. He asked for certain nobles by name, and,
when told that they had retired to their estates, drew attention to the
bourgeois aspect of the Court circle, adding sarcastically, 'Are there
no Jews and Jewesses here?' When a merchant's wife ventured to rally
him for not acknowledging her curtsey, he replied, loudly enough for
Matilda to hear, 'I cannot understand how my Ambassador should have
been guilty of such an oversight—for I desired him to present to me
every lady of rank. He must have forgotten.' He acknowledged Struensee's salutes, but refused to speak to him; and his brief meeting with
Christian—they were brothers-in-law—convinced Matilda and her
lover that the King was becoming unpresentable, and that such visits
must not be repeated. With his dogs and his servants, Christian was put
in the charge of Brandt, who found him extremely trying, and ended
by leaving him in the care of two valets and a Negro slave. He then
began to show signs of violence—and was dealt with accordingly.

NOTE

1. R. Murray Keith, *Memoirs*, p. 205.

XI

Crisis

ON FEBRUARY 12th, 1771, Gunning informed his Government that 'alarming reports' were being circulated about Christian's health, adding that although great pains had been taken to explain away 'very unpromising symptoms', the King's mental decline was now public knowledge. It was said, he concluded, that Struensee's assistant, Dr Berger, had been ordered to drug him into semi-consciousness. In fact, Struensee and Matilda were making every effort to conceal his condition, in order to keep up the illusion of his personal absolutism.[1]

This was becoming increasingly difficult, especially during Brandt's absences. On one occasion, he had no sooner left the King's apartments, when a page began, 'Your Majesty must make me a groom of the chamber,' and presented Christian with the necessary paper, which he signed. Shortly afterwards, the servant whose duty it was to light the stoves came in, to be greeted by his master with 'My good fellow, would you like to be a Chamberlain?' With an embarrassed grin, the man murmured that he would not mind. 'Then you shall be,' said Christian. 'Come with me,' and, taking his hand, led him into the throne-room, where Matilda was receiving guests. The courtiers made way. Then Christian called out, 'I appoint this man my Chamberlain.'

Matilda appeared to concur, and coaxed her husband from the room. Next day, Struensee sent for the stove-lighter, and asked him whether he would not prefer a more practical gift—what about a small farm and some capital? The new chamberlain was only too glad to exchange an empty honour for a good living, and made no objection when he found himself established many miles from Copenhagen.[2]

It was then agreed that Christian must no longer have access to the state apartments; but Brandt's carelessness made it easy for him to escape; and one day, when Matilda was holding a levee, he suddenly appeared, called for silence, and recited a long poem—*A Warning Ode to Princes*, by Klopstock—of peculiar aptness to his own situation. He then saluted the company, and, bursting into a roar of laughter,

FREDERICK VI *(Juel)*

THE CASTLE OF CELLE

THE PRINCESS LOUISE
OF AUGUSTENBURG *(Juel)*

MEMORIAL TO CAROLINE
MATILDA AT CELLE *(by Oeser)*

walked out of the room. Pale and shaking, Matilda tried to behave as if all was well. When she consulted Struensee, he advised her to make a great feast in Copenhagen, during which she and Christian would appear on the balcony of Christiansborg. The people were to be admitted into the courtyard, where the fountains would run with wine, sheep and oxen be roasted whole and medals distributed, together with largesse.[3]

These celebrations had the effect required, and Struensee further distracted the public by instituting a new Order, that of Queen Matilda, to be conferred on both sexes, to the number of twenty-four persons only. He himself headed the list. 'The Order', his proclamation concluded, 'will be worn with a pink ribbon, striped with silver. The men will wear it round the neck, and the ladies will fasten it in the shape of a bow on the left breast.' The badge of the Order—of which a specimen is now in the Rosenborg Museum—consisted of an enamel medallion set in diamonds, enclosing the letters C.M., surmounted by a crown and surrounded by a wreath of laurel.[4]

In April of this year Gunning was replaced by Sir Robert Murray Keith, a severe and outspoken critic, whom Struensee resolved to placate by producing Christian at balls and operas, so attended as to be unobtrusively restrained. Sir Robert was on the look-out, however, and reported the King's escape from his guardians, when he would be found wandering distractedly about the palace; he then had to be led back to his rooms.[5]

The Ambassador was horrified by Matilda's hunting dress—smalls, a beaver hat which concealed her hair, scarlet coat, cravat and spurs—but succumbed to her charm. ('She is an angel,' an old Chamberlain told him.) He described Struensee as 'a mushroom minister', and his contempt alarmed the dictator, who decided to pay him special attention. He began by taking Sir Robert to see young Fritz, as he called the Prince of Denmark, whom they found playing with Little Karl—they were dressed alike, which pained the envoy—and beating a drum.[6]

The Englishman's censorious attitude convinced Struensee that better care must be taken of Christian, and he sent for Reverdil to look after him. The King remembered his old tutor, and seemed pleased to see him; presently he lapsed, much to Reverdil's distress, mistaking him, first for Brandt, and then for a French actor. As Reverdil waited, hoping for recognition, Christian burst into a speech from *Zaïre*, and then sank into unintelligible muttering. After a pause, he announced,

H

in a pleased tone, 'Struensee is the Queen's *cicisbeo*,' adding, 'Does the King of Prussia sleep with Matilda?' 'Who is the King of Prussia?' asked Reverdil. 'Struensee,' Christian replied; a few minutes later, he spoke at length, and quite sensibly, about his visit to England. 'I was like a god there,' he said.⁷

On another occasion, they were out of doors, when the King told Reverdil that he thought he had better commit suicide—'But how can I do it', he went on, 'without making a scandal? And if I do, shall I not be even more unhappy? Shall I drown myself?' he pursued—they were walking by the lake—'or knock my head against the wall?' Reverdil, observing his expression—one of teasing anticipation—realized that he was hoping for a horrified protest, and replied, 'Do as you think best.' Next day, Christian suggested that they should go for a row. Suddenly, in a sad voice, he announced, 'I should like to jump in—and then be pulled out, very quickly.' He continued, in German—he and Reverdil had always spoken French together—'I am confused. There is a noise in my head. I cannot go on.' He understood nothing that Reverdil said, and did not seem to desire his company. At intervals he would ask for Struensee or the Queen, but took no interest when they did appear. Later, he required Reverdil to read to him, and chose a scene from a play about Mary Queen of Scots, in which Darnley's murder of Riccio on the grounds of the King's jealousy, was presented. Christian, muttering to himself, appeared not to be listening; then he said, '*I* should not have been jealous.'⁸

One evening, Reverdil read him a passage from Tacitus. Here he was not so successful, for he read it ten times running, while Christian continued to mumble, staring at the ground. Reverdil asked Berger what treatment he was being given. 'Cold baths and quinine,' replied that functionary. Reverdil thought these remedies brought on Christian's fits of giddiness, and suggested carriage exercise, which the King seemed to enjoy. They were driving slowly through the park of Fredericksberg, when Reverdil heard a gardener say, 'At least, he will be safe with that man. *He* won't ill-treat him.'⁹

While Reverdil was in charge Christian led a more or less peaceful life, for the ex-tutor's patience did not fail; and at this time, the King entered a phase of comparative although temporary sanity. When Brandt accompanied him and Reverdil on their drives, he shrank into a corner of the carriage, and seemed glad when they got back to the palace. Brandt then told Reverdil that he himself could no longer be of use to Christian, whose mania now recurred, together with his

day-dreams about suicide ('Shall I throw myself out of the window?')
and schemes for attacking Brandt.[10]

Struensee was too busy to attend to this problem, for Matilda's
child was due in a few weeks, and no announcement had been made.
Nor was it, until her labour began, on July 1st, 1771. No member of
the royal family, no Minister or official was summoned to attend the
birth, which took place at Hirschholm in the utmost privacy. Struensee
and Dr Berger delivered the baby, a girl, who was called Louise
Augusta. Berger long remembered that Struensee held Matilda in his
arms throughout her sufferings, and that during the worst pangs her
eyes were fixed upon him. The news was then proclaimed with the
usual publicity from the balcony of the Christiansborg palace and the
principal churches of Copenhagen. Matilda recovered within a few
hours, and three days later went out riding. Her horse stumbled and fell
into a ditch, but she remained seated, pulled it out and rode on.[11]

The press then burst into indignant protests about the man who had
'shamelessly dishonoured the King's bed, and introduced his vile
posterity' into the royal house. Struensee replied to this charge by an
acknowledgment, from Christian, of the Princess as his own child; and
a fortnight later another statement from the King made him Privy
Cabinet Minister and a Count. A supplementary order invested him
with absolute power in Christian's name. 'The orders issued in this
way', the proclamation concluded, 'shall have the same validity as those
drawn up by Our hand. They shall be immediately obeyed.' Thus, in
the event of Christian's final collapse, Struensee would openly take his
place. Unofficially, the King had abdicated. With the Queen-Dowager
and his half-brother, Christian then stood sponsor to the Princess
Louise. Juliana and her son dared not refuse his command—issued,
naturally, at Struensee's instigation—that they should support the
child's legitimacy. The courtiers called her 'the Mamsell'.[12]

Gunning, now on the point of departure, advised his Government
to countenance Struensee—because, he explained, when the King's
madness resulted in Matilda's becoming Regent, she would be ruled by
her lover. George III then transferred Gunning to Berlin, and Murray
Keith was left in charge.

The envoy decided to take a tactful but firm stand with the favourite.
'I shall be equally cautious', he assured George III, 'not to court too far
or to disgust this gentleman.' He then discovered that he could do
neither. The Queen never saw him alone; he had to wait on Christian
in the presence of witnesses; and Struensee's secretary, Count Osten,

said that his master could not see him, but that he might join the King
and his suite at supper. Keith sat down with twelve other guests to a
meal of eighty dishes served on gold plate. The 'man mountain' or
'grand Vizier', as he called Struensee, did not appear, and the Ambassador was horrified by the informal gaiety of the company, and the
lack of attention he himself received. 'The scenes that pass here', he
wrote, 'are often ridiculous, and sometimes wicked, as well as des-
picable.' In a letter to his father he described the climate, society and
politics of Denmark as 'equally uncomfortable'. He had made no
friends, was cold-shouldered by the Court circle and dreaded the
winter.[13]

Reverdil—whom Keith ignored, as a middle-class professional—was
even more disapproving. He noted that Christian believed the Princess
Louise to be his child and delighted in the festivities which celebrated the
christening. Reverdil was appalled by the free and easy life at Hirschholm, which he found 'bourgeois and ignoble', and especially disliked
the procedure at meals—when the servants, having brought in the
dishes, left the room until rung for—but could not help being amused by
the conversation when Struensee and the Queen were present, although
her habit of listening only to her lover and never taking her eyes off
him seemed quite ridiculous. On one occasion, something was said
about revolution; in that event, Matilda went on, they would all
have to think of how best to earn a living; she would become a singer.
(Not a bad idea, Reverdil considered, for she sang very well.) 'I should
have a farm and study philosophy,' said Struensee: and Brandt settled
for a career in the theatre. One of Matilda's ladies said that she should
like to be an artist's model. 'You have a defect which would make
that impossible,' Brandt remarked. Reverdil was disgusted. The lady
did not seem to mind; but Struensee reproved Brandt for his discourtesy. Christian remained vacant and inattentive; when he began
to fidget and mutter, Matilda signed to Reverdil to lead him from the
room.

Later that afternoon, they all went out for a walk. Christian was
escorted by Reverdil and a lady; Struensee gave Matilda his arm; and
the rest, Brandt leading them, followed in couples. Reverdil observed
that when they returned Struensee and the Queen fell back, and were
not seen again for some hours. Shortly afterwards, two of Matilda's
ladies, Mesdames Hornes and Brun, who seemed genuinely concerned
for their mistress's reputation, confided in Reverdil, and asked his
advice.[14]

They began by describing the presents Struensee had given the Queen —a pair of scented garters and his miniature; she wore his portrait round her neck during the day, and at night concealed it in the book she read in bed, before placing it under her pillow. He had a key to her rooms, which he entered by a secret staircase. These women so often saw him coming in and going out, that they decided to ask Matilda to be more cautious, but, dreading the interview, they were in tears before it began. Finding them thus distressed, Matilda made inquiries, and as they continued to weep, kissed Madame Brun and persuaded her to explain. She was then told that Queen Juliana and the whole Court knew of Struensee's visits and gifts, and that at any moment he might be arrested. Matilda said that she would speak to him, adding, 'Do you think that if we saw one another less frequently the gossip would die down? If I no longer saw him at all, that would cause more talk.'

When she consulted Struensee, he pointed out that she was being blackmailed; her ladies were simply angling for a bribe. Matilda had not thought of that; enraged, she told them that their warnings were treasonous. 'In old days', she said, 'such an attack would have been punished by the loss of your tongues'—and thereafter, they told Reverdil, she became bitterly hostile.[15]

Matilda and Struensee then cut down their meetings—for a fortnight—and evolved a scheme by which they saw one another more secretly. The Queen began to confide in Mademoiselle von Eyben, to whom she described Struensee as the saviour of Denmark. His latest reforms, those of the consanguinity and marriage laws, impressed Reverdil, who observed, 'Struensee was only concerned with the public good; but he was wrong in thinking that one can reform a nation through decrees, which are extremely vulnerable, when issued by a person who has seized power.' He added that if Struensee had persuaded Christian to sanction the new laws before he went mad, his position would have been unassailable. Now, all his efforts were condemned, and he was suspected of planning to imprison, not only the King, but also Queen Juliana and her son, whom Reverdil visited at this time.[16]

The Queen-Dowager said that Struensee had encouraged Matilda to neglect the Prince of Denmark, and was angry with Reverdil when he told her that they were always together, and that Matilda was constantly seen carrying the baby Princess, while Little Karl and the Prince hung about her. He admitted that Struensee's economies were not always judicious. His order to stop the building of a vast church, which had been begun in the previous reign, had caused serious unemployment, besides giving the clergy another weapon against him. And Reverdil thought that Matilda degraded herself by letting Struensee choose what dresses she should wear, and telling her how much to spend on her clothes.[17]

He then obtained an audience with Struensee, in order to plead with him for the Queen-Dowager and her son: but his arguments were ineffectual; although Struensee was well aware of the harm they might do him, he would not placate them. The former heir-presumptive, described by a contemporary as 'ugly, disagreeable, false, cowardly and proud', had little or no following; also, he seems to have been slightly mental. Reverdil thought that Struensee relied too much on Matilda's popularity. ('She has but to appear to please and soothe the people,' said one courtier.)[18] Meanwhile, he noted that she no longer troubled to protect her husband from Brandt's ill-treatment, partly because the King insisted on provoking it. In fact, he preferred Brandt's bullying to Reverdil's gentle approach and attempts to reason with him. Struensee's attitude seems to indicate his approval of Christian's indulging his aggressive instincts in this manner.

They were all at dinner when Christian, who had been muttering to himself for some time, suddenly turned to Brandt, and in what Reverdil describes as a highly theatrical style, announced, 'I am going to thrash you, Count—do you hear me?' Brandt made no reply. Struensee and Matilda then drew Christian aside and seemed to be scolding him. The King left the room, summoning Reverdil to follow. Later that day, Struensee told Reverdil that he should have reprimanded his former pupil, and himself informed Christian that he had wilfully and without cause insulted Brandt. 'He is a poltroon,' Christian replied, 'and will submit to insults.' 'Your Majesty will soon see that that is not so,' said Struensee. 'He is determined to revenge himself.'

Brandt then entered Christian's apartments, dismissed his attendants, challenged him and gave him the choice of weapons. Christian rejected swords and pistols, and they decided to fight with their fists, with the result that the wretched lunatic was soon writhing on the floor and begging for mercy. He then complained to Reverdil, who protested, first to Brandt and then to Struensee. 'The Count completely forgot himself,' he told the latter. 'I did not think he would go so far—I will tell him that it must not happen again,' Struensee promised. To Brandt he said, 'It is well—now we shall have no more trouble'—but he protected the King thereafter, greatly to Brandt's annoyance. Struensee then made Brandt Grand Master of the Wardrobe, but this did not satisfy the Count, who began to consider going over to Queen Juliana's faction. Finally, he decided to stick to Struensee and Matilda.[19]

NOTES

1. Wilkins, *A Queen of Tears*, vol. I, p. 319.
2. Ibid.
3. Ibid.
4. Op. cit., p. 320.
5. Murray Keith, *Memoirs*, p. 201.
6. Op. cit., p. 209.
7. Reverdil, *Mémoires*, pp. 260–9.
8. Op. cit., pp. 195–228.
9. Ibid.
10. Op. cit., p. 260.
11. Murray Keith, op. cit., p. 197.
12. Wilkins, op. cit., vol. I, p. 325.
13. Murray Keith, op. cit., p. 199.
14. Reverdil, op. cit., p. 208.
15. Op. cit., pp. 208–9.
16. Op. cit., p. 230.
17. Ibid.
18. Falkensjold, *Mémoires*, p. 112.
19. Reverdil, op. cit., pp. 290–1.

XII

Conspiracy

SHORTLY AFTER the birth of his daughter and the assumption of his title, Struensee acquired a coat of arms, which he designed himself. It comprised, among other symbols, rivers, fields, palm-leaves, a crown, helmets, two beavers holding a shield and an owl with a key in its beak. To this absurdity he added a gilded coach and new liveries of scarlet and white for his valets and running footmen, who wore diamond badges. Such ostentation, said his contemporaries, resembled the bursting conceit of the frog in the fable, and the madness of grandeur which precedes the loss of all sense of proportion.

In fact, Struensee's private conversations show a mood of uncertainty and doubt, which he was attempting to conceal by a display designed to impress the common people. The courtiers mocked him; but those for whom he had done most, seeing these signs of greatness and power, may well have felt that he was there to stay—until they heard that his valet, appearing in his new finery for the first time, had fallen downstairs, broken his nose and covered his diamond badge with blood.[1] No omen could have been more depressing; and Struensee's comment—'As God wills,' uttered with a shrug—was another proof, the courtiers said, of his intolerable arrogance.

Yet he was increasingly aware that his dictatorship could not last much longer. He told Reverdil that he was weary of it, and would like to retire. Asked why he did not do so, he said, 'I have considered it—but there is the Queen, whom I love. If I leave her, she will become the victim of intriguers and evil persons.' He continued to speak of Matilda in a manner that convinced Reverdil of his devotion. He then confided in Brandt, who advised him to stay. 'Where else', said the Count, 'could you be Prime Minister, the King's friend and the Queen's lover?' These considerations and the pursuit of his reforms weighed less with Struensee than the Queen's dependence on him; but he desired leisure (his choice of a country life and the study of philosophy was presumably an expression of genuine feeling) and he may have found Matilda's uncritical adoration somewhat taxing. One evening, speaking of a courtier who had just made a rich marriage, he said, 'Bielke is wiser than any of us. He is established—and when we are all in gaol, he will have pity on us, and send round basins of soup.' It is evident that Struensee was prepared for a downfall which would begin with a term of imprisonment and end in exile and tranquillity. Having been born and educated in a comparatively civilized milieu, he did not visualize a more violent fate, for he had never really grasped the savage hatred, the barbaric standards and the furious jealousy of those who surrounded him. Relying only on the Queen, he trusted none of them; and he seems to have believed that the sister of George III—then, with Louis XV, another ally, the most powerful monarch in Europe—would provide all the protection he needed. His attitude was rather one of resignation than of fear.[2]

Reverdil, alternately gloomy and hopeful, then asked for a second visit to the Prince of Denmark, on whose chilblains he had already reported. The child was neither shy, nor disobedient nor plaintive; but the Swiss thought that his formal education was being neglected. At the age of four, when, according to contemporary standards, he should have been able to speak fluent German and French, he could only express himself in an odd mixture of Danish and German. He now had another companion besides Little Karl, and they all seemed happy enough, playing in the garden, bathing and being generally independent. Reverdil deprecated his not being taught to read and write till after his sixth birthday: but that, Dr Berger told him, was Struensee's order, and part of Rousseau's system.[3]

Returning to his study of Struensee's administration, Reverdil found much to criticize. The dictator was becoming increasingly dogmatic. He thought only of giving orders and seeing that they were carried out, when it would have been wiser to persuade and reason; and he had fallen into the fatal habit of refusing to see anyone likely to disagree with him, particularly those responsible for the forces. When a band of Norwegian sailors, who had been idle and unpaid for eight weeks, decided to protest, Struensee was more alarmed than he need have been by their demonstration, partly because, having entrusted their treatment to a subordinate, he was taken by surprise when they appeared at Hirschholm in what seemed a dangerous humour.

It was said afterwards that when they heard the sailors were approaching the palace, the Court party prepared to fly, and that Struensee, the Queen and Christian left by a secret way before they arrived.

Reverdil, who was there, gives the lie to this accusation. Struensee, believing that they intended to besiege the palace, told the dragoons to be ready to defend it, and to disperse the Norwegians by force, if necessary. When they announced that they had come merely to protest about their pay, they were enraged by the sight of the soldiers: and their leader said that if the dragoons laid hands on them, they would defend themselves with their knives, having no other weapons. They were then told, as from the King, that they would be paid, and returned, peaceably, to Copenhagen.

Meanwhile, Matilda, more alarmed for Struensee than for herself, had packed up her jewels; she laid out her riding-habit, had her horse harnessed and went to bed, having ordered a patrol to surround the palace till daylight. This precaution was sensible enough; for Queen Juliana's faction, hearing of the sailors' plan, had decided to support them and use their march on Hirschholm as the preliminary to a general uprising, which would end in the arrest, imprisonment and execution of Struensee and Brandt. The citizens of Copenhagen seemed ready to co-operate—but did not do so.[4]

Struensee then announced that on September 28th, when the Court would have left Hirschholm for Fredericksberg, a great feast would be held there, presided over by the King and Queen. Nothing more was heard of mutiny or revolution; and Struensee asked Reverdil to consult with and advise his brother, whom he had entrusted with the economic administration of the kingdom, including the fisheries and the reorganization of forestry, mines and agriculture. Reverdil was much impressed by Karl August, whom he thought more adaptable than Struensee. They agreed that a regime detested by the majority could not succeed; but when Struensee was approached, he pointed out that, once in motion, his machine could not be halted; in fact, he had become so set in his ways, that he would not consider rescinding a single one of his reforms.[5] He was haunted by the thought of Matilda's danger; and her fears for him had increased, with the result that they both, with Christian and Brandt, left Hirschholm for Sophieberg, a castle some miles away; from there they planned to go on to Elsinore, but eventually decided to return to Fredericksberg.

One of the Queen's ladies, Madame von Bülow, who may have wished to draw attention to herself, then announced that during the feast at Fredericksberg Struensee and Brandt would be assassinated. Once more, Matilda urged departure to Elsinore; but further inquiries reassured her, and the party, attended by five thousand people, took place without mishap, except that Christian refused to attend it. When it was known that he, Matilda, Brandt and Struensee had remained at Hirschholm, the two Ministers were reviled as cowards. In fact, if they had appeared, they would have been seized and murdered; for Queen Juliana's plot had been reorganized with this intent, and then betrayed to Struensee, who told Reverdil that though there seemed to be no danger of revolution, one might break out at any moment.

A placard announcing the outlawry of Struensee and offering a reward for his assassination was then discovered in one of the main streets of Copenhagen. At Matilda's desire, he consented to leave the country; a few days later, concluding that the placard was a hoax— the citizens of Copenhagen treated it as such—he changed his mind. Keith reported that Struensee 'unexpectedly betrayed signs of personal fear', as if shocked that the great man should wish to avoid being lynched or shot. That he remained where he was—he accompanied the Queen into Copenhagen twice a week, returning the same night— shows both courage and common sense.[6]

He now had to deal with the furious rivalry of Brandt, who, wavering between keeping his post and deserting to Queen Juliana, openly defied his authority. Brandt and Count Osten sent for Reverdil, in order to discuss with him a plot for forcing the dictator into resignation and exile. It would have been well for Struensee if it had succeeded.

When Reverdil arrived, Brandt was not there. 'Would you', Osten began, 'be willing to come to the rescue of the State, which is in great danger?' Reverdil agreed about the danger, various aspects of which— Struensee's methods, the resultant economic upheavals, the fatal estrangement from Russia and Great Britain—were discussed at length; but he pointed out that he had no personal grudge against Struensee, who had sent for him to look after the King. 'I must therefore remain neutral,' he concluded. When Osten suggested sending for Bernstorff to take over, Reverdil said that he was sure to refuse. 'What will be the end of all this, then?' Osten exclaimed. 'The only possible end would be a rupture between Struensee and the Queen,' replied the Swiss, and Osten, violently irritated by this statement of an impasse, dismissed him.[7]

Next day, Brandt told Reverdil that Osten was a fool and a rogue. 'He wants us to take the chestnuts out of the fire for him,' he said, and described the plot for Struensee's arrest as impracticable and absurd, adding, 'I could console the Queen for his loss.' (Brandt's vanity was such that he really believed this to be possible.) He then reported Osten's plans to Struensee, who, hearing that Reverdil had considered them, said, 'He is an honest man. If he did attempt to arrest me, I should still think well of him, because he would do so on principle.' Reverdil, much struck by Brandt's report of what he describes as Struensee's 'grandeur of soul', decided to have nothing to do with any plot, but to try and heal the breach between Juliana and Matilda. Naturally, he failed.[8] He then found out that the talk of Struensee and the Queen being brutal to Christian was false. The King spent a good deal of time alone, or with his pages and a female Turkish slave, formerly the property of the Queen, whom Christian knocked about, but who was protected by the pages. 'The King', Reverdil adds, 'liked to be beaten, but was never seriously hurt while I was at Court, except when he challenged Brandt. But that disgusting scene was not repeated.'[9]

Reverdil believed Brandt to be the dictator's most dangerous enemy; yet Struensee was fond of him, and, when the Count continued to complain, told him to put his grievances in writing. Brandt then wrote, 'Yours is a reign of terror. No tyrant ever claimed such power, or used it as you do. Even the Queen fears you'—with a great deal more to the same effect, adding that he must now resign his post—in other words, that he was about to go over to Queen Juliana—and would leave for Paris, where he proposed to live on his pension, which must of course be doubled. He then threatened suicide, in the event of his requests being refused. 'My position', he concluded, 'has become intolerable, and can only be resolved by the use of poison or steel.'[10]

Struensee replied with extraordinary mildness. The tone of his letter, one of immense length, was that of a physician to an hysterical patient. 'You are discontented', he told Brandt, 'because Countess Holstein [the Count's mistress] has been unkind to you.' He refused to give Brandt any more money, and desired him, in conciliatory terms, to stay where he was. In fact, he knew that Brandt had no intention of leaving; when the Count implored him to rescind some of his most unpopular decrees, he replied, 'I shall withdraw nothing which benefits the State.'[11]

Struensee was then warned by Keith and Reverdil that he was in great danger, and should leave the country. 'I may meet with the fate of Concini,' he said to the latter, recalling the assassination of Marie de Medici's Italian favourite by the courtiers of Louis XIII; but he was not serious. The worst that could happen, he still believed, was disgrace, imprisonment and exile.[12]

Nevertheless, the strain was beginning to tell. Formerly abstemious, Struensee now ate and drank to excess, had put on weight, and was known as 'the great ox' by the people. While still able to exercise his charm and maintain a certain elegance, he had become dependent on stimulants; he slept badly, and his hitherto amazing memory had begun to weaken. Keith, an unwilling admirer, wrote of him that 'his genius has wasted itself by the hasty strides he made ... He has formed no steady plan.'[13]

Matilda, increasingly anxious, but more than ever devoted to him, now abandoned all discretion, and said to her ladies, 'Do you love someone? If you do, you should love even under torture, or the pains of hell.' 'But if the lover is unfaithful?' one suggested. 'Then I should go mad—or kill myself!' cried her mistress, adding. 'How fortunate you are, to marry where you wish! If I were a widow,' she went on, 'I would marry him I loved, and give up my throne and my country.' Fingering a jade cross she always wore, she told them that it was the gift of 'a very intimate friend'. 'The King?' someone asked. Matilda burst out laughing. 'Oh yes, who else?' she replied. After a pause, she continued, 'I know what they say of me, I don't care—to be unfaithful to a husband one has been forced to marry is not a crime.'[14]

Two of her ladies, Mesdemoiselles Bleckenberg and Schitt, assisted by a maid, Anna Petersen, and a lackey, Hemsten, then organized a watch on the Queen and Struensee, the details of which they recorded, in the event of being asked to retail them. They began by stopping up the lock of her bedroom door with wax—this was removed during the night—and scattering powder on the secret stair leading up to it; this enabled them to trace footsteps which reached the bed itself. Here they found the sheets stained and tossed about, and a man's handkerchief, also stained, which they kept. They then noted Matilda's daily morning drives, alone with Struensee, which might last several hours, and 'overheard' her complaining to him about his frequentation of other women, with his joking reply that in future he would 'only dance with old ladies'. When they found her sitting with him on a sofa, she ordered them out of the room; she was expecting the King, she said, and must see him alone. On several occasions they saw her naked in bed—this was after Struensee's departure—and sometimes she dined alone with him, sitting up in bed, while he sat on the end, in order, she told them, to examine and prescribe for her. In the same way, they would breakfast together, taking tea or coffee on alternate days. When these ladies commented on the bruises on Matilda's throat and breast,

she laughed and said it was nothing. (Through the keyhole, they saw
Struensee massaging these injuries.) The candles in her bedroom often
burned throughout the night; and one morning, the pocket of Struensee's coat was discovered to be stuffed with her handkerchiefs, all
stained and crumpled. Finally, they found out that she had given him
her miniature and a number of valuable rings. She was in the habit of
'consulting' Struensee at frequent intervals, and when this happened,
the times of his arrival and departure were observed and recorded.[15]
It may be that Matilda's mother had behaved in something after this
fashion with Bute; in any case, she had been more fortunate in her
attendants, none of whom were employed as spies; and she herself
would have been incapable of her daughter's maniacal recklessness.

In the autumn of 1771 Rantzau decided to join Queen Juliana, but in
such a manner as to give the impression that age and infirmity necessitated his withdrawal from the political scene. He therefore took
formal leave of the King and Queen, and retired to his estates; later, he
secretly approached the Queen-Dowager, to be told that she had not
made up her mind as to how a *coup d'état* should be effected. Actually,
she was afraid that Rantzau might report her plans to Struensee: for she
knew that he had written to Bernstorff with a scheme for uprooting
the dictator—one in which she was not included—and had been
rejected by the ex-Minister. She had come to the conclusion that to
employ Rantzau was to take too great a risk, and so did not commit
herself. As Osten and Gahler were also disaffected and might come over
to her, it seemed best to wait until she was sure of them, in which case
Rantzau could be relied on, and a *coup d'état* brought about with the
support of the majority.

Among the spies, traitors and scoundrels who infested Struensee's
administration, there were a few persons of integrity, Reverdil being
one; but his resolve to remain neutral and his unofficial position made
him powerless. The dictator's most influential supporter was a Colonel
Falkensjold, whose memoirs reveal a stubborn—although sometimes
critical—loyalty. He was intelligent and hard-working, but neither
subtle nor disingenuous—as it were, an eighteenth-century Colonel
Newcome, whose courage was unquestioned. With certain reservations, he approved of Struensee's reforms; and his record shows that
the dictator retained the support and gratitude of a large number of the
Danish people. The Colonel describes Struensee's administration as
excellent; he was particularly impressed by his chief's treatment of the
Prince of Denmark, who had been languid, invalidish and disagreeable,

and had now become 'alert, healthy and good'.[16] Although appalled by Matilda's besotted rashness, he admired and pitied her.

Meanwhile, the Ministers of George III were so out of touch with the situation as to believe that Bernstorff might oust Struensee. To their suggestions on this point, Keith replied that Her Majesty's 'partiality' for him was merely increased by opposition, adding, 'In the five months I have passed [here] I have not had the honour of exchanging ten sentences with the Queen.'[17]

Struensee now found that not only Fredericksberg and Hirschholm but the capital itself must be strongly guarded, in the event of a general uprising; and during October and November these precautions were carried out with Matilda's approval and consent. Neither she nor her lover had imagined that Christian would take in what was going on; but early in December he sent for Struensee in great alarm, and asked why his palaces were bristling with cannon and patrolled night and day by armed men. 'That is for the better protection of Your Majesty's royal person,' Struensee replied, 'your subjects having become rebellious and disaffected. If they are not checked, there will be a revolution.' 'But what have I done?' Christian exclaimed, bursting into tears. 'Why should they hate me?' To this appeal there could be no reply save from Queen Juliana, whose propagation of rumours about Struensee's evil intentions was ceaseless and ingenious.[18]

Struensee then told Falkensjold, who was responsible for the Foot Guards, that they must be merged into other regiments for the general strengthening of the army. The colonel objected, but was overruled, and obeyed orders. On Christmas Eve the King's command for what the Foot Guards looked on as their degradation was read out, and they were told to hand over their colours for distribution among the other regiments. They refused, and a free fight between them and their rivals took place. The Foot Guards marched to the Christiansborg palace, drove away the sentries, killed one and wounded several others. They then proceeded to Fredericksberg to see the King, whom they met halfway, driving out with Reverdil, a postilion and a single equerry.[19] They saluted him, and went on to the palace, where they stated their demands; either they must be discharged, or remain in their former positions. Struensee discharged them—mutinous troops were worse than useless—formally, in writing; when they saw his signature instead of the King's, they refused to accept dismissal. Struensee then told them that unless they did so, he would storm the Christiansborg palace, where the other mutineers were installed, and remove them by force. They remained obdurate, and at midnight he was obliged to obtain Christian's signature to the discharges, with a bonus of three rix-dollars for each man.[20]

Keith, feeling responsible for the Queen's safety, implored Struensee to resign, in vain. Rantzau reappeared in Falkensjold's quarters, and, presumably in order to protect himself in the event of Queen Juliana's conspiracy failing, told him of her plans. 'If that is true, you should report them to Count Struensee himself,' the Colonel coldly replied. 'He will not listen to me,' said Rantzau, and went away. He then drew up a forged document, as from Struensee, outlining a plot to dethrone the King, and to imprison—for life—Queen Juliana and her son. When shown this paper, she decided to act. The arrest of Struensee and Matilda was planned for the night of January 16th, 1772, during the course of a masked ball at the Christiansborg palace. It was to be organized and led by Count Rantzau.[21]

NOTES

1. Wilkins, *A Queen of Tears*, vol. I, p. 336.
2. Reverdil, *Mémoires*, p. 288.
3. Ibid.
4. Op. cit., p. 283.
5. Op. cit., p. 273.
6. Wilkins, op. cit., vol. II, p. 24.
7. Reverdil, op. cit., pp. 293–5.
8. Ibid.
9. Ibid.
10. Wilkins, op. cit., vol. II, p. 6.
11. Reverdil, op. cit., p. 298.
12. Ibid.
13. Wilkins, op. cit., vol. II, p. 6.
14. *Procès de Caroline Mathilde*, pp. 61–85.
15. Ibid.
16. Falkensjold, *Mémoires*, p. 188.
17. Wilkins, op. cit., vol. II, p. 34.
18. Op. cit., p. 37.
19. Reverdil, op. cit., p. 312.
20. Op. cit., p. 314.
21. Nors, *Court of Christian VII*, p. 180.

XIII
The Masked Ball

REVERDIL'S ACCOUNT of the events preceding the night of Queen Juliana's *coup d'état* shows that, acute though he was, he had long ago been deceived as to her character, and continued to be so. Having been Prince Frederick's tutor before he entered Christian's service, his loyalty to the Queen-Dowager, who had treated him well, sustained his belief in her virtues. That her gentle and retiring manner, her piety and her seeming friendliness towards Christian and Matilda might conceal bitter jealousy and a taste for intrigue, did not occur to Reverdil, whose sense of propriety was offended by the licence of Christian's Court and Struensee's domination. He saw Juliana as a disinterested patriot, whose only desire was to rescue Denmark from the rule of an adulterous Queen-Regent and an atheistical revolutionary. Juliana's modest address had been so long assumed that it had ceased to be a pose; her standards of social conduct were Reverdil's own; and so he was completely taken in by what seemed to him her correct attitude towards Matilda. He declares that she had always been kind to the younger woman; it was Struensee who wrecked a relationship which would otherwise have become even more genial in the course of time.[1]

Reverdil did not know till later on that the conspirators, now headed by the Queen-Dowager and her son, were seven in number: Judge Guldberg, Prince Frederick's secretary; Colonel Koller and General Eichstedt; Beringskjold, formerly a spy, who had been dismissed by Struensee; Jessen, a wine-merchant, who knew all the secret entrances and stairways of the Christiansborg palace; Suhm, the historiographer-royal, who had more influence with Juliana than any of the others; and, of course, Count Rantzau. He was still mistrusted by her; but his account of Struensee's designs convinced her faction that she and Frederick were really in danger of an imprisonment that might end in execution.

On January 8th, 1772, the Court returned to Copenhagen. That night, there was a ball; next day, Matilda, Christian and Struensee went to the play, and two days later, the Queen, attended by her lover, held a levee. She had just received a letter from George III, imploring her, for the last time, to dismiss him and to recall Bernstorff. This plea, almost humble in tone, was never answered.[2]

The conspirators, meeting in a house next to the palace, then decided to seize Matilda and Struensee in the small hours of the 17th, when the bustle of the masked ball would help to conceal their movements. They intended to make Christian proclaim a new Government, after signing an order for the arrest of his wife, Brandt, Struensee, Falkensjold and Karl August. As Koller and Eichstedt were due to command the soldiers guarding the palace, Matilda and her supporters would be neatly trapped.

Struensee had decided that the ball should be unusually magnificent. It took place in the theatre, the auditorium having been made level with the stage; the boxes were newly gilded and hung with purple silk curtains; the dais for the orchestra was illuminated with coloured lamps and banked by hot-house flowers.

At ten o'clock Struensee appeared, the Queen on his arm, dressed in a blue velvet coat and rose-coloured satin breeches, the Order of Matilda glittering on his breast. She wore a gown of white brocade, embroidered with pink roses, and a diamond necklace and stomacher. (These are now in the Rosenborg Museum.) They entered the royal box, where the King, refusing to dance, sat down to cards. Struensee and the Queen, laying aside their dominoes, then opened the ball. Reverdil, having just visited Queen Juliana, who told him that she was not going to attend it, joined them. He observed that Matilda was in great beauty and the highest spirits. Struensee, equally serene, summoned him to sup with them at midnight.

This was Matilda's most triumphant and happiest hour. Whatever fears she had had for her lover were dispersed; and he, surrounded by sycophants and toadies, seems to have been convinced that immediate danger of a revolution was at an end. Together, they had reached a point where indiscretion and rashness combined to make them parade their relationship. Despising censure and heedless of warnings, they gloried in their union. Paradoxically, this shared attitude was the result of their contrasting temperaments and backgrounds.

At twenty, Matilda's character might have been assumed to have reached maturity. It was not so. She was simple, passionate, credulous and child-like. In many ways she had hardly changed at all since her fourteenth birthday, when she was told that her marriage to Christian was being arranged. Her upbringing, a combination of discipline and indulgence, would have successfully prepared almost any girl for private life. In the case of a future queen, it was fatally mistaken.

Matilda had grown up without the faintest sense of public responsibility, while being trained to regard herself as a privileged person; her belief in the divine right of her dynasty was unconscious and inherent, quite apart from the fact that Bute's frequentation of her mother and the Princess-Dowager's contempt for popular opinion ('poor, deluded people') had provided the worst of examples. Matilda was not stupid; but her development had been halted, first by being wrenched out of a happy home, and then by her sufferings at her husband's hands. Also, like other members of her family, she was unadaptable, obstinate and abysmally naive. Her bursts of chatter to her ladies about her love for Struensee, and her indifference to being discovered with him in highly compromising circumstances, show her as having become slightly unbalanced; and her behaviour in this respect was also in the Hanoverian tradition. With the same recklessness, her great-grandmother had continued her relationship with Königsmarck, despite all warnings, and so brought about his murder; similarly, the Princess-Dowager's obsession with Bute had contributed to his disgrace and exile. As Queen of Denmark and the sister of George III, Matilda could not visualize being dealt with as Sophia-Dorothea had been; and she was incapable of giving up the fascinating creature of whom she had made an idol—although, according to Falkensjold, she and Struensee did, for a short time, consider separation. Her strength of purpose reinforced his self-confidence, producing a common optimism —a 'nothing can happen to us' attitude—which carried them along at a speed they were unable to gauge, while the standards of the Danish Court enhanced what seems to have been rejection of, rather than indifference to, the conventions.

Struensee's participation in this headlong rush to ruin was mainly caused by his awareness of his own abilities, and the limitations of his early surroundings. As he had never met anyone cleverer than himself —and could hardly conceive of such a person—so he assumed that the worst he had to fear was a set-back ending in the retirement for which he now longed; he may even have imagined sharing it with his mistress, just as Königsmarck had planned to elope with the Princess Sophia-Dorothea in order to live happily ever after in Saxony. Struensee saw the Danes—not unreasonably—as an underdeveloped people: a herd he could direct, and had directed, by substituting a modern for a semimedieval regime, and thus ultimately benefiting the majority. His reading having imbued him with what would now be described as socialistic principles, he had no awe, much less fear of, the ruling classes. Success, first with women, then with Christian, and finally the conquest of Matilda, had led him to believe that he could do anything he thought desirable—as indeed, he had, for a short time. These triumphs were, in his view, the inevitable outcome of a genius acknowledged and deferred to, as much by his enemies as by his allies. Furthermore, most of his contemporaries and all his intimates took licence for granted. So it was that, with regard to the Queen, he behaved as if he were in the position of Louis XV or Catherine the Great, whose disregard of sexual morality was proverbial—and accepted. Struensee chose to ignore the fact that his rank made imitation of their conduct a crime against the State he had reformed and now ruled. His three years' residence in Denmark had not provided an apprenticeship, because he had shot out of obscurity into a dominion which became absolute within a few months; he was therefore in the position of a man transported, as if by the stroke of a wand, from the earth to the stars. He forgot that he was still, socially and politically, a terrestrial being. With a beautiful and devoted woman, who was Queen of that higher sphere, in his arms, this seeming aberration was neither so unnatural nor so arrogant as his adversaries chose to think.

Struensee and Matilda, glancing down at friends and enemies, saw them through the wrong end of a telescope—diminished and negligible; the voices reaching them from that distance became fainter and fainter, until, on the night of January 16th, 1772, they were hardly audible. Struensee put them out of his consciousness much as he would once have relegated the murmurings of his patients when they left his consulting-room, to be dealt with in due order on the resumption of his working day. That those he now directed might turn to destroy him did not seriously trouble him, even when, in the outbreaks he diagnosed and prescribed for, they threatened to do so. All his life, he was guided and ruled by his training as a physician—the sort whose attitude towards his cases is kindly, objective and slightly inhuman.

At eleven o'clock the party in the royal box was joined by Prince Frederick, who appeared nervous and flushed. 'You are very late, brother,' said Matilda, adding, 'Is anything the matter?' 'I have had business to attend to,' the Prince replied. 'You should have been enjoying yourself at the ball, instead of troubling about business,' said the Queen with a smile. Frederick made no reply, and she took Struensee's arm for the next dance.[3]

Meanwhile, Koller and Guldberg were strolling about, and presently Koller sat down to take a hand at cards. Struensee came up and asked him if he were going to dance. Koller looked at him smiling. 'Not yet,' he said. 'My time to dance will come later.' Struensee then returned to the royal box for supper.[4]

Here, the party consisted of himself, the King and Queen, Brandt, Reverdil and Countess Holstein. Prince Frederick reappeared, only to be told that there was no room for him; he then joined the other conspirators at the buffet, who informed him, in great alarm, that Rantzau had not arrived—did he intend to betray them?

Some hours earlier, Rantzau had called at the house of Karl August, to find that he had gone out to dinner. The servants said that he would probably return at ten o'clock in order to change his dress for the ball. Punctually at that hour, Rantzau called again; this time, he saw the elder Struensee's valet, who told him that his master, in his domino, was dining with General Gahler, and would therefore not be back till the ball was over. Rantzau left a note for him, which ran, 'I must see your brother before midnight. If you do not arrange this meeting, you will repent it for the rest of your life.' He then returned to his own lodging, and went to bed, after telling his servants that anyone who called on him but Karl August must be informed that he was incapacitated by a severe fit of the gout.[5]

At midnight, the supper party in the royal box was concluded and Christian taken back to his rooms. Madame Holstein suggested that when the ball was over, the others should come to her apartments for a last glass of wine, but the Queen decided that she did not want to stay up so late. (If she had accepted, the *coup d'état* might have been postponed, or even have failed altogether.) Matilda and Struensee then returned to the ballroom, where they danced till three o'clock. Their withdrawal was the signal for the ball to end. Within half an hour the theatre was empty, and the servants were putting out the lights.

This was the moment agreed on by Juliana's group for a final consultation. As the absence of Rantzau indicated that he was going to inform on them, Beringskjold rushed to his house. He burst into the Count's bedroom, and ordered him to attend the Queen-Dowager immediately. 'I cannot move,' said Rantzau, 'I am crippled with the gout.' 'Your chairmen must carry you, then,' Beringskjold replied. 'I have dismissed them for the night,' said Rantzau. 'I will find others,' the ex-spy persisted, and summoned a couple of soldiers. Rantzau was helped to dress, lifted into his sedan chair and carried to Queen Juliana's house. Meanwhile, Karl August, returning to his rooms, read Rantzau's note, and said to his valet, 'That summons will keep. The Count is often agitated about some trifle or other,' and went to bed.[6]

Koller and Eichstedt, who had left the ballroom some hours earlier, then prepared to arrest Struensee, Brandt, the Queen and several others. Each had an order, signed by Prince Frederick and his mother, which they showed to the senior officers on guard. 'The King', it declared, 'is surrounded by enemies. His royal person is in danger, and so his loving brother and stepmother hereby command Colonel Koller and General Eichstedt to arrange for your help in the arrest of Count Struensee and Count Brandt.' Although they knew that such an order had no validity without Christian's signature, the officers swore to obey it. Koller then summoned the junior command, and gave them similar instructions. This ensured the closing of the trap, and all the officers returned to their posts.[7]

Koller and Eichstedt, reporting to Juliana and Frederick, were desired to join them and the other conspirators in earnest prayer for the success of the *coup d'état*. The seven plotters rose to accompany the Prince and his mother to Christian's apartments, taking with them orders for the arrest of their victims.

It was now four o'clock. The palace was dark and deserted. Jessen guided them through the secret, unguarded passages, and they reached Christian's rooms, to find the valet occupying the ante-chamber fast asleep. When woken, this man, Brieghel, a person of great bulk and strength, refused to let them disturb the King. As they stood, helplessly gazing at him, Guldberg dropped the candle. Queen Juliana tottered and nearly fell, and Prince Frederick sank into the nearest chair, trembling all over. None of them dared attack Brieghel, lest he should give the alarm. (Presumably, they were not sure of the officers.) Then Rantzau, miraculously recovered from his gout, intervened with cool authority. 'We have come', he told Brieghel, 'to save His Majesty from his enemies. The whole city has risen, and the palace may be stormed at any moment. You will be well rewarded, if you let us in to rescue your royal master.' 'Do you promise me', said the valet, 'that you mean no harm to His Majesty?' Receiving a solemn oath to that effect, he unlocked the door, and the conspirators entered the bedroom. Drawing aside the bed-curtains, Juliana roused Christian, who started up with a shriek of terror. She reassured him, with tears, and declarations of loyalty. Then, seeing the men standing behind her, he exclaimed, 'For God's sake! What have I done? What do you want?' and sank back on his pillows. Rantzau desired Brieghel to give him a glass of water, Juliana renewed her assurances, and Rantzau explained that the people had risen against Struensee and the Queen, and were about to storm the palace.

Sobbing and moaning, Christian cried, 'Terrible—terrible! Where shall I go? What should I do?' 'Sign these papers,' said his stepmother, placing them on the coverlet and handing him pen and ink, 'and Your Majesty's life will be saved.'

Christian glanced at the one nearest his hand, and, seeing his wife's name, threw aside the pen; he then began trying to get out of bed. He was pushed back, the pen thrust into his hand, and he signed everything put before him, including the appointment of Eichstedt and Koller to supreme command, 'for the safety of King and country'. The order for Matilda's arrest, which is in French and still preserved, ran as follows:

Madame—I have found it wisest to send you to Kronborg, as your conduct obliges me to do so. I am very sorry, it is not my fault, and I hope for your sincere repentance. CHRISTIAN.[8]

It was then decided that Koller should arrest Struensee. To Rantzau fell the agreeable task of seizing the Queen. Armed with some of the necessary documents, the Colonel and the General set forth on their respective errands.

NOTES

1. Reverdil, *Mémoires*, pp. 327–8.
2. Wilkins, *A Queen of Tears*, vol. II, p. 47.
3. Murray Keith, *Memoirs*, p. 283.
4. Nors, *Court of Christian VII*, p. 183.
5. Reverdil, op. cit., p. 333.
6. Ibid; Nors, op. cit., p. 185.
7. Wilkins, op. cit., vol. II, p. 61.
8. Nors, op. cit., p. 189.

XIV

The Arrests

IT WAS now essential that Queen Juliana should wait while Christian got dressed, and should then conduct him to her own rooms, so that neither Matilda nor Struensee could reach him; for if they did, it would be the work of a moment to prevent him signing any further orders. She and Prince Frederick therefore remained with him and Brieghel, in order to impress upon him the danger he was in from Struensee, the Queen and their faction. This was easily done, and within half an hour or so he was cut off from his wife and her lover in the Prince's apartments. Reassured as to his safety, he settled down to signing a quantity of orders which, besides disposing of Struensee and Matilda, reversed the laws ensuring the former's dictatorship, while handing over the administration of the Kingdom to his stepmother and half-brother.

This delighted Christian. There was nothing he liked so much as signing orders; it made him feel busy and important. When Juliana explained that Brandt would be among those arrested, all his fears vanished. He was a little doubtful about the elimination of Struensee; but when told that his former physician had treated him quite as badly as Brandt, he signed the warrant with alacrity. Now, at last, Juliana said, he had regained the power those evil men had taken from him. The next orders—one to the Governor of the Castle of Kronborg and the village of Elsinore requiring the 'close confinement' of the Queen, and another to the head of the royal stables for two coaches and an escort of soldiers—gave the poor creature an even stronger belief in his own firmness and efficiency. Hearing that there would be several executions, carried out with the usual brutality, Christian became quite gleeful.[1]

Meanwhile, Koller had collected three officers and a party of soldiers, whom he led to Struensee's apartments. On the way, he made them promise to shoot the Prime Minister in the event of himself being killed first. Finding the outer door locked, they tried to force it, thus rousing the valet, who refused to let them in. 'Open, in the King's name, under pain of death!' Koller shouted, and the frightened youth (he afterwards stated that he had been woken from a nightmare) obeyed.

They entered to find the candles still burning, and Struensee in bed, holding the book over which he had fallen asleep. He sat up and said, 'What is this?' 'You are the King's prisoner,' Koller replied, drawing his sword. 'Dress yourself, and come with me.' 'Do you know who I am?' Struensee exclaimed. Koller burst out laughing. 'I know well enough,' he said. 'You are the King's prisoner.' 'Where is your warrant?' Struensee demanded. Koller, who had failed to bring it, replied, 'It is with the King—but I can answer with my head that I am carrying out His Majesty's orders.' As Struensee did not move, he thrust his sword against the Minister's breast. 'I have orders to take you, dead or alive,' he announced. 'Which shall it be?' Struensee leant back. 'I must have time to think,' he said calmly. 'You are to come at once,' he was told. Struensee replied, 'I will first take a cup of chocolate.'

Koller shook his head. Struensee then got out of bed, remarking, 'You will at least allow me to dress myself?' 'You have two minutes to do so,' said the Colonel, signing to the soldiers to surround his prisoner, who began to resume the clothes he had left on a chair two hours earlier—the rose-coloured breeches and the blue velvet coat on which the Order of Matilda still glittered.

Flinging on a fur cloak, he was then taken to the guardroom, where his arms and legs were bound, and, surrounded by armed men, pushed downstairs and into a coach. 'What crime have I committed?' he asked Koller, who did not answer. In a few minutes they reached the Citadel, where the Governor was waiting for them. As they descended, Struensee, with his usual care for underlings, said to Koller, 'Give the coachman something,' and the Colonel produced a dollar. Glancing vindictively at the prisoner, the man said, 'I would willingly have driven you for nothing.'[2]

By the time Struensee entered the Citadel, he had recovered his poise. Removing his cloak, he said to the Governor, 'I suppose you are surprised to see me here?' 'Not at all,' replied that functionary, 'I have been expecting Your Excellency for a long time,'—and sent for a gaoler to conduct the prisoner to one of the cells used for the lowest criminals.

Struensee asked for his valet. 'I have not seen him,' replied the warder. 'Where are my clothes?' 'I have not seen them either.' 'Bring me my cloak,' said Struensee peremptorily, 'I don't intend to be frozen to death.' The man did not move, and Struensee, glancing round the cell, which contained only a truckle-bed and a stool, continued, 'Bring me a sofa.' 'There are no sofas here,' said the grinning warder, 'you ——'

This epithet, discreetly censored in the official report, destroyed what remained of Struensee's composure. He burst into a torrent of abuse, and, trying to reach the door, was seized and held. The gaoler then described him to the Governor as violent. 'Chain him to the wall,' was the answer, and this was done, while Struensee protested that he was being treated '*en canaille*'. The warder, having no French, merely laughed and left him.³

Struensee was unaware that Brandt had been placed in a cell below, after a similar attempt at resistance. His greeting to the Governor was, 'I must apologize for visiting you so early,' and the reply came as insolently. 'Not at all—my only regret is that you did not come earlier.' 'Upon my word, these are fine rooms!' Brandt continued. 'You will soon see that we have even finer ones,' he was told, and was then taken to the smallest and darkest cell in the building. 'The Governor spoke truth,' Brandt remarked, and, drawing a flute from his pocket, began to play. His insouciance contrasted favourably, the Governor thought, with Struensee's rage; and so he was not chained.⁴

A few hours later, Struensee's valet, now also a prisoner, was admitted to his cell. (In the confusion of the arrest, he had managed to hide his master's watch and jewels.) He knelt, weeping, at Struensee's fettered knees, and kissed his hand. Struensee bent to kiss his cheek, and, using the familiar second person singular, said gently, 'My poor fellow —I meant to provide for you. I delayed it too long, and now you are my companion in captivity. Do you forgive me?' 'O God!' the young man exclaimed, 'if only I had not opened the door, Your Excellency could have escaped'—referring to the secret staircase which led to the Queen's apartments. He was then removed and, some months later, set free.⁵

As Struensee's suite was exactly below Matilda's, she had been woken by the noise of his arrest; but the sounds were so confused as to make her think that the party suggested by Madame Holstein was being held there. She looked in on the infant Princess, and, finding her undisturbed, returned to bed, after sending down one of her attendants to ask Struensee's guests to make less noise. The woman did not come back; as Matilda fell asleep immediately, she was unaware of her disappearance.

At half past four, she was roused again by another woman, who fearfully told her that the passage was crowded with men in uniform. Matilda got out of bed and asked what they wanted. 'Count Rantzau is there, with several officers,' she was told. 'He demands admittance in the King's name.' 'In the King's name!' Matilda repeated; then, beginning to grasp the situation, she ordered the woman to fetch Count Struensee. 'The Count has been arrested.' 'I am betrayed—lost!' Matilda exclaimed. 'But let them in—traitors! I am ready for anything they may do.'

Rantzau, followed by half a dozen officers, then entered the antechamber. Without uncovering, he produced Christian's letter and read it aloud. 'Give it me,' said Matilda, 'I must see it for myself.' Having done so, she threw it on the floor and went on, 'This is treachery, with which the King has had nothing to do,' adding, 'Leave me, Count—I am not presentable.' Rantzau sat down, stretched out his legs and said, 'I must beg Your Majesty to obey the King's orders.' 'His orders!' repeated Matilda with a wild laugh. 'He can know nothing of them— your villainy has made use of his madness. No—a queen does not obey such a command!'

Rantzau said, 'My commission does not allow delay'—and signed to some of his group to seize her. She retreated into the bedroom to find a dressing-gown. Returning, she moved to the door, to be halted by one of Rantzau's men. She said, 'Till I have seen the King you dare not touch me. Let me go—I must, I will speak to him'—and once more advanced, to be held back by another officer. Shaking herself free, she exclaimed, 'How dare you? Go—I'm not afraid of you!'

As she moved past him, she was seized by three officers. Furiously struggling, she called for help, and then, wrenching herself away, rushed to the window, smashed the glass, and was trying to throw herself out when she was grasped from behind by a soldier. She turned, and pulled at his hair with such violence that he fell on his knees. He was followed by another, whom she also struck down.

As his assistants hung back, Rantzau, still seated, apologized for his insistence, adding that he would have to answer for it with his head if she did not yield. 'Where is Count Struensee?' Matilda demanded. 'There is no longer any such person,' Rantzau replied. 'And Count Brandt?' 'Those birds are caged,' was the answer.

Seeing that his subordinates still hesitated, Matilda dashed past them and ran along the passage to Christian's suite. Here she banged on the doors which Juliana and Frederick had locked behind them an hour earlier. Returning, she was seized by five officers. She managed to extricate herself, with the result that her gown was torn off, leaving her half naked. 'Your Majesty must excuse me,' said Rantzau, looking her up and down, 'but my duty forces me to resist your charms. Pray dress yourself,' he went on, signing to his men to carry her back to the bedroom. As they set upon her, Matilda fainted.

Rantzau then sent for Count Osten, who waited for the Queen to be restored and dressed. When she appeared, he told her that she was to go to Kronborg, where her stay would be short, and that she was being sent there for her own safety. He added, 'The people have rebelled against Your Majesty's authority.' 'What have I done to the people?' Matilda exclaimed. 'I know that there have been changes—but I have always done what I could'—and burst into tears.

'Your Majesty must forgive me,' Rantzau put in, with the same mocking courtesy, 'that my gout'—pointing to his feet—'prevents me from escorting you to Kronborg.' Osten said, 'You yourself considered going there during the mutiny of the Norwegian sailors.' 'I will not go without my children,' Matilda declared. 'The Crown Prince', Osten replied, 'cannot be moved. But as you are still nursing the Princess Louise, you may take her—and two of your women.'

After some further argument, Matilda, surrounded by an armed escort and followed by a nurse carrying the baby, eventually consented to leave. Rantzau said, 'You see, Madam, that my feet fail me. But my arms are free—and I beg the honour of conducting Your Majesty to your coach.' 'Go—traitor! I loathe you!' Matilda cried. She then walked down to the courtyard, where the coaches were waiting. Taking the Princess, she got into the first, accompanied by Mademoiselle Mosting, one of Queen Juliana's employees, and Captain Castensjold, Prince Frederick's equerry, who sat opposite her, his sword drawn. The nurse and the bed-chamber woman entered the second coach; both vehicles were surrounded by a guard of thirty armed dragoons.[6]

No record survives of Matilda's behaviour during the journey from Copenhagen to Kronborg, which must have taken some three hours; and as Mademoiselle Mosting had been ordered to report all she said, it can be assumed that she was silent, shocked into exhaustion by her struggles. From later accounts, it seems that she was rather concerned for Struensee than for herself or her children. Her sanguine and credulous temperament no doubt led her to believe Osten's promise that she would not long remain in a confinement which was merely protective, and that she would eventually rejoin her son. Also, she appears to have visualized Struensee's fate as one of imprisonment and disgrace; that he would be accused of high treason did not, then, occur to her.

It was still dark when Matilda left Copenhagen. By the time the coaches passed the lake surrounding Hirschholm, it would have been light enough for her to see the outlines of the palace where she, her lover and their Court had held their revels. She seems to have sat still, clasping her child, speechless and dazed. Pine forests, snow-spread fields, scattered cottages and farms, peasants trudging to work in the merciless cold of a northern winter, provided a grim setting for the gilded coaches and the scarlet-clad dragoons, whose drawn swords made a steely barrier between the Queen and the country she no longer ruled. She had, of course, no conception of what awaited her.

At the outer gate of the fortress the officer commanding her escort handed over the instructions given him by Queen Juliana and signed by her stepson, and the drawbridge was raised. The coaches crossed the ice-bound moat and drew up in the vast, unlit courtyard. The Governor, General Hauch, then took charge of Matilda's party. Juliana's orders had forbidden her the occupation of the state apartments. Carrying the baby, she was ushered into a small, octagonal, heavily barred room, overlooking the Sound; it had neither fireplace nor shutters, and contained a pallet bed, a *prie-dieu* and two stools; its base was battered by the waves. Beyond was the guardroom, now crowded with soldiers and warmed by log-fires and stoves. Matilda sank on to the bed and began to cry. Presently the ration issued to prisoners was brought her, but she refused it, until her women, who were admitted from time to time, pointed out that the Princess was dependent on her, and she forced herself to eat a little; meanwhile, the child and its nurse were established in a heated room. Matilda was then left alone till night. At nine o'clock she was escorted to the other side of the castle, so as to feed the baby again. Glancing out of the window, she saw a blaze of light over Copenhagen, and asked the reason. Mademoiselle Mosting, who had had orders not to leave her, replied, 'Those are the illuminations celebrating your and Count Struensee's arrest.' Matilda turned upon the grinning woman, and slapped her face; after a burst of wild sobbing, she fainted and was carried back to her room, reviving to weep again.[7]

She was presently joined by Mademoiselle Arensback, another of Queen Juliana's spies, and roused herself to ask about Struensee. 'He is in the Citadel,' she was told. 'Is he in irons—has he enough food?' Matilda inquired, and receiving no answer, pursued, 'Does he know that I am at Kronborg?' Mademoiselle Arensback could not say. Next day, Matilda became calmer, and it was observed that she had regained her dignity. She behaved with courage and patience, and made no complaints, nor any demands for the treatment to which her rank entitled her.[8]

In Elsinore and throughout the countryside, it was believed that Holger Danske, the unconquerable and deathless hero of Danish legend, was also imprisoned, in the cellar of the castle. 'He is clad', Hans Andersen was told, a century later, 'in iron and steel, and leans his head upon his strong arm. He has been sleeping there for a thousand years. His long beard hangs down over the marble table, and has grown into it. He sleeps and dreams—but in his dreams he sees everything that happens up here in Denmark ... But when once a danger comes, then old Holger will rouse himself, so that the table shall burst when he draws out his beard! Then he will come forth and strike, so that it shall be heard in all the countries in the world.'[9]

When it was known that Holger Danske had not risen to rescue the Queen, the country people assumed that she must be guilty of the crimes of which the State, guided by Queen Juliana, was preparing to accuse her.

NOTES

1. Reverdil, *Mémoires*, p. 336; Wilkins, *A Queen of Tears*, vol. II, p. 67.
2. Wilkins, op. cit., vol. II, p. 70.
3. Ibid.
4. Ibid.
5. Nors, *Court of Christian VII*, p. 190; Murray Keith, *Memoirs*, p. 243.
6. Falkensjold, *Mémoires*, pp. 155–7; Reverdil, op. cit., pp. 336–7; Murray Keith, op. cit., p. 267.
7. Reverdil, op. cit., p. 338.
8. *Procès de Caroline Matilde*, pp. 61–85.
9. Hans Andersen, *Fairy-Tales and Other Stories*, p. 338.

XV

Revolution

DURING THE next few days Queen Juliana and Prince Frederick were very busy. Not only were they guarding Christian—much to their annoyance, he kept on asking for Matilda—but after their announcement of Struensee's arrest, which was made between five and six on the morning of January 17th, they had to summon the police to seize and imprison a number of people in Copenhagen; for the rejoicings at the downfall of Struensee's government took the form of destroying the red-light district of the city, besides the houses of those suspected of supporting him. Sixty buildings, including several brothels, were burnt down, and the occupants of the latter, described by Reverdil as 'les nymphes de ces asiles impurs', were made to run the gauntlet, stripped and flogged.[1]

There were some—the humble and the obscure—who deplored Struensee's fall; of the few who were articulate, one was Gaiter-Catherine, whom he had caused to be released from her prison in Halle a year earlier, and another was Brockdorff, a servant of Christian's, who had saved his master from drowning and been left unrewarded until Struensee gave him a pension. 'God bless him!' Brockdorff exclaimed, adding, 'And may his sins be forgiven!'[2]

Besides watching Christian, organizing the re-establishment of the old Council of State, reversing Struensee's decrees and unobtrusively taking on the dictatorship of the kingdom, Juliana had to arrange a series of public appearances for Christian, in order to convince the people, firstly, of his sanity, and secondly of his release from Struensee's domination. This involved a number of drives through the city, during which the King, accompanied by herself and his half-brother, was wildly acclaimed. No one seems to have minded (perhaps they did not even observe) that he could not make a single gesture of response, and that, when pushed on to the balcony of the Christiansborg palace, he neither waved nor bowed and that his expression remained one of idiot blankness.

Yet Juliana persisted. As she could not trust her son to do anything on his own without making a fool of himself, she organized several theatre galas, ordered Te Deums to be sung in all the churches on January 19th, decided what honours and rewards should be given the conspirators, and had to consider how best to meet Sir Robert Murray Keith's threat of a declaration of war from George III.

Keith's dispatch to that monarch described his sister's imprisonment as flagrantly illegal, in that she had not yet been accused of any crime, and was being brutally treated. Juliana, realizing that invasion by an English fleet would bring about her own downfall, hastily ordered that Matilda should be moved to the state apartments, suitably attended and served, and allowed to walk in the gardens of Kronborg. In order to show her care for the Queen's spiritual welfare, she sent two of her favourite preachers to the castle, whom Matilda refused to see. Forced to attend chapel morning and evening, she had to submit to their sermons; these were couched in dramatically insolent terms, as expressed in texts from the prophet Isaiah. 'Hell from beneath is moved for thee to meet thee ... Thy pomp is brought down to the grave ... Thou art cast out ... like an abominable branch.'3

Meanwhile, the riots increased. Cellars were broken into, bonfires became a serious danger, the royal stables were attacked, and the police asked for military aid. Queen Juliana dared not, at first, use this form of prevention, her aim being a semblance of liberalism in contrast to Struensee's tyranny; nor could she employ her son, who was enjoying a brief popularity, to make an appeal to the people. She therefore desired his chamberlain to express the King's gratitude for their support, and to suggest that they should now retire to their homes. They replied by raiding the pawnbrokers' shops; and so the soldiers were summoned, followed by the heralds, who once more read messages of thanks from Christian, concluding, 'His Majesty regrets that you have let your zeal outrun your discretion.' Even then, the streets had to be patrolled, day and night, by the local militia. Rioting did not cease until January 24th.4

The next problem was that of Christian's guardianship. When consulted, he rejected all his stepmother's candidates but Count Osten, who refused the post. Queen Juliana then appointed Koller as the King's 'personal attendant'. A far more brutal keeper than Brandt, the Colonel led the poor lunatic a miserable life, and denied him to all visitors. Again and again, Murray Keith requested an audience, with no result. Juliana would not hear of it; for she knew that any mention of Matilda would drive Christian into a fit of violence, which would be reported to George III. At all costs, his brother-in-law's insanity must be concealed, so that Matilda could be presented as having first provoked and then betrayed the husband who had always been kind to her.[5]

Keith's dispatch describing the Danish revolution reached England on January 28th; George III then sent him the Order of the Bath, together with instructions to insist on an audience with Christian. An appointment was made; but when Keith arrived at the palace, he was received by Osten, who told him that the King was ill, and eventually he had to give his master's letter to Queen Juliana. Meanwhile, Dieden, the Danish envoy to the Court of St James's, was not received by George III. In fact, that monarch had been so disgusted by Matilda's liaison with Struensee—it does not seem to have occurred to him that his and his mother's insistence on her marriage to Christian might have contributed to her downfall—that he shrank from defending her; and so nothing was done to prevent her trial for adultery, although it was known that this might result in a charge of high treason. He therefore played into Queen Juliana's hands. She then desired Pastor Münter, still the most popular preacher in Copenhagen, to describe the horrors of Struensee's regime in a sermon delivered at Christiansborg, which concluded, 'Our King is once more ours, and we are again his people.' This was followed by an open letter to Christian from the historian, Suhm, on the same lines, with the result that Juliana's employees paraded the streets, shouting, 'Justice on Matilda!'[6]

Christian's twenty-third birthday, January 29th, was celebrated by the performance of two French plays, *L'Ambitieux* and *L'Indiscret*, based on Struensee's relationship with the Queen. The cheaper seats had been sold twice over, and this produced a riot. Panic ensued, Christian rushed out of the theatre, Juliana fainted, and it was reported that Brandt, Struensee and Matilda had escaped and were approaching Christiansborg at the head of an army.

As soon as the situation became quieter, Juliana sent for Reverdil—he had been arrested on the morning of the 17th—apologized and said that a mistake had been made. She added, 'If only I could have spared those others! But the Queen has forgotten what is due to her sex, her birth and her rank. We should have done nothing, my son and I, if the safety of Denmark had not been in question. But God helped me. I have no fears for myself.' She advised Reverdil, whom she knew to be devoted to Matilda, and apt to interfere on Christian's behalf, to

K

leave Denmark. He did so a few weeks later, never to return. Juliana then summoned Prince Charles of Hesse to help her organize the Government.[7]

Meanwhile, Struensee had attempted and failed to commit suicide. Preparations for his, Brandt's and Matilda's trials were set in hand, hers for adultery, and those of the men for high treason. Her pleas for rescue to George III availed her nothing, and were later destroyed, with all her letters. Juliana's propaganda resulted in Matilda being likened to that Old Testament queen who tired her head and painted her face and was thrown from a window to be eaten by dogs. Vengeance, rather than justice, was what Juliana desired. The judges were chosen with this end in view, as was the Commission sent to Kronborg to take down Matilda's statements. She had been much shaken by the increasingly savage attacks of the preachers; strongly guarded, she was made to sit directly beneath the pulpit during discourses which lasted for two hours. She became very pale, but neither fainted nor tried to move. In privacy, she only gave way when the baby Princess began to wail; then their tears flowed together. She made no further inquiries about her lover. and so knew nothing of Struensee's treatment, which had been designed to break him down before he left the Citadel to face his examiners; and he did not know that she was a prisoner. He thought of her as he had left her on the night of the ball—in charge of the kingdom, and of a husband who would sign anything she desired. He must therefore have concluded that he had only to deny their relationship, and that she, having followed his example, would eventually effect his release and the exile he himself had planned less than a year ago.

This belief enabled him to withstand the cruelties used upon him. Chained to the wall all day, he was put to bed in another set of chains attached to a heavy weight. As he began to get over the shock of his arrest his attempts at suicide ceased, and he submitted without complaint to being fed by his gaolers. This phase of his imprisonment lasted five weeks. He was then released from the wall, allowed to shave, dress himself decently, fettered again and escorted to the Governor's lodging, where the irons were removed. This brought on a trembling fit, which the Commissioners ascribed to fear; but Struensee was not intimidated; he had grown so used to the weight of his chains that he found it difficult to stand without them. He then prepared to answer the first interrogation, which lasted from ten in the morning till two in the afternoon, and was resumed from four o'clock until seven.[8]

Questioned as to his seizure of power, he defended himself by pointing out that he had obtained the King's signature to all his decrees. He said that he had never bullied nor allowed anyone else to bully Christian, standing up for Brandt with more loyalty than truth, and describing Christian's bouts of violence. His judges then accused him of brutalizing the Prince of Denmark. Struensee explained his methods, and dwelt at some length on the improvement in the child's health and behaviour. The matter of his embezzlement of State funds was raised; having once more asserted his innocence, he was taken back to his cell.[9]

Next day, the Commission accused him of illicit relations with the Queen. Their leader, Braem, was so enraged by Struensee's cool refutations that he burst into a torrent of abuse. 'Pray calm yourself,' said the prisoner, 'and remember that it is I, not you, who am in danger.' Braem retorted that instruments of torture were ready in the next room, and that confessions could be forced from obstinate criminals. 'That would avail you nothing,' Struensee replied, 'because I have nothing to confess'—and was again dismissed.[10]

On the third day, the Commission informed Struensee of Matilda's arrest and imprisonment, and of her forthcoming trial for adultery. Then his whole aspect changed. He put his hands over his face and burst into passionate weeping. As they watched and listened they heard such broken phrases as 'the person I loved best in the world'—'What have I done'—'Disgrace—shame'—and glances of triumph were interchanged.

At last Struensee looked up and asked if he might retire to think over this terrible news. His request was refused, and he was desired to admit his guilt; a full acknowledgment, he was told, might result in a reprieve. While he remained speechless, trying to collect his thoughts, Braem said, 'As the Queen has confessed to your intimacy, you would do well to follow her example.'

After a short pause, it became clear that Struensee did not believe in Matilda's confession; in fact, he went so far as to say so. The clerk of the court then gave him her statement, signed, he was told, not under duress, but freely, and, it was implied, without the faintest concern for his safety. He read it, and was convinced. Then he said, 'It is true. Our intimacy began in the spring of 1770, and has continued ever since. We tried to give it up—and were unable to do so'—and again broke down.[11]

Four days later, he supplied details, adding, with tears, that he had sometimes been harsh to Matilda, and that he had suggested leaving Denmark, but was persuaded to stay, 'and submit to the Queen's will'. He dwelt on the circumstances of a love he could no longer deny with the despairing frankness of one without hope. The Commissioners then renewed their inquiries.

'Was the state of the Queen's bed such that no doubts could be entertained as to what had taken place?'

'Yes. I must admit that—but I do not remember that it happened more than twice.'

'Were you aware that the Queen's women had warned her, and did that fact affect your conscience?'

'The Queen told me that her maids had spoken about certain rumours—but she denied them, and, after reprimanding the women, ordered them to be silent.'

'Who are the go-betweens in this unlawful affair, and in whom have you confided?'

'There have been no helpers or go-betweens. I have no recollection of having directly confided in Count Brandt as to how far matters had gone between the Queen and myself ... The first intimacy took place in the Queen's cabinet.'

Struensee then described Christian's complaisant attitude, his own daily têtes-à-têtes with the Queen and her refusal to heed his warnings. 'I plead guilty to the charge,' he concluded, 'and I would gladly suffer any agony as long as the Queen and my friends could be spared.'[12]

The Commission, having acquired Struensee's signature to the evidence they needed, handed it over to those about to confront Matilda. She had, of course, made no confession of any kind; her statement was forged.[13] A fortnight passed while they made the charges watertight by collating them with the evidence of the waiting-women and footmen. On March 8th they set off for Kronborg, headed by Stampe, the Attorney-General, Schack-Rathlou, formerly Minister of State, Count Otto Thott, dismissed by Struensee in 1770, and Judge Juell-Wind.

Shortly after the news of Matilda's arrest reached England, the Princess-Dowager, who had been seriously ill for some time, but had appeared in public as usual, died, having forbidden her attendants ever again to mention her daughter's name. Sir Robert Murray Keith then asked Count Osten if he might break the news of her mother's death to Matilda, and was denied. He made several other attempts to see her, and finally managed to write to her, pointing out that a trial would be illegal, and that she should refuse to answer any questions. She replied that what she most feared was assassination. When Keith reported this possibility to George III, and Parliament raised the matter of his sister's treatment, Lord North said that His Majesty had desired him not to discuss 'so delicate a matter', thus indicating that the King was convinced of his sister's guilt and was not going to act. The Opposition then attacked the King and North, and 'Junius' declared that 'an insignificant Northern potentate is honoured by a matrimonial alliance with the King of England's sister ... A confused rumour prevails that she has been false to his bed ... Our hopeful Ministry are however, quite silent ... ', and went on to denounce North's 'shameless remissness'.[14]

The fact that Matilda's case was being discussed all over Europe did not affect George III's attitude; he merely ceased to appear in public, or to enter into the matter, giving his mother's death as an excuse. Meanwhile, Keith's efforts on Matilda's behalf resulted in Osten's telling Dieden that as the Queen was guilty, her removal from Christiansborg—nothing was said about her imprisonment—was in order. A few days later, a letter to George III signed by Christian and composed by Osten and Juliana begged the English King to 'suspend judgement' until his brother-in-law wrote again. George III then asked for 'fair treatment' for Matilda, and once more desired Keith to interview Christian. Again, the envoy was put off, and Juliana, counting on George III's inactivity, completed her plans for the Queen's trial, while informing her brother that she was being treated as became her station, and would be examined by unbiased judges.

Armed with Struensee's confession, the Commissioners entered Kronborg without warning, and, having established themselves in the guardroom before a table set out with pens, ink and paper, sent to inform Matilda that they awaited her pleasure. Dressed in a state gown, she eventually appeared, attended by her women, to be faced by a group of men she knew to be her enemies. They rose and bowed. She sat down, indicating that they should do the same.[15]

Those who had expected to find her in tears or hysterical, were considerably taken aback by her dignity and composure. When Schack-Rathlou began to cross-question her, her denial of his right to do so, and refusal to incriminate herself in the slightest degree, brought matters to a standstill. She was told that these continued and pointless refutations would result in the Princess Louise being taken from her; still she remained firm.

Schack-Rathlou then stood up and said, 'Your Majesty having refused to acknowledge your guilt, it is my duty to inform you that Count Struensee has confessed to your having committed adultery.' 'Impossible!' Matilda replied. 'And if he has, I deny it!' The Commissioner then read out Struensee's statement, which she denounced as a forgery. Schack-Rathlou handed her the paper. She read it—and, recognizing the signature, fell back in her chair, her face in her hands.

Schack-Rathlou paused. Then he said, 'Madam—if this confession be true, no death can be cruel enough for such a monster'—adding that Struensee had already been condemned to execution. Matilda fainted. Having been revived by her women, she gripped the arms of her chair, in an attempt to rise. Failing to do so, she leaned forward and began, 'If I were to confess—would the King spare Struensee? Could I save his life?' 'Surely, Madam,' the Commissioner replied. 'That would be adduced in his favour, and thereby alter the situation. You have but to sign this'—and he produced a paper in which Matilda's adultery was acknowledged.

Still she hesitated—was this a trick to entrap both her and her lover? Then she said, 'I will sign'—and took the paper. She had got as far as writing 'Carol—' when something made her look at Schack-Rathlou. Throwing down the pen, she exclaimed, 'You are deceiving me! Struensee has not betrayed me, I know it—he could not!' The Commissioner put his finger on Struensee's signature, and Matilda collapsed again. In a frenzy of impatience, he thrust the pen into her hand and guided it on to what she had begun to write. Half dazed, she scribbled '—ine Mathilde'.[16]

The Commissioners then rose, collected their documents and left the guardroom. Matilda was carried back to her apartments. As soon as she regained consciousness she sent for the little Princess. She seems to have guessed that her confession would be used to condemn Struensee—who had betrayed her. He, brooding over her confession, prepared himself to die. The fact that he was no longer chained, allowed a change of clothes and an improved diet, showed him that, having signed his own death-warrant, he was to be treated as a State prisoner. Neither he nor Matilda was ever told of the trick—one of the oldest in legal history—that had been played upon them. Each died convinced of the other's treachery.[17]

NOTES

1. Reverdil, *Mémoires*, p. 340.
2. Murray Keith, *Memoirs*, p. 215.
3. Reverdil, op. cit., p. 347.
4. Wilkins, *A Queen of Tears*, vol. II, p. 93.
5. Op. cit., vol. II, p. 100.
6. Op. cit., vol. II, p. 97.
7. Reverdil, op. cit., p. 370.
8. Op. cit., pp. 394–5.
9. Falkensjold, *Mémoires*, p. 183.
10. Reverdil, op. cit., p. 395.
11. Nors, *Court of Christian VII*, p. 212.
12. Op. cit., pp. 211–12.
13. Ibid.
14. Wilkins, op. cit., vol. II, p. 125.
15. Falkensjold, op. cit., p. 207.
16. Op. cit., pp. 206–9.
17. Ibid.; Reverdil, op. cit., pp. 396–8.

XVI

The Trial of the Queen

THE COMMISSION had now obtained two admissions of guilt from Matilda, one forged, the other genuine, and one from Struensee. This evidence, quite apart from that provided by the Queen's attendants, should have been enough to condemn them out of hand. But these gentlemen had overreached themselves; for the fact that Matilda would be able to prove her first confession to be a forgery might throw doubt on the other two. The outcome of her trial was therefore still in the balance; and there were more aspects in her favour, besides that of the forged confession. One was the danger of interference from England, another her popularity with the Danish people, of whom only a minority, paid by Juliana, desired her punishment. The last difficulty was the lack of visual evidence; for no one had actually seen her and Struensee in bed together. Both in the Court circle and beyond it, there was of course no doubt about their relationship; it had been openly conducted for two years. His fate, that of execution for high treason, was in any case ensured by his seizure of power and his institution of laws abrogating Danish custom and tradition.

In an earlier age, Matilda's adultery would have brought about either imprisonment for life or execution. Now, if the charge against her could be proved beyond question—and this was not certain, in view of the fact that she might plead having been bullied and frightened into a false admission—her divorce and 'honourable confinement' would follow. She would then be incarcerated in circumstances which would, sooner or later, cause her death.

Reverdil, who composed but did not publish till later on, a lengthy defence of the Queen, thought that Christian's complaisant attitude towards Struensee, and his insistence on his establishment as Matilda's *cicisbeo* should be put forward.[1] This plea could not have been considered, any more than the King's treatment of Matilda in the early days of their marriage; for the monarch was sacrosanct and therefore incapable of error. Nor was his lunacy even mentionable; as he had not abdicated, he must be perfectly sane.

Meanwhile, Juliana's employees were slightly hampered by the necessity of staging an ostensibly fair trial, of which the evidence must appear incontrovertible; they could not conduct cross-questioning and summing-up in secret, as in the sixteenth century. So they had to appoint a lawyer of repute for Matilda's defence. This man, Uhldal, was an advocate of experience and distinction. In their first interview, he explained to his client the conditions of the trial, and described such loop-holes as would be available.

He told Matilda that she would not be allowed to appear at the hearing; nor would he be allowed to cross-examine those giving evidence against her. The procedure was based on her husband's charge of adultery, and, as he could not be present, neither could she. The witnesses—some fifty in number—would read out their statements and then withdraw. Uhldal added that, as Matilda's rank gave her certain privileges, he might be able to persuade the authorities to let her confront her accusers—did she wish to do so?[2]

In view of the fact that she would not be cross-examined either by Uhldal or by Bang, Christian's advocate, and must therefore remain silent, Matilda decided not to attend the trial; privately, she confessed herself unable to deny the charge of adultery. Uhldal then asked her for a public version of her conduct. She replied, 'I may have been imprudent—but cannot youth be my excuse?' When he raised the question of her signed confession, she said, 'Although I seemed to acknowledge my guilt, I was in too much distress. Now I am calmer, I know that I am innocent.' Uhldal appears to have suggested that she should appeal to Christian, and together they evolved the following plea—'My husband has granted me much, and I hope he will also, through the mouth of his judges, acknowledge that I have made myself not unworthy of him.'[3]

On March 14th, 1772, the trial opened in the great hall of the Court of Exchequer in Copenhagen with a prayer read by the Bishop of Zeeland. The thirty-five judges, who now completed the Commission, were formally released from their oath of allegiance to the sovereign; it was announced that this ceremony ensured their trying the case without prejudice. Christian and Matilda would be heard through their respective advocates, not as rulers, but as simple citizens. Queen Juliana was thus able to impress on George III that his request for a fair trial for his sister had been scrupulously observed. In fact, as long as Matilda remained in Kronborg, and was therefore unable to appeal to the people or to her husband, and thus cause a revolution in her favour, Juliana could be virtually sure of her condemnation. She was already making arrangements for the Queen's imprisonment—for life —in the castle of Aalborg in Jutland, which had been set in order a month earlier.[4]

When the preliminaries of the hearing were over, the witnesses for Christian gave their evidence. None was called for Matilda. During the next ten days her attendants described their observation of her and Struensee's relationship, and retailed her talk about love affairs. This was followed by the reading out of Brandt's statement, in whom Struensee had confided. 'But', the Count added, 'this confidence was unnecessary, as every word and look that passed between Struensee and the Queen showed their attachment.' Brandt's statement then described Matilda's jealousy, her quarrels with Struensee and their reconciliations. Bang then rose to make his indictment.

'Only the command of my King', he began, 'could induce me to speak against the Queen.' He went on to urge the necessity of faithfulness to a royal bed, in view of the danger to the succession, emphasized the incontrovertibility of the evidence, and asked, 'Can we submit to the doubtful heritage of the Queen?' He concluded with a declaration of 'deep regrets and profound reverence for Her Majesty', adding, 'I submit that the King's personal right, the honour of his House and the security of the nation simultaneously demand that the justice and loyalty which animate this Commission should, in accordance with the law of God, the law of nature and the law of this country, dissolve the marriage tie which binds Christian VII to Her Majesty Caroline Matilda.'[5]

After an interval of ten days, Uhldal defended his client in a speech which lasted four hours. It was emotionally inspired, magnificently delivered and entirely devoid of any appeal to reason. He said that their confessions had been forced from Struensee and Caroline Matilda, and that her attendants' evidence was the merest gossip and therefore could not be proved in Danish law. As no witness had seen them sleeping together, the accusations were based on guess-work. His Majesty had encouraged and approved their friendship; as he was in the habit of visiting the Queen at night, he may have been mistaken for Struensee—this plea seems unworthy of any reputable lawyer—and her talk of love to her maids was, of course, quite impersonal. He added that the interchange of presents between Matilda and Struensee was customary in Court circles. Uhldal wound up with a burst of rhetoric which reduced his defence to absurdity. 'How could Her Majesty have so broken her marriage vows? Count Struensee betrayed her to save himself. It is impossible that Her Majesty could have been so imprudent. All the evidence is conjectural.' He then repeated Matilda's declaration of innocence, and added, 'How I wish that I could reproduce the emotion with which those words were spoken! Can it be believed that Her Majesty could so far have forgotten herself? I hope that I have now proved the innocence of the Queen. I venture in Her Majesty's name to submit that Her Majesty Queen Caroline Matilda be acquitted from His Majesty the King's accusation in this matter.'[6]

Four days later, judgment was given against Matilda, and her divorce pronounced, with the result that Christian was now free to marry again. Her sentence depended on his pleasure. Then, to the fury of Queen Juliana, the legitimacy of both her children was confirmed. That lady's plans for her son's succession seem to have been based on the grounds that, in 1767, Matilda had taken a lover, who was the father of the Prince of Denmark.[7]

This judgment deprived the trial of all meaning; for if Matilda had committed adultery, then both her children were more than likely to be illegitimate. (The portraits of Princess Louise, painted in her twenties, show a striking resemblance to Struensee.) Meanwhile, these findings were not made public: but the verdict was sent to the governors and viceroys of the provinces. In this, Christian stated that he had set aside his wife for the honour of his House and dynasty, but gave no reason for having done so. Queen Juliana then arranged that Matilda's degradation should be announced to the foreign ambassadors in a solemnly ceremonious manner. They were received by the principal courtiers and the Grand Chamberlain—who were dressed in deep mourning—at the Christiansborg palace, told that His Majesty was wifeless, and that his ex-consort's name would be omitted from the public prayers. Matilda was dead in law.[8]

Uhldal then left for Kronborg to break the news of her condemnation to the Queen. She said, 'I expected as much—but what will become of Struensee?' Uhldal replied that he would be sentenced to execution. She burst into tears, and 'shook all over', according to the advocate. Then she said that she had been the cause of her lover's misfortunes. 'Tell him', she sobbed out, 'that I forgive him for the wrong he has done me.' She no longer cared, Uhldal thought, what happened to her; all she asked was, that if she were allowed to live, her daughter should remain with her. She submitted without protest to the decree of divorce, not realizing that it might entail her separation from the Princess, who was not yet a year old.[9]

There were many objections to the acceptance of this child's legitimacy. But as she had been acknowledged by Christian and sponsored by Queen Juliana and her son, to cancel her status would have fatally weakened the plans for the succession. For if the Princess Louise's legitimacy was in question, then so also was that of the Prince of Denmark; and the newly restored Council were determined that he and not his half-brother, who was universally disliked, should inherit the throne. The general—and correct—belief was that Struensee had fathered the Princess, and that the Prince of Denmark was Christian's son. Shortly after her mother's arrival at Kronborg, Louise developed measles; naturally, her recovery was a disappointment to those who considered that Struensee had foisted her on the royal house.

In the intervals of nursing her daughter, Matilda spent much time in private prayer. Hitherto, her religious observance had been conventional and unthinking. She had always taken the existence of the Deity for granted. Now, in need of help from that source—all others having failed—she was forced rather than led into a spiritual frame of mind, which did not become natural to her till later on. She seems not to have been influenced by her lover's agnosticism; and he may not have cared to meddle with her faith, accepting it as the corollary to her rather childish temperament.

Waiting for the outcome of his trial, Matilda dared to hope that he would not be condemned to death: for Uhldal, in whom she still believed, was defending him. But the advocate knew himself confronted with an insuperable difficulty. His client was guilty of fornication with the Queen-Consort, and of high treason, to which capital crimes he had confessed. He had two defences: Christian's signature to all his decrees, and Matilda's 'insistence' (this was Uhldal's idea) on his becoming her lover. That of Christian's insistence on their relationship could not, of course, be put forward. When Uhldal raised the point of the Queen's advances to him, Struensee refused to discuss them; the reminder of her affectionate and demonstrative manner to him at the masked ball so unhinged him that he became speechless.[10]

On April 8th the divorce and Matilda's proposed removal to Jutland were made public, causing violent indignation in England. Keith then put her case before the Council with ingenious logic. As she was no longer the King's wife, or Queen of Denmark, then George III was responsible for her as an English subject, and she was free to go whenever and wherever he thought suitable. If this demand was ignored, Keith went on, war would be declared. His statement resulted in Matilda's departure to Aalborg being indefinitely postponed, and she remained at Elsinore, while George III made no attempt to rescue her, and the English people, maintaining her innocence, bombarded him with letters of protest. One of these desired him to send a fleet to Denmark to save his 'illustrious sister' from 'a parcel of frog-eating rascals', and to 'batter down Elsinore, and make Copenhagen feel the force of English resentment. I'd have our bombs fly about their ears,' the writer continued, 'and set fire to their already flame-coloured hair.'[11] It was horribly cruel, another correspondent pointed out, to imprison anyone in a castle haunted by Hamlet's ghost and 'battered by the waves'.[12] Horace Walpole, having little use for the House of Hanover, merely told a friend that there was 'the devil to pay in Denmark', and was much amused by the useless attempts at secrecy of the Danish Government.[13]

By this time, Christian, so long deprived of his wife, had become increasingly difficult and rebellious. As his demands for her return were disregarded, he determined to find her for himself. Hearing that she was at Kronborg, he managed to escape from his keepers, reached the stables and ordered a coach to be made ready. He was about to get into it when his captors caught up with him, and he was taken back to his apartments. He then seems to have relapsed into a state of lunacy, interspersed with outbursts of grief, and unanswered requests for Struensee.

Meanwhile, the ex-dictator, knowing himself doomed, continued to prepare his defence under Uhldal's direction. He had accepted a cruel death, calmly and without fear. His trial, which he was not allowed to attend, was set for April 8th. But on March 1st he had been subjected to an ordeal for which he was not prepared, and which he tried, in vain, to resist. And then, gradually, a complete and startling metamorphosis of his outlook, principles, and even his character, was accomplished through the efforts of his bitterest enemy.

NOTES

1. Reverdil, *Mémoires*, pp. 403–6.
2. *Procès de Caroline Mathilde*, pp. 61–85.
3. Ibid.; Nors, *Court of Christian VII*, p. 231.
4. Wilkins, *A Queen of Tears*, vol. II, p. 150.
5. Op. cit., p. 153; *Procès*, pp. 61–85.
6. Wilkins, op. cit., vol. II, p. 167 (Uhldal MSS.).
7. See p. 62 above.
8. Wilkins, op. cit., vol. II, p. 173.
9. Ibid.
10. *Procès*, pp. 61–85.
11. *Calendar of Home Office Papers*, 1772.
12. Wilkins, op. cit., vol. II, p. 124.
13. Walpole, *Letters*, vol. VIII, p. 14.

XVII

Struensee's Conversion

TOWARDS THE end of February 1772 the Governor of the Citadel asked Struensee if he would like to talk to a clergyman. During his youth and, later, in his days of power, the prisoner had had to listen to what he always described as the melancholy and tiring discourses of the Lutheran pastors. He therefore refused, adding, 'I and all divines differ very much in opinion, and I have no inclination to dispute.' Then, realizing that a Government order would enforce the arrival of a visitor of this kind, he resolved to 'receive him civilly', however great his distaste, but to warn him that there was no hope of his conversion. A week later, he was told that, by the King's—i.e. Juliana's—order, Pastor Münter had come to 'look to the welfare of his soul'.

In his own opinion, at least, Münter was the John Knox of the eighteenth century, and he regarded his mission as a challenge, and also as the opportunity to crown his career. Anticipating greater hostility than he actually found, he was naively amazed when Struensee began to yield during their third interview. After his victory, effected through thirty-eight conversations over a period of seven weeks, was achieved, he wrote an account of it, which he called *A Faithful Narrative of the Conversion and Death of Count Struensee ... to which is added the History of Count Enevold Brandt*. This book, published in 1774, and consisting of two hundred and sixty-five closely printed pages, became a bestseller of staggering proportions. It was translated into twelve languages, and the German edition alone ran into twenty thousand copies.

The *Narrative* is composed of talks between Struensee and Münter, in which the author's discourses and questions are not quite equalled in length by his pupil's replies. A first reading gives the impression that Münter has in fact invented the whole book. No human being, not even one possessing a Johnsonian memory, could possibly have recalled all that speechifying. As if aware that he would be accused of manufacturing his story, Münter prefaced it by protesting too much about his integrity, with the result that his public was divided into two sections, one denouncing his efforts as a pack of lies, the other receiving them as proof of his powers. Neither party was right; the disentanglement of Münter's propaganda from Struensee's opening defiance and his return to a long discarded faith, is a complicated but not impossible task.

After each interview, most of which lasted several hours, Münter wrote down all he remembered of these talks, adding to them according to taste, in the style which had made him famous. Some twentieth-century biographers have described him as a narrow-minded bigot, Juliana's tool and a 'fanatical thunderer', adding that Struensee, that 'miserable turncoat', was hoping to save his life by his so-called conversion, while his admissions were reported by Münter to his accusers, so as to ensure his condemnation.

These judgments are not well founded. Reverdil, who knew Münter, and had often heard him preach, described him as pompous and calculating, but not corrupt. The circumstances of Struensee's downfall, of his imprisonment and of his expectation of death by being broken on the wheel, contradict the picture created by those who choose to ignore his upbringing, his tastes and his courage. For five weeks he had been chained up like a savage beast, so helpless that he had to be fed, and deprived of the most primitive amenities. He had remained stoical, until he was told that he had been betrayed, without scruple or hesitation, by the woman he loved. The conditions of his confinement improved with his confession of their relationship; but during the next seven weeks he was allowed neither books nor writing materials, and was left alone to think over the past and contemplate the horrors awaiting him. He endured—and remained outwardly calm. When questioned, and no doubt taunted, by his guards, he replied that he was not afraid to die; and throughout this stage of his imprisonment he behaved with extraordinary coolness. What he most missed was distraction—of an intellectual kind; and this was provided by Münter, on whose visits he very soon came to depend; for the pastor brought him books, writing materials, and, later, enabled him to communicate with his family and friends.

Swollen with conceit, intolerably verbose and incapable of a single original idea, Münter was nevertheless a courteous and warm-hearted man. While representing the worst aspects of Lutheranism, he was just able, every now and then, to listen to and even understand, another person's point of view. Within a very short time he and Struensee became friends; and this is not really surprising, because, until Münter arrived, the fallen Minister had been bullied, insulted and, as he thought, traduced. Now, he was encouraged to recollect, reason and argue in tranquillity with someone who was neither spiteful nor gloating over his fate, and who guided him back into the past. The degrading and hideous present temporarily vanished; and in their talks together the intellectual agnostic reverted to his days of unquestioned faith and quiet family life. Struensee had lost everything. Humiliation, treachery and the thought of death by torture were his only companions. He faced them bravely, until Münter, after reviving the influences of his upbringing, set before him a vision of life in the next world. Gradually, Struensee accepted it—and so achieved another kind of moral and mental stability.

And there were times when he could not but be amused by his new friend's simplicity, his chatty references to the supreme figures in the divine hierarchy, and his total inability to deal with the most obvious criticisms of the Christian faith. To these, Münter's only riposte was to recommend yet another religious work, which he at once supplied. And books—books of any kind—were what Struensee needed above all else. Those brought to him were what was then described as metaphysical and philosophic: his favourite reading, together with the works of Rousseau, Voltaire and Helvétius, on whom the Reverend Jerusalem, Cramer and Gellert vociferously declared war. Study of their attacks on the free-thinkers absorbed him; he told Münter that, with certain reservations, he found them admirable. Gratitude forbade criticism, and produced an appreciation which may have been partly assumed.

Their first talk was not, from Münter's point of view, very satisfactory. 'Does he come by command?' Struensee asked; and in contemptuous resignation received his visitor 'with a sour and gloomy countenance', doubtless remembering Münter's diatribes during his dictatorship and his joy at the success of the *coup d'état*. As soon as they were alone, Münter began, 'Good Count—you see that I come to you with a heart that is sincerely affected for you. I know and feel my obligations towards an unhappy man, whom God, I am sure, never intended to be born for such a misfortune. I sincerely wish to make my visits, which I am ordered to pay you, agreeable and useful.' Struensee thanked Münter and shook hands with him; it was the first time since his arrest that he had been kindly addressed. When the pastor said,

L

'Should it happen that accidentally in our conversations a word should slip from me which perhaps may appear offensive, I declare beforehand that it was never said with such a design, and I beg that, in such instances, you will overlook my precipitation', Struensee, still 'not very favourable', replied, 'Oh! you may say what you please.' Münter at once launched into an immense and compassionate discourse, concluding, 'I come not for my own sake, but only with an intent of being useful to you. I am your only friend.' It was true. Struensee's eyes filled as he stared at his former adversary in silence. So their discussions began on a basis of trust.

Münter, an essentially practical man, had decided that Struensee's views on death in general and his own in particular must be defined. Struensee said that he had 'no hopes at all' of survival in this world, or in that to come. Having ascertained his belief in a First Cause, Münter said, 'It will always be out of your power to prove that there is no eternity.' 'I do not find the idea of total annihilation so terrible as I have found it was to many,' Struensee replied, and went on, 'I think it will be impossible for me to renounce any of my principles. I am far from being a Christian, although I acknowledge and adore a Supreme Being.' It seems likely that 'adore' was added by Münter; in any case, Struensee, perhaps unwittingly, had lost his advantage. Given the existence of a Supreme Being, why should He not have bestowed immortality on His creatures?

During their next talk, Jerusalem's *Meditations* were discussed, and Struensee confessed himself partly 'brought over' by that production. Münter then began to arouse his pupil's consciousness of error (Struensee was far from being a conceited man) and to work up his remorse. This was not difficult. Struensee had had weeks to reflect on his own arbitrary methods, his self-seeking and his responsibility for the ruin of the Queen and their friends. A reassuring prospect of divine forgiveness was offered him; but he continued to criticize Christianity as a means of everlasting happiness—'since it is so little known amongst mankind', he explained, 'and so few keep its precepts—which are quite impossible. I have so many of these doubts', he added, 'that it will be the most difficult thing to satisfy them all.'

Münter could only reply by falling back on another religious book, and in their next interviews began to work on Struensee's fears—what about eternal punishment in the life to come? As this attack did not have much effect, he reverted to the hope of God's forgiveness, and described the joys of existence in the next world. 'It is extremely difficult to come to any certainty on this point,' Struensee replied, and expressed his doubt of the Supreme Being's clemency.

Münter could always answer for his Maker's good will; he had done so for years. He then touched on the life of Christ, and, having left Struensee with a copy of the New Testament, began their next talk with 'How do you like the man?' Struensee, as if amused by this gossipy opening, replied, 'His morals and His personal conduct are excellent.' Münter said gravely, 'He was a good and a divine man, and one that deserves great credit. Even Voltaire does justice to His moral character. And Rousseau was quite charmed with Christ's morals—and with His death.'

If Struensee restrained a smile at this point, Münter did not observe it. He then began to speak of the prisoner's past, his debauchery and his dealings with women. Both men enjoyed these recollections, which were gone into at length—and here again, the possibility of Münter's inventive power arises. 'During the whole inquiry,' he wrote, '[Struensee] did not leave off crying.' Whether or no, his tears did not prevent his admission—surely one of some complacency – of having been 'a dangerous seducer. None among those I attacked', he went on, 'was at last able to resist me.' He denied having practised homosexuality, and so Münter hurried on to the next point, that of the sin of self-indulgence. But Struensee was more interested in the dogmas of the Christian faith. Why, he asked, had Moses never mentioned the immortality of the soul? And what about the Trinity, and Christ's claim to be the son of God? Münter took refuge in the Mystery slogan, 'for which', he added, 'you are not yet prepared, as it is above your understanding.' He then—not unnaturally—found it advisable to leave.

It was now time for Münter to break down Struensee's composure, and then heal the wounds he had made by promises of an agreeable existence in eternity. He began by producing heart-broken letters from his victim's parents, which brought on tears of remorse. Then came the opening stages of the pastor's triumph. Since Struensee had admitted that there might be a life beyond the grave—he could not be sure—why did he not take the final step, and thereby depart from this one in joyful anticipation?

In fact, Struensee had deceived himself, when he said that he did not fear permanent annihilation. His temperament was in one sense that of an egoist, in that, while courageously facing a horrible death, he could not face the thought of lasting extinction. Like many of those who, having ignored or even rejected the idea of immortality, then find

themselves deprived of all they most care for, he could only be consoled—and retain his sanity—by belief in a future life. Instinctively
seizing on one of nature's most popular remedies against despair, he
yielded to the alluring prospect of what certain groups now describe
as the Hereafter. (A hundred years later, he might have been able to
communicate with its occupants: but the Lutheran creed did not
countenance such activities.) So he accepted the vision of himself
continuing to exercise his talents in a higher sphere — one without
coups d'état, anxiety or betrayal. The temptation was irresistible, and he
cannot be blamed for giving way to it, doubtfully at first, and then
with conviction. Swallowing the opiate in hurried gulps, he began to
look forward to this new existence—at its worst, it would be a vast
improvement on the present—until Münter warned him against
exaltation, and was reassured.

Then came another set-back. Struensee admitted that Jesus Christ
was an admirable character, and, 'His resurrection', he said, 'seems to
me probable. But it appears to me a little odd that He, after the
resurrection, did not show Himself to His enemies.' For Münter, a
firm anti-Semite, it was the work of a moment to deal with this
objection. 'It would have been of no use', he glibly replied, 'and would
never have convinced the Jews, on account of their obstinacy,' and told
Struensee, rather sharply, that he ought to pray more. He then gave
him Bonnet's *Philosophic Explanation of the Arguments of Christianity*,
to which he added Claparède's *On the Miracles of the Gospel*—for why
should he do all the work?—and departed in a high state of satisfaction.

All this time, the trials of Struensee and Brandt were proceeding,
and every now and then Uhldal reported on them to his client. At
some point, Struensee realized that he was not to be broken on the
wheel. After his right hand had been cut off, he would be beheaded.
He made no comment on this exercise of Queen Juliana's mercy: but
henceforward his attitude towards eternity became characteristically
practical. With Münter's help, he composed an account of his conversion, which might be compared to the action of one taking out an
insurance policy with the Deity. He described himself as quite sure of
divine compassion, and seemed to revel in the tasteless pronouncements
of religiosity. Here again, Münter may have been more responsible
for this production, which he published with his *Narrative*, than he
cared to admit. He points out that the original MS. is in Struensee's
handwriting, and declares that there was no question of its being dictated, adding that he hopes he has not over-persuaded himself as to the

sincerity of his pupil's conversion. This rather naive admission throws a new light on their duets. That Struensee had reverted to type, in fact, to the influences of his early youth, did not occur to Münter.

At no point, according to the *Narrative*, did Struensee mention the reforms which had so horrified its author; nor did he justify himself by referring to the benefits he had bestowed on his adopted country. Münter's account of his attitude shows, merely, a cringing penitent; but any other version of their talks would have prevented the success—perhaps even the publication—of his book. He knew what his readers wanted, and he supplied it in full measure. Struensee's relationship with the Queen was also avoided; he referred to her only once, obliquely, as an unnamed person who had had too high an opinion of his talents. 'My former life', he added, 'seems like a dream.'

On April 21st their thirtieth interview took place. Münter had begun to worry about Struensee's calmness—could it be natural? He said, 'This week, in all probability, will be the last of your life.' Struensee replied, 'I hope I shall meet my death without fear. I am only apprehensive that you will be much affected by this shocking scene, and I should wish you not to accompany me to the scaffold.' 'No, my dear Count!' Münter exclaimed. 'I am your only friend, and I dare not leave you. I will assist you—and the only recompense I expect is, that you will die like a Christian.' A day was then arranged for the prisoner to take the Sacrament. On April 25th Uhldal entered his cell. He said, 'Good Count, I bring you bad news'—and produced a copy of the sentence.

'I expected nothing else,' said Struensee. 'Let me see.'

'He read,' Münter says. 'I fixed my eyes upon him with great attention—but I did not observe the least alteration in his countenance. After he had read it, he gave it to me. It was as follows: "According to Danish law, it is hereby declared just and right that Count Johann Struensee, for his due punishment, and that he may be an example to terrify others, has forfeited his honour, his life and his estates. He shall be degraded from his dignity as Count, and from all other dignities which have been conferred upon him. His coat of arms shall be broken by the common hangman. Likewise, shall Johann Struensee's right hand, and afterwards his head, be struck off, his body be quartered and laid upon the wheel, and his head and hand be stuck upon a pole." '

Struensee then discussed the course of his trial with Uhldal. Hearing that Brandt would suffer the same fate as himself, he was much distressed. As soon as they were alone, he desired Münter to speak to him 'as little as possible' on the scaffold. He went on, 'I shall certainly do as much as lies within my power to direct my thoughts towards God. I shall not take any leave of you. I know and feel how much I owe you.' He then gave Münter letters to be delivered to his parents and friends after his death; among these, was one of forgiveness to Rantzau.

Two days later, the Governor of the Citadel told Münter that his prisoner had 'kicked with his feet, gnashed with his teeth and gnawed his fingers' during sleep. Asked about these demonstrations, Struensee replied with a pious cliché, thus putting an end to further inquiries. When Münter spoke of the circumstances of his execution, he replied, 'I am far above all this, and I wish my friend Brandt may be the same. Neither honour nor infamy can affect me any more. It is not my *all* which will be laid upon the wheel. It would be the same', he added, 'if I was to undergo a painful operation for my health.' He then compared his execution to the sufferings of Jesus Christ upon the Cross. This piece of arrogance and ineptitude may have originated with Münter. On the other hand, Struensee was now sufficiently far advanced in a mingling of complacency and fanaticism to have produced it himself.

So ended the moral defeat of a brilliant and remarkable man by a third-rate demagogue. Yet in his last moments—which Münter, catering for a sadistic public, describes in detail—Struensee behaved as became one who had once ruled a kingdom.[1]

NOTE

1. B. Münter, *A Faithful Narrative*,
    pp. 1–253.

XVIII

Release

THE FATE of Struensee's supporters had now to be decided. With the exception of Brandt, none was condemned to death, and most were exiled. A few were sentenced to terms of imprisonment—Falkensjold for life; he was released four years later. Judge Guldberg thought that Brandt was not guilty of high treason; but when he suggested to Queen Juliana that he should be imprisoned or exiled, he was overborne, first by Rantzau and then by the King. Christian said that he would not sign the warrant for Struensee's execution unless it was accompanied by Brandt's; and Rantzau supported him. Partly through the intervention of Frederick the Great, Karl August Struensee was allowed to leave Denmark unpunished, and later became one of that monarch's Ministers. It was then decreed that the executions of his brother and Brandt should take place early on the morning of April 28th. Having signed the warrants on the evening of the 27th, Christian, with all his Court, attended a gala performance at the opera. This was followed by a banquet at the palace of Christiansborg.

The arrangements for the executions met with what seemed, at first, a number of insuperable obstacles. It was obvious that, unless the forces were called in, both Struensee and Brandt might be rescued on their way to the scaffold, or even snatched from it. Brandt was universally disapproved of, but not hated; and the common people had begun to realize that in submitting to Juliana's rule they were exchanging King Log for King Stork.

So four thousand sailors, armed with pikes and supported by fifteen hundred soldiers, surrounded the Osterfeld, where a scaffold twenty-seven feet high had been set up, after a series of delays; for the workmen usually employed in these tasks had gone on strike. Their leader told the authorities that to further such a deed would cause their own early deaths. Blacklegs, at three times the current wage, were called in, and the scaffold was completed a few minutes before the headsmen took up their positions. As the wheels on which the victims' limbs were to be exposed had been stolen on the evening of the 27th, two from one of the royal carriages were substituted at the last moment. Meanwhile, some fifty thousand people had come in from the countryside to watch the executions, and were camping out in the adjoining fields; they were then allowed into the Osterfeld, which was surrounded by armed men. Thousands of troops lined the route from the Citadel to the scaffold.

Pastor Münter's account of Struensee's behaviour on the last morning of his life is one of awestruck admiration and genuine surprise, mingled with doubts as to his pupil's attitude of mind. Surely he should have shown more remorse? Such unbroken fortitude was not quite suitable; nor was his care for his appearance. Münter entered his cell to find him dressed in the velvet coat and satin breeches of the masked ball. He had slept for some hours, and was now talking quietly to the officer who was to drive him to the place of execution. He told Münter that when he awoke he had trembled violently; that seizure passed, he had begun to read and was now quite composed. He added, 'I am sure I shall remain so.'[1]

Münter's account of their penultimate interview must be taken with extreme caution. He may or may not have used this time of waiting to deliver a discourse on the Eighth Chapter of St Paul's Epistle to the Romans; the exercise of his professional talents at such a moment would not have been beyond him. But it is difficult to believe that there would have been time, let alone inclination, for Struensee to hold forth at length and apparently without a pause, about sin, immortality and God's mercy. When Münter's turn came round again, he stressed the need of the condemned man's repentance, warning him against 'inward pride' and adding, 'You are to do nothing merely for the sake of being applauded by the spectators on account of your resolution and composure.' As this was exactly what Struensee had decided to do, he replied reassuringly in a speech which again seems to reveal Münter's inventive powers, and hinted that he would prefer not to be spoken to on the scaffold. The pastor said, 'The scaffold is neither for you nor for me the place for speaking much,' while reserving to himself the right to make the appropriate remarks during Struensee's last moments. 'Now', he writes, 'the doors of the prison opened—for which the Count himself never, but I very often, had looked with a fearful expectation.'[2]

Struensee's chains were resumed before he left his cell to enter the coach. Münter, preceding him in another vehicle, waited below the scaffold, where Brandt, with Dean Hee, was preparing for death with the utmost coolness and numerous declarations of piety. Among the thousands of spectators watching the executions from a distance was Queen Juliana. Armed with a telescope, she had established herself in one of the tower rooms of the Christiansborg palace. In later years, when asked why she preferred this small and inconvenient suite to any other, she said, 'These rooms are dearer to me than my most splendid apartments, for from the windows I saw the remains of my bitterest foes exposed upon the wheel.'[3]

Meanwhile Münter, realizing that Struensee was to die after Brandt, ordered the coachman to turn his carriage round, so that the prisoner should not be forced to witness his friend's execution. Struensee, pale but composed, said, 'I have already seen it,' adding, 'Pray do not mind me—I see you suffer,' and prepared to mount the scaffold, pausing to salute those spectators whom he knew with his accustomed grace. His chains made the long ascent difficult, and he was trembling as he faced the masked headsmen, who had thrown sand on the blood-stained platform and were now re-sharpening their axes. Münter, following him, continued with a series of questions as to his beliefs, which Struensee, according to the pastor, answered in the approved style. His chains were then struck off, his coat of arms broken and his death warrant read aloud. Helped by the executioner, he began to undress, producing a handkerchief to bind his eyes. 'It is not necessary,' said the man, took it away and guided him to the block, which, Münter observed, 'was stained and reeking with the blood of his friend'. The last words Struensee heard from him were 'Go in peace whither God calls you—His grace be with you.' When his hand was cut off, he fell into convulsions, and had to be held down before being beheaded.[4]

All this time, Queen Juliana had been in ecstasies, calling out, 'Now for the fat one!' as Struensee came into view. Her only regret, she told her attendants, was the absence of Matilda; she would have liked to see her dismembered corpse thrown into the cart with those of her lover and his friend, and her head exposed on a pole in a field beyond the city. Here, those of Struensee and Brandt remained until 1775, when they were stolen by a party of English sailors.[5]

Münter left the scaffold to report his triumph to the Queen-Dowager, who was able to produce a few tears, and said, 'I feel sorry for the unhappy men,' adding that she had had no feelings of personal enmity against Struensee, and that her conscience was clear. She then gave Münter a diamond snuff-box as a memento of the occasion—but her rejoicings were slightly damped by Christian's laments for Matilda, and his inquiries about Struensee.[6]

And then at last Sir Robert Murray Keith was allowed to visit Matilda. He was told that when she received the news of Struensee's execution she fainted, recovering to sit in frozen silence for several hours. His account of his first interviews with her was destroyed by the orders of George III.

That monarch's position with regard to his sister was a difficult one. He felt it his duty to rescue her from the perpetual imprisonment planned by Juliana. But Queen Charlotte refused to allow her to come home; she said that, rather than receive her, she herself would leave the country. After much Anglo-Danish wrangling, which concluded with preparations for the bombardment of Copenhagen, George III was told that he might remove Matilda from Elsinore. He agreed with his wife that she must not return to England. Where, then, could she be established as became a royal princess and the sister of an English king?

Matilda herself assumed that she would be allowed to live in England, and welcomed by those who had championed her cause. She did not know that the Government's plan for an invasion had enraged the Opposition, nor that they were now staging a campaign against her, of which the principal theme was her adultery. 'Yesterday', announced the *General Evening Post* of April 30th, ' ... men were crying printed papers, containing the most scandalous rumours and impudent reflections on the Queen of Denmark. The worst prostitute that ever Covent Garden produced could not have had more gross abuse lavished on her.'[7]

Although she was now living as became her rank, Matilda was still cut off from her former subjects, who had begun to desire her restoration; some of them even sympathized with her for the loss of her lover. Queen Juliana was much annoyed by these protests—and further put out by Christian's confusion of mind. He had forgotten signing Struensee's and Brandt's death warrants, and continued to ask what had become of them. Recalling an execution game he used to play with Brandt, in which a roll of paper was substituted for the axe—they had taken turns to kneel at the block—he was under the impression that this process had merely been repeated. While fearing and disliking Brandt, he had enjoyed that game, and wanted to play it again—so why could not Brandt be sent for? When told what had happened, and of his own responsibility for the executions, he burst into tears, and a

little later asked once more for the return of both men—and for
Matilda. He refused to accept the divorce; she was his wife, and they
ought to be together.

This attitude was shared by his humbler subjects; their mistrust and
resentment of Struensee had vanished with his execution. His prolonged
and cruel death, and the clumsiness of the headsman had so disgusted
them that they left the Osterfeld in silence; and, far from rejoicing at
the elimination of someone they had thought of as a tyrant, they were
now turning against the restoration of the regime he had destroyed,
and asking that Matilda should replace Juliana.[8] This convinced the
Queen-Dowager that Matilda must go before a counter-revolution
removed her own group from power. She agreed not to publish the
decree of divorce, and consented to the restitution of Matilda's title.
Keith then said that Matilda's allowance must be continued, and that
she should leave with a salute of guns; but he had to yield over her
going away without saying farewell to her son, and to her being
parted from the Princess Louise. The Council said that, as the legitimacy of both children had been acknowledged, they must remain in
Denmark. Keith warned Matilda of this decision; she continued to
believe that it would be impossible for the Danish Government to
separate her from her daughter, whatever their official decree.

Meanwhile, the discussions as to where Matilda should live continued. Lüneburg was considered, but rejected, as being too near the
Danish frontier. Finally, George III suggested Hanover, still an English
colony, of which the Viceroy was his brother-in-law, Prince Charles of
Mecklenburg-Strelitz. Queen Charlotte intervened with a strong
objection to the capital as a residence; it was too gay and social a
centre, she said, for an immoral young woman: and she urged Prince
Charles, who commanded the garrison there, to support her, in spite
of the fact that the city contained three unoccupied palaces. George III
then selected Celle, as being sufficiently remote from any diversions.
A pretty, medieval town, set round the banks of the Aller, it was
governed by another brother-in-law, Prince Ernst, a lively young
bachelor, who was eager to welcome Matilda. The castle, one of great
splendour, had not been inhabited since the death of her ancestor, Duke
George William, in 1705. So it was decided that she should be established at the hunting-lodge of Goerde, some fifteen miles away, while
her new home was renovated. There she would have a miniature Court
and an allowance of eight thousand pounds a year.

When Keith told Matilda that an escort of two sloops and a frigate would be calling for her, and that she was no longer a prisoner, but the guest of the Danish Government, she did not recognize the euphemism—there could be no question of her leaving Kronborg for Copenhagen—and burst into tears of relief. Neither of them realized that the unrest in the kingdom was such that if she had gone to Aalborg, her restoration would almost certainly have followed, and thus her reunion with her children. Matilda pictured herself imprisoned there in misery and danger, and seems not to have known of its amenities or of its pleasant surroundings. Her only wish, apart from the possession of her daughter, was to leave Denmark as quickly as possible.

Keith then told her of the other concessions he had obtained from Queen Juliana. The exception, he added, forgetting the guardianship of the Prince and Princess, was the proclamation of her innocence. Matilda replied that time might clear her character. She should continue, she said, to wear mourning for her 'murdered reputation'. She had enough sense not to deny categorically that she and Struensee had been lovers.

Juliana then offered to return the jewels Matilda had been given as Queen-Consort. She refused them; she would accept nothing from a husband who had cast her off without a hearing—she did not know that he was always asking for her—or from a country where she had been condemned by her enemies. All she wanted to take away were her own jewels, her books, her wardrobe and her bibelots. These were to be packed up and sent to Celle.

Although she was now free to receive visitors, Matilda's manner of life had changed from that of social intercourse to one of solitary study. Mistrusting everyone, she shrank from company, and took to reading with passionate absorption. 'Our library will be exhausted if the Queen continues thus,' said General Hauch, and asked Sir Robert Murray Keith to help supply her. Matilda's other interest was the welfare of the prisoners of Kronborg, to whom she sent dishes from her own table, and presents of money. When Hauch objected to her condoning the offence of a spy in this way, she replied with a quotation from Voltaire —'Il suffit qu'il soit homme, et qu'il soit malheureux.' Her chief occupation was, of course, the care of the Princess, now ten months old. Keith, who saw her daily, observed, 'A more tender mother than this Queen was never born.'

So the weeks went by; and as Matilda walked up and down the castle ramparts, looking out for the English ships, there came no sign of her deliverance. She told Keith that until she saw the British flag she would still feel herself in danger. She might be seized and sent to Aalborg; anything might happen to change Queen Juliana's mood.

She need not have concerned herself. Juliana longed to see the last of her. Only so could she be sure of retaining her hold over Christian and the Government; for the people had begun to hate both her and her satellites' repressive measures. Eventually, some of the laws promulgated by Struensee had to be restored, for fear of an outbreak.

On May 27th, 1772, the *Southampton*, the *Seaford* and the *Cruiser*, Captain McBride Commander, were sighted rounding the point off Elsinore. Matilda, who was at dinner, ran up to the ramparts to see them enter the harbour. Yet her relief was shadowed by despair, for Keith, who had taken a house near Kronborg and had orders to leave with the English squadron as her minister in attendance, had at last convinced her that she would have to part from the Princess Louise.

He now walked down to the harbour to welcome Captain McBride and bring him to the Queen. Their meeting was smoothly formal, until the Captain asked her when she would be pleased to sail. Then she put her hands over her face and burst into tears. The bewildered sailor heard her gasp out, 'My children!' as she rushed from the room. Presently one of her ladies came with a message asking him to forgive Her Majesty's breakdown; she would be ready to leave in three days' time.[9]

Queen Juliana then dispatched a party of noblemen to wait on Matilda and wish her godspeed. She received them with cold dignity in the presence of the English officers, who refused to shake hands, and replied to their compliments by turning their backs. Matilda arranged for parting presents to General Hauch's staff, and gave him a sum of money to distribute amongst the prisoners. She was told that, in order to avoid Copenhagen, her escort would proceed to Stade, where her Danish suite would be replaced by Baroness d'Ompteda as mistress of her household, two ladies-in-waiting, two chamberlains, three pages and some thirty maids and valets—all from Hanover. Passing the Cattegatt and the Skaw, she would land at a German port and thence travel to Goerde.[10]

She was in the midst of her last preparations when a coach, escorted by mounted dragoons and containing two ladies of Queen Juliana's household entered the courtyard of the castle. They were ushered into Matilda's apartments by General Hauch, who announced that they had come to fetch away the Princess Louise.

The Queen seems to have been in the habit of playing a game with the child in which she would snatch her up, put her down and seize her again; this had become one of Louise's greatest pleasures. So when Matilda took her from the nurse's arms, covered her face with kisses, and, weeping, repeated the process, the baby smiled and stretched out her arms in high delight. On this occasion her treat was prolonged until Juliana's emissary stopped it—for the agonized mother, turning back again and again for one last caress, was aware, not only that years would pass before she and her daughter were together once more, but that this parting might well be permanent. Finally, yielding to the inevitable, she tore herself away, sobbing out, 'Let me go — now I have nothing—nothing!' and rushed through galleries and ante-chambers, down to the courtyard. Blind with misery, she reached the harbour, and, as the cannon fired, boarded the *Southampton*.[11]

She had so delayed as to increase her sufferings; for the wind having changed, the squadron could not at once stand out to sea—and the Princess and her attendants were to remain at Kronborg till morning. Matilda leant over the rail, gazing at the lights of the castle till late that night, resuming her watch with the dawn. Then the ships sailed slowly along the coast, making little headway; for several hours the towers of Kronborg were still visible.

So, six years earlier, Matilda, an unwilling bride journeying towards a hidden destiny, had watched the English shore diminish and sink away. Her desolation now seemed complete and lasting. Yet the most dramatic phase of her whole life was still to come.

NOTES

1. Münter, *Narrative*, p. 194.
2. Op. cit., p. 196.
3. Wilkins, *A Queen of Tears*, vol. II, p. 211.
4. Münter, op. cit., pp. 204–5.
5. C. F. L. Wraxall, *Life and Times*, vol. III, p. 95.
6. Wilkins, op. cit., vol. II, p. 212.
7. Op. cit., p. 222.
8. C. F. L. Wraxall, op. cit., vol. III, p. 153.
9. Wilkins, op. cit., vol. II, p. 235.
10. Falkensjold, *Mémoires*, p. 231; C. F. L. Wraxall, op. cit., vol. III, p. 152.
11. Ibid.

PART III
Celle

I

Exile

BY THE end of May 1772 Caroline Matilda had lost her lover, her reputation, the care of her children, her position and the esteem of her brother and his family. She retained youth, health, beauty, an adequate though not lavish income, and the prospect of installation in a Court where she would be treated as became her rank. Presently she gathered that she would be allowed, under supervision, to visit the environs of Celle; her communication with the outside world by letter was so censored as to prevent any attempt to appeal to her Danish supporters, whose numbers increased with every week of Queen Juliana's rule. In a material sense, Matilda had no cause for complaint; morally, she was disgraced, living in the shadow of adultery, divorce and dismissal.

She spent four months in the hunting-lodge of Goerde, while the castle of Celle was being made ready for her. This temporary home was well appointed, even luxurious; but its loneliness—the nearest house was some fifteen miles away—and its gloomy forest setting made a bitter contrast with her existence in Denmark. She was completely isolated, without any distractions, and no pursuits but those she evolved for herself. No visitors were allowed, until her sister Augusta, and her brother-in-law, Prince Charles of Brunswick-Wolfenbüttel, arrived for a short stay.

Socially, this visit produced complications, for the Prince was Queen Juliana's nephew; and he seems to have been desired by his aunt to report on Matilda, while Augusta made it her business to find out what plans she had for escape and restoration. Matilda was glad of their company; some time passed before she realized that she could neither confide in nor trust them.

Augusta was still very unhappy in her marriage; for her husband's neglect and brutality were widely known. She was aware that she had become an object of pity—perhaps of ridicule — in the Courts of Europe. But his accompanying her to Goerde was a sign, in her view, that they were on better terms. The fact that she began to set a watch

M

on Matilda did not prevent a renewal of their childhood affection; they had always got on well together and still did so, if only on a superficial basis.

Augusta was stirred to indignation by the cruelty and spite of Juliana's behaviour. It was then arranged that she should come regularly to Celle as soon as Matilda settled in there. By and large, her companionship was to become an asset, although with reservations; her husband looked forward to her leaving him at frequent intervals.

Matilda's description of her treatment by the Queen-Dowager combined with her charm of manner to influence the Prince of Brunswick-Wolfenbüttel in her favour; such loyalty as he had for his aunt was forgotten as he listened to what seems to have been a remarkably fair account of her machinations. Matilda had not the least desire for revenge; she submitted without protest to all her losses but that of her children; for she looked on the possibility of her restoration simply as a means of rejoining them. Presently she managed to correspond with Struensee's family; but her letters have not survived, and there is no record of her referring to their relationship, or even mentioning his name.

Her twenty-first birthday passed uncelebrated in Goerde. It is unlikely that she troubled to contrast the monotonous routine of that retreat with the gaieties of Copenhagen. The splendid palaces, the glittering canals, the pastel-coloured houses of its citizens, the lakes and islands of that lost kingdom had been, for her, a background merely, for her children and her lover. She left behind a few ruined and imprisoned supporters, a crowd of dissatisfied and half-heartedly loyal subjects, but not a single friend; freed from an insane husband and his fiercely hostile family, she was at peace and unmolested. Yet the focus of her life was gone—as it seemed, for ever; so she resigned herself to filling in time with private hobbies: books, music, needlework, cards— and religion. Her former, conventional piety soon became the mainspring of thought and action. The pastor of Lüneburg visited her regularly, and every Sunday conducted a service for her and her household. She came to depend on his ministrations and, so far as it was possible, to be consoled by them. She appears not to have suffered from remorse, or from any consciousness of having sinned. She never complained of her fate, and refused to pose as a tragic figure, remaining outwardly philosophical and unembittered. She expected nothing more of life; and so the long-planned welcome waiting for her at Celle came as a wonderful surprise.

On October 20th she and her suite began their journey to that city, while Sir Robert Murray Keith left for England, where he was warmly thanked by George III for his efforts on her behalf. The King then made it clear that, having established his sister in her own Court, he would do nothing more for her. Denmark and England were still allies; she must therefore be permanently set aside. The information he had received over the last two years convinced him of her guilt, which he neither admitted nor denied. Meanwhile, because the cause of, and the evidence for, her divorce remained hidden from the general public, they were able to condemn or stand up for her, as they chose. The English people looked on her as a martyr, unjustly cast out by a group of fiends. The majority on the Continent thought that she had been monstrously used; and among these the most compassionate were the citizens of Celle—or Zell, as it was then called.

The inhabitants of this formerly important city longed for the re-establishment of royalty. The vast, lemon-coloured castle which dominated its surroundings had been the principal residence of Matilda's ancestors, the Dukes of Brunswick-Lüneburg, Hanover, Calenberg and Celle; but since the death of Duke George William it had been uninhabited for sixty-seven years, and the prestige of its people had been, in their view, thereby diminished. Now, that lost grandeur was to be magnificently restored by the installation of a queen; so they planned to acclaim her, not only as their sovereign, but as a spotless heroine and an illustrious victim, who could claim descent from Henry the Lion, and thus from her namesake, the wife of Henry II of England.

Some weeks before her arrival a public holiday was promised. The carvings and mottoes on the houses were repainted, speeches and verses prepared, and music for the train-bands specially composed. As the great day dawned, the country folk crowded into the town, the inns were full to bursting, and the local militia, heavily rosetted and carrying their banners, marched to and fro in strenuous rehearsal.

The sun shone in a cloudless sky: and there was just enough breeze to display the royal standard on the tower of the castle. At the west gate, the Mayor and the principal burgesses, dressed in blue velvet and mounted on elaborately caparisoned horses, had assembled long before Matilda was due, while the humbler citizens lined the route to her new home; then, unable to wait any longer, they marched out to meet her.

They had to stand in the road for what seemed a long time before a courier appeared to tell them that Her Majesty was on her way. At last, her coach came in sight; it was drawn by six Hanoverian greys and accompanied by postilions in liveries of scarlet and gold; an escort of cavalry rode between this equipage and the carriages containing the royal suite.

The foremost merchant of Celle then advanced, and Matilda ordered a halt. Kneeling, he presented her with a poem ('To us returns the sun of golden days, God Save the Queen shall be our song'), and a concourse of mounted citizens and militia escorted her to the main gate of the town. Here, Herr Würning, the Mayor, was waiting with another ode, printed on white satin ('Through us, O Queen, Zell utters her rejoicings'), and after its numerous verses had been recited, the trumpets blared out. As Matilda entered the city the people thronged about her, cheering and throwing flowers. So her progress was halted to a walk: but she would have no one turned away; bowing and radiant, she progressed past the town hall and over the drawbridge to the castle. In the courtyard, Prince Ernst of Mecklenburg-Strelitz, surrounded by his staff, was waiting to hand her out and escort her up the great staircase to the state apartments, where she was served on the knee with wine and sweetmeats. She held a reception lasting some two hours; then, slightly overcome—for she had not expected such a prolonged and vociferous welcome—she withdrew to rest and change her dress for a banquet. It was reported that she said to the Baroness d'Ompteda, 'Thank God, my brother's subjects do not believe me guilty'—but the remark may be apocryphal. At this time, Matilda never referred to her trial, or to its outcome. She had resolved to live in the present, and did so with apparent serenity—for a little while.[1]

During the banquet Matilda became aware that Celle was brilliantly lit up, and decided to go out, on foot, to see the illuminations. The informality of what became her habitual approach to her subjects was thereby inaugurated, and from that moment onwards she was worshipped. She could do no wrong; and as she and her suite paused to inspect the 'devices', the bonfires, the beribboned maypoles and the dancing people, she burst into exclamations of gratitude and delight. Escorted by Prince Ernst, she walked about till ten o'clock, and then went to bed, a little tired, perhaps, but happier than she had been for a long time. Next day, she was able to go round her new home.

The castle of Celle, formerly a late medieval fortress, had been entirely rebuilt by Duke George William in the fashionable baroque style, with the exception of the Gothic chapel and the gallery overlooking it. In the 1680s he had inserted a theatre, now the oldest in

Germany, but in such a manner as not to break away from the original outline, which had been set round a huge quadrangle. The general effect was one of stateliness, without gloom or mystery, the impression given being rather that of a pleasure-dome than of a palace. Seen from across the moat (this, and the drawbridge, created the rumour that Matilda had once more been cruelly incarcerated), the façade of the castle appears subtly irregular: some towers are domed and circular, others octagonal. In the eighteenth century, the slope leading down to the grey-green waters of the Aller was planted with avenues of limes and beeches.

Matilda's apartments occupied the south side of the quadrangle, next to the chapel, the principal features being a picture gallery, which separated the dining-room from an octagonal cabinet, and the ante-chamber leading into the bedroom, boudoir and library. These rooms were hung with canvas painted in the Chinese manner with birds and flowers. From the boudoir a few steps led down into a passage, and thence to her pew in the gallery, overlooking the choir.

No suite could have been more conveniently planned. But, in the picture gallery were some rather disturbing reminders of such passion and despair as had come within Matilda's recent experience. It was impossible for her to walk from one end of it to the other—and she had to do so several times a day—without being aware that her tragedy repeated, although in a lesser degree, that of her great-grandmother, the spoilt, exquisite, harshly victimized wife of George I. Sophia-Dorothea's earliest portrait, one of startling unconventionality, then hung there, flanked by those of the parents who had cast her off. There, as a child, she had first known the handsome Swedish page, who, ten years later, became her lover, and who had paid with his life, as Struensee had, for the brief raptures of an adulterous union. In a white gown, her dark hair loose on her shoulders, the sixteen-year-old Princess leans forward, smiling; under one arm she carries a mass of wild flowers and grasses; it is as if she had just run indoors from the river. She looks untameable, and faintly sinister—an enchantress un-aware of her own power: a Morgan le Fay whose spells have not yet materialized: an innocent Nimue. That such a creature should be imprisoned for thirty-three years for a single lapse was inevitable; once freed, she might still have been dangerous: unlike her descendant, who had finished—for ever, as she believed—with intrigue and scheming.

Matilda might have achieved contentment, if she had not so longed for her children, and been haunted by the thought that they would be taught to hate and condemn her by the woman who was now their guardian. A few days after she reached Celle she was able to consult Sir Robert Murray Keith, who visited her on his way to Vienna, about this aspect of her situation. He had been desired by George III to produce a full report of her attitude and behaviour. 'You cannot be too minute and ample on all points of your mission to Zell,' Lord Suffolk, then Foreign Secretary, told him. 'A thousand little circumstances which would ... be passed over on other occasions will be interesting on this ... The more conformable your accounts are to this hint, the better they will please.'[2]

If Sir Robert, that well-intentioned and totally unimaginative man, had not been ordered to give a detailed report on Matilda, his account of her state would hardly have been worth reading. As it is, his letter to Suffolk shows that George III was both anxious and remorseful about his sister. Now that she had left Denmark without mishap, and all danger of her arriving in England was removed, the King wanted to make her existence in Celle agreeable and — within reason — one of comparative freedom. He therefore wrote to her affectionately, promising to do everything possible for her happiness in a material sense, while making no attempt to receive her, either publicly or through a private visit.

In the first of two audiences Matilda spoke gratefully, according to Keith, of her brother's 'fraternal affection and friendship'. She replied, he adds, 'frankly and explicitly', to his questions 'upon any subject that arose'. Keith's limitations and his diplomatic training prevented his referring to the past, or to Struensee, and he was too discreet to ask about the Queen's hopes and plans for the future.[3]

George III's first demand related to Matilda's correspondence with her supporters in Denmark. 'I have no wish', she told Keith, 'for any correspondence or connection there, beyond what concerns the welfare and education of my children.' She then spoke of their being influenced against her. Keith replied that they were too young for such treatment to have any effect, adding, with characteristic ineptitude, that as they grew older 'more candid instructors and the dictates of filial duty would break in upon their minds'. He may have known what he meant to convey by this statement. It reduced Matilda to tears.[4]

Next day, she told the envoy that she wanted to hear from her brother himself about her future—how could they confer through a third person? As George III had made up his mind neither to see her nor to be informed of her side of her case in a letter, Sir Robert replied with another vague reassurance as to his master's good will, and changed the subject. Was Her Majesty pleased with the improvements in the castle—and was she well and cheerful? Matilda said that she would like a suite prepared for the Princess Augusta, whose plan was to visit Celle every week. She added that both her sister and brother-in-law had been disgusted by Queen Juliana's treatment of herself, to which Keith made no answer. He goes on, 'Her Majesty talked to me of several late incidents at the Court of Denmark, but without appearing to take much concern in them. She mentioned, with a smile, some of the paltry things that had been sent as part of her baggage from Denmark, adding that this new instance of their meanness had not surprised her. But the Princess of Brunswick, who happened to be present when the baggage was opened, expressed her indignation.' Matilda then asked for a selection of English books to be dispatched to Celle, and sent messages of thanks to Suffolk and several other Ministers 'for the zeal they had shown in the late unhappy transactions relating to Denmark and to herself'.[5]

After Keith's departure to Vienna, George III pursued his highly injurious policy of secretiveness about Matilda's misfortunes. This resulted in a flood of journalistic gossip and scandal which none of his envoys was able to prevent. Mr Woodford, who had succeeded Keith at Copenhagen, described these publications as detestable, and tried, vainly, to get them suppressed. The Danish Minister for Foreign Affairs agreed to co-operate, but failed to do so. Pamphlets and 'true accounts of the late melancholy and unfortunate transaction' continued to pour out from the secret presses of Denmark, Germany and France, and so reached England. No penalty affected their distribution, which was partly organized by Count Rantzau, with Queen Juliana's approval.

So Matilda found herself helpless and unprotected. Although she could not have denied her adultery, she could have defended herself by describing Christian's progress from mental degeneracy to madness, and its effect on their marriage; but as he was still, officially, a reigning sovereign and England's ally, this was impossible. All she could hope for was a revolt against Juliana's regime; and even that might not necessarily bring about her own rehabilitation. She showed common sense and self-control in building up what became a full, useful and fairly satisfactory life in her miniature kingdom. Augusta's visits were a help. And then, suddenly, an old and once treasured friend appeared in Celle—Madame de Plessen, whose firm belief in her former mis-

mistress's innocence was sustained by her having left Denmark before Struensee arrived there. This lady's view—that a person of Matilda's rank must be incapable of error—was not contradicted. Her loyalty was too valuable to be assailed. She assumed, as did many others, that Matilda had been the victim of her husband's and his stepmother's cruelty—and of Struensee's ambition.

NOTES

1. Wilkins, *A Queen of Tears*, vol. II, pp. 234-4.
2. Op. cit., p. 249.
3. Murray Keith, *Memoirs*, p. 162.
4. Ibid.
5. Ibid.

II

Queen of the Castle

REVERDIL'S LENGTHY defence of Matilda denouncing the pamphlets
and broadsheets which described her orgiastic exploits had little effect.
Naturally, the general public preferred to visualize her as having been
given up to the pleasures of the alcove, and now being justly punished,
rather than as a young woman who had been pitchforked, when
scarcely more than a child, into an impossible position, and who was
thereafter unable to resist temptation. In any case, the fact remained
and could not be denied by those who had frequented her Court that
she had broken her marriage vows, blatantly and unashamedly. Until
the future Frederick VI grew up to look like his father, he was thought
of by many as illegitimate; and Princess Louise was universally
acknowledged to be a bastard.

Temporary conventions made it as impossible for George III to
receive Matilda as for her to proclaim her wrongs—although a more
tolerant and less henpecked man might have consented to hear her
version of those disastrous six years in a private interview. As it was,
her husband alone continued to stand up for her and to ask for her
return. In his moments of lucidity Christian was accustomed to say
that this was the only occasion he knew of on which a divorce had
been desired by neither of the parties concerned; and more than once
he signed an order concluding, 'Christian by the Grace of God King
of Denmark etc., in company with Juliana Maria by the grace of the
devil'.[1] Meanwhile, Matilda's and Struensee's 'own and true confessions' of their Cytherean adventure continued to circulate throughout
Europe, agreeably supplementing the rather tattered repetitions of the
'private lives' of Louis XV and the Empress Catherine.

This blackening of Matilda's reputation did not lessen Juliana
Maria's difficulties. With Judge Guldberg as her principal Minister, she
struggled on, giving way here, repressing there, and becoming more
and more resented by the Danish people. The Crown Prince would
not be of age to take over the regency for another nine years; and even

then, Juliana and Guldberg might refuse to declare Christian incapable of rule. In fact, their intention was to shelter behind his sovereignty until he died, while endeavouring to replace the heir by his half-brother. This proved to be impossible. The elder Prince never became a responsible figure; and his unpopularity increased as he matured.

Suddenly, Juliana became afraid that when the Crown Prince reached his majority he would take it upon himself to revenge his mother. So in the winter of 1772 she evolved a scheme by which he was to be deprived of the succession. She spread reports of his having inherited his father's lunacy; these were ineffectual, and she resorted to keeping him in the background as much as possible. Her Ministers disagreed among themselves about this and her other policies, and her hold on the Government was sustained with increasing difficulty; she then made overtures to those of Matilda's supporters who had not been imprisoned, and gave them places at Court; but she could not appease the general public, who had begun to look on Matilda as an innocent victim; some of the nobles wanted her to be reinstalled as regent until her son came of age.

Meanwhile, it began to dawn on Matilda that she was more fortunate than other royal ladies who had been imprisoned for real or suspected gallantries. Apart from Sophia-Dorothea, who had been deprived of her title, and was known as the Duchess of Ahlden from 1694 until her death in 1727, there were Elizabeth Christina of Brunswick-Wolfenbüttel, who was shut up in the castle of Stettin, and Augusta Elizabeth of Tour and Taxis, whose brother had set George III the example by incarcerating her in the fortress of Württemberg.[2] Indeed, the chastisement of such erring wives as these was an ancient custom, spreading over Europe, the most famous being that of Dante's Maria Pia of Lucca. When Matilda renewed her Italian studies, she may have come across that unfortunate lady's cry of despair from the *Purgatorio*:

> Ricorditi di me, che son' la Pia—
> Siena mi fè: disfecemi Maremma ...

So Matilda decided to change her way of life to one of middle-aged respectability. She gave up riding—this had a deplorable effect on her health and looks—and no longer danced. She dressed soberly but richly, and followed a daily routine from which she rarely diverged. In her only surviving letter to Augusta she describes getting up at seven thirty to walk by the river. After breakfast, which she took out of doors in fine weather, she was dressed for the day, and held a private reception. She then walked again, or drove out over the bleak, flat countryside till dinner at two o'clock, retiring to read, sing and play the harpsichord, or work at her embroidery before taking another turn in the garden. She might wander about the town, sometimes shopping, sometimes visiting the families of its poorer inhabitants—her charities became a permanent occupation—before returning to dress for the evening, and to meet her guests for supper. This was followed by a concert, cards or a play. At eleven o'clock she went to bed, pausing on starlit nights to gaze through the great telescope from one of the towers. She learnt a good deal of poetry, and read till a late hour in German, French, English and Italian.[3]

This monotonous existence was varied by church-going in Celle, and by the parties she gave for the children of its inhabitants. Every now and then, parties were given for her by her suite. In one of her letters to Baroness d'Ompteda she writes, 'Madame de Plessen, having wished to celebrate my birthday, gave an illumination in the garden, but ... the bonfire would not burn. The whole town was illuminated.'[4] She made special shopping expeditions on market days; but the choice of goods from outside Celle was sadly limited. Presently she sent for a company of players from Paris. She preferred comedies. One evening she was faced with a drama which presented a situation resembling her own, wherein a mother's separation from her children was the theme. Matilda rushed from her box, to walk, sobbing out her misery, in the rainy and windswept garden. Her ladies dared not follow her, and an hour went by before she returned. Nothing was said on either side; after that, one of her courtiers went through the travelling players' pieces before they were put on.[5]

Matilda's need for the company of children increased as the months went by. She would stop and talk to any she met in the street or in the market-place, and very soon became part of their lives; they looked forward to meeting the kind, pretty lady their parents called the good Queen, who was to be seen every fine day, strolling with a single attendant from the booths to the French Garden, and who herself came to see that they were properly cared for when they were ill or in straits for money. Matilda held another kind of court in the French Garden. There she could sit and chat with the townsfolk, who at first were a little in awe of her; then, feeling the sincerity and frankness of her approach, they found themselves talking to her as to a friend; but there must have been some who became aware of the sadness lying beneath her pleasant, easy manner, and some who found it odd that anyone so gracious and gentle should give the impression of being lonely.

Yet Matilda was by no means friendless. The Baroness d'Ompteda and Madame de Plessen were agreeable and affectionate if not very interesting company. When her former Mistress of the Robes took a house in Celle they met almost every day. Travellers of distinction and repute had the entrée to her receptions; she had many resources and plenty to do; on her visits to Hanover she was lavishly entertained.

Nevertheless, it was a makeshift life. Born for motherhood and the care of a family, Matilda was very unhappy —not all the time, for she could be gay, as in her more richly filled days—and whether she still mourned her lover or not, she had to live with the recollection of his treachery; for as she was never told of the trick played on them both, she may have come to believe that all along he had made use of her. She did her best; but sometimes it was difficult to appear as became a privileged great lady. While deceiving such as Keith about her real state of mind, she gave herself away to more perspicacious observers.

One of these was a Mr John Moore who, making the grand tour with the Duke of Hamilton, was received at the castle in the spring of 1773. He and the Duke spent several evenings there, and Moore, prepared to pity the 'ill-fated' Queen, soon found that he had cause to do so. 'She seemed', he wrote, in his *View of Society and Manners in France, Switzerland and Germany*, 'in better spirits than could have been expected. Though she was in perfect health and appeared cheerful, yet, convinced that her gaiety was assumed and the effect of a strong effort, I felt the impression of melancholy which it was not in my power to overcome all the time we remained at Zell.' He then described the amenities of Matilda's Court, her 'genteel' attendants, the devotion of her ladies and her dependence on the Princess Augusta. 'The moment she goes away ... the Queen becomes a prey to dejection.'[6]

It was at about this time that Matilda decided to try to fill the gap in her life by adopting a child. Her choice fell on a four-year-old orphan, Sophie von Benningsen, whom she took into her household to educate and care for as her own. Yet that hideous loss remained. She had no news of her son and daughter. She knew only that they were alive.

Then, through an unknown adherent, a picture of the Crown Prince, now in his sixth year, arrived. She hung it opposite her bed, and talked to it sometimes. Once, the Baroness d'Ompteda found her

doing so; before she could retire, Matilda, the tears streaming down
her face, repeated the verses she had adapted to suit 'my sad case'. They
were halting, commonplace, a mere jangle; but for a long time the
Baroness could not get them out of her head.

> 'Eh! qui donc, comme moi, goûterait la douceur
> De t'appeler mon fils, d'être chère à ton coeur!
> Toi, qu'on arrache aux bras d'une mère sensible,
> Qui ne pleure que toi, dans ce destin terrible!'[7]

In a further search for distraction, Matilda turned one of the octagon
towers into a miniature library for her specially favourite books—there
is no record of their titles—which she hung with green damask. Here
she took music lessons and sat at her needlework with Augusta. When
the Princess left for Brunswick, she wrote to her of her longings and
deprivations—and of Augusta's children. 'My peace of mind', she told
her sister, '[is] continually disturbed by … this cruel and unnatural
separation … I have not once wished to be again an enthroned queen.
Pray give my love to the dear Augusta [her eldest niece] and all her
brothers. Charles is, I understand, like his father, born a warrior,
nothing but arms, swords and horses can please his martial tastes …
Tell George, Augustus and William that I have some presents I shall
send them.'[8] Matilda added that planning the castle gardens had become
another resource. She gave the head gardener daily instructions, and
observed that his men worked 'with a contented mind … I see everybody happy around me,' she wistfully concluded. Although she knew
that Augusta still spied on her, she clung to the sister who shared her
memories of the good times at Kew and Carlton House.

The presentation of Matilda's forebears then began to irk her. In
the chapel, her box faced the portraits of Duke George William and
the beautiful Éléonore d'Olbreuse, first his morganatic wife and then
his consort. The last Duke and Duchess of Celle were shown kneeling
on either side of a triptych; it was impossible for Matilda to avoid the
spectacle of the parents who had treated Sophia-Dorothea, their only
child, more harshly than George III had treated her. She moved her
seat to face the pulpit; behind it was a fresco of St Peter denying his
Lord.[9]

In fact, Matilda was living in an oasis. And as those who pause in
such places for rest and refreshment expect to move on to a long-
planned destination, so she began to take to heart the rumours of
Denmark's discontent and the shakiness of Juliana's authority. That

state of affairs could not last much longer. A large number of Matilda's supporters had now settled in Altona, the frontier city, and were organizing a revolution. At the slightest hint of an arrest, they had only to cross a couple of streets to be in Germany. None of them had as yet approached Matilda, nor she them. All either side needed was a competent and courageous intermediary.

NOTES

1. Wilkins, *A Queen of Tears*, vol. II, p. 269.
2. Nathaniel Wraxall, *Memoirs*, vol. IV, p. 179.
3. Wilkins, op. cit., vol. II, p. 259.
4. Op. cit., vol. II, p. 261.
5. Op. cit., vol. II, p. 259.
6. J. Moore, *View of Society and Manners*, p. 179.
7. Wilkins, op. cit., vol. II, p. 258.
8. N. Wraxall, op. cit., vol. III, p. 169.
9. Wilkins, op. cit., vol. II, p. 248.

III

Nathaniel Wraxall

IN THE spring of 1773, Mr Nathaniel Wraxall, a young man of good family and moderate wealth, decided to leave the West Indies and come home. He was then twenty-two, and had been doing well enough to make a successful career in the Islands; but he desired fame and adventure. Arriving in Bristol, he discovered that a thirteenth-century ancestor had become Bailiff of that city. This inspired him to try for a similar distinction by setting out on a north European tour and writing a book about his experiences.

After visiting Sweden and Russia, Wraxall reached Copenhagen in the late summer of 1774, and there heard the whole story of Matilda's misfortunes. He determined to go to Hanover, and so obtained an introduction to the exiled Queen. While visiting the court of Princess Augusta's brother-in-law, the Duke of Mecklenburg-Strelitz, he had come to the conclusion that to reinstal Matilda would make him famous. She was young, beautiful and persecuted—what more could a knight-errant desire? Of course she was innocent. He had made up his mind on that point before setting out for Celle.

In later life, Wraxall produced a defence of Matilda's character which he had not troubled to evolve when he first approached her. Arriving in early youth at a 'dissolute' court, she had been 'indiscreet' —no more—after marriage to a man 'whose vices rendered him unworthy of her, surrounded by bad examples and abandoned to her own control before the empire of reason could operate'.[1] Although he knew all about Struensee's share in her downfall, Wraxall decided not to connect him with Matilda's fate, and so never mentioned him in his correspondence. Her innocence was essential; without it, a chivalric attitude would be untenable.

Wraxall was a high-minded but egocentric enthusiast; and such persons generally lack either humour or perspicacity. When his father, with whom he corresponded regularly, implored him not to romanticize his hopes and plans, he was outraged by the implied criticism. He knew that he was in the right; and as to any reward—that was a negligible consideration. He saw himself as the saviour of a queen. Nothing else mattered.

In this frame of mind, he arrived at Celle on September 18th, 1774, and began by introducing himself to Matilda's Chamberlain, Baron von Seckendorf, who conducted him to the castle and presented him to Baroness d'Ompteda, and other members of the Court. With them, he waited in the gallery for a quarter of an hour. Princess Augusta then came in, and engaged him in a talk which was interrupted by the entrance of Matilda. 'She gave me', Wraxall complacently recalls, 'her hand to kiss, and began conversation with me directly.'[2] He sustained his part well enough; but he had received a shock of which the memory haunted him for the rest of his life.

Terror, grief and nervous strain had produced a sad change in Matilda's appearance. She had what the eighteenth-century faculty described as a plethoric physique; this, her sufferings and her having given up riding and dancing, had caused her to put on weight; also, she may have become a compulsive eater, as often happens with deprived persons. 'She was very fat', Wraxall says, 'for so young a woman'—too fat, that is, even for the taste of an age in which slenderness was at a discount, and 'plump' a complimentary adjective. Desperately attempting a description of beauty, the poor young man continues, 'Her features are pretty, and her teeth small, even and white,' regretfully adding, 'She resembles His Majesty George III infinitely in face.'[3] (By this time, that monarch had greatly coarsened, as was the case with all his family.) If ever Wraxall had seen himself as romantically inclined towards his heroine, that dream was now shattered. Some ladies might be exuberantly framed, and yet remain objects of admiration; but fat—alas! Wraxall noticed Matilda's flame-coloured dress with approval, in spite of the fact that it must have drawn attention to what he later gallantly described as her not unpleasing embonpoint.

They were now joined by Princess Augusta, and Prince Frederick's forthcoming marriage was mentioned. Matilda said—it was her only lapse into spitefulness—'He was an unknown youth when I was there.' Presently she told Wraxall that Hirschholm was her favourite palace. Augusta hastily put in, 'Tell me about the Queen-Mother. She's my aunt, but no matter. Say what you will, be free—and for the King, how is he?' Wraxall does not record his reply, but says that he spoke frankly. Matilda then asked about his travels; and after that, she brought herself to speak of her children. 'How do they dress the Crown Prince?' she said. His clothes were described, and she passed on to other subjects. 'She was very gay,' Wraxall adds, 'and seemed in no way a prey to melancholy,' apparently forgetting that they were surrounded by her courtiers. 'How old are you?' she went on, and hearing the answer, said, 'You are then exactly the same age as I am.' Princess Augusta observed that her sister was considered to resemble George III, and some discussion on this point ensued in English and German. Wraxall asked the Queen how many languages she spoke, and was told, five—Danish, English, French, German and Italian. Then Augusta began to speak of her brother Gloucester's mistress, and after they went into dinner said that Wraxall might have been mistaken for a Frenchman. 'You don't take that as a compliment, do you?' the Queen inquired. 'Indeed, no, I am too proud of my country,' Wraxall replied. 'Macaronies—' Matilda began, and stopped. Was she thinking of Struensee's status as her *cicisbeo*? ' 'Tis all over now,' said Wraxall; 'the word is quite extinct in England.' Matilda, amused and inclined to tease him, went on, 'But tell me—were you not a little bit of a one, while it lasted?' 'No, Your Majesty,' Wraxall replied.[4]

The young man's gallant address, his elegance and courtliness combined with his good looks to make an excellent impression on both ladies, and he was bidden to a reception on the following day, when all three talked together for nearly an hour, 'on fifty subjects', says Wraxall, principally those of Catherine the Great and the Russo-Turkish peace. Later, he was walking in the covered market, when he perceived Matilda, dressed in one of her favourite pink gowns and a white bonnet. Her only jewel was a small locket. 'Her face', he adds, 'is very handsome. They are His Majesty's features, but all softened and harmonized. Pity she is so large in her person.' He then showed her his medals of the Empress of Russia, with other souvenirs of his travels, and they parted very well pleased with one another. His only regret was that he had not been able to speak to her in private. When he came to take leave, she said, 'If you see Mr Mathias,'—the British Minister in Hamburg, Wraxall's next stop—'ask him how soon I may expect the French players.' Somehow, he was led to believe that a more vital matter was in question. A few days after he reached Hamburg his longed-for adventure began.[5]

That city was only half a mile from Altona, where a number of Danes exiled by Queen Juliana had taken refuge. They were to be seen at the opera, the cafés and the private houses of Hamburg most nights

N

of the week; and so it was that Wraxall, dining with the English consul on September 28th, always remembered that date as inaugurating his plans. Among his fellow guests were Baroness de Bulow, the Baron and Baroness von Schimmelmann, and Monsieur Le Texier, who had been Christian VII's Treasurer during his English visit. All these persons besieged Wraxall with inquiries about Matilda. Having answered them, he spoke with great indignation of the injustice of her fate.

Three days later, he was called on by Le Texier, who described the *coup d'état* of 1772 in detail. Matilda's future was not mentioned; but Wraxall got the impression that he had been tested. On the following night, they met again, apparently by chance, at the opera; here Le Texier suggested that they should foregather the next morning, 'in a manner which seemed to indicate that he had some communication to make of importance', and a time was fixed.

At Wraxall's hotel Le Texier made further inquiries as to the kind of life Matilda was leading. He then began a sentence which he did not finish. At last he said, 'Would you be disposed to render Her Majesty a service?' 'I am ready to engage hand and heart in her cause,' Wraxall replied. 'You are then the person whom we want,' said Le Texier, and went on to explain that a plot had been formed by a large group of exiles to remove her from Celle, 'and invest her with supreme power during the King's incapacity'. He added that so far they had not been able to approach the Queen, 'beset as she is by spies', of whom Augusta was the chief. 'Your arrival', he went on, 'offers a means to approach her. Will you undertake the commission?' Eagerly, and with many assurances of his dedication to the project, Wraxall agreed, and Le Texier said, 'I am satisfied, and will make my report without delay to those by whom I have been sent.' As he reached the door, he added, 'Expect to hear further from me,' and went out.[6]

Two days later, Le Texier introduced Wraxall to the younger Baron von Schimmelmann, and left them together. Von Schimmelmann said, will tell you why I and the persons with whom I am acting are compelled to restore Queen Matilda,' adding that none of them expected or desired any reward for their efforts, and that they had no intention of revenging themselves on Queen Juliana's adherents. 'This enterprise has dangers,' he went on, 'but it demands the exertion of every good subject,' and described the abuses of Juliana's regime. He referred obliquely to Matilda's connection with Struensee. 'Adversity instructed her,' was his explanation.[7]

Von Schimmelmann then said that, apart from Matilda's co-operation in their scheme, his party must be assured of her trust in their
abilities. 'My affairs', he went on, 'call me to Copenhagen, where my
presence may be eminently useful to the cause. But I will tomorrow
introduce you [as an agent for Matilda] to the Baron de Bulow, and
from him you will receive your instructions.'

Wraxall's interview with that gentleman was to follow the pattern
of a cloak-and-sword romance. When he reached Celle, he would
himself compose a letter to be secretly conveyed to the Queen,
together with a seal, which she would recognize as de Bulow's. 'In
particular,' his instructor went on, 'beware of the Princess of Brunswick, who is attached to the interests of the family with which she is
allied.' He then raised the most difficult aspect of the whole situation
—the co-operation of George III. 'Without his approbation, if not
his aid,' he explained, 'we cannot long maintain, though we may
effect, a revolution.' He concluded by assuring Wraxall of their belief
in his courage, efficiency and discretion. After some further discussion
about details, Wraxall prepared to return to Celle, which he reached
on October 9th, where he heard, 'not without concern', that Princess
Augusta was still staying at the castle.[8]

He then approached Baron von Seckendorf, and told him that he
had been entrusted with a letter from Mr Mathias to the Queen in
reply to her inquiries about the French players. He was bidden to
dinner at the castle, and thus had to face what seemed an insurmount-
able difficulty—how could he give Matilda the letter proposing her
restoration without her sister's or her courtiers' knowledge? 'Its
contents', he records, 'might agitate the Queen, perhaps so powerfully
as to excite an emotion ... betraying the nature of my errand.' Finally,
he evolved what he considered was a practical, although risky, means
of communication.[9]

Wraxall may have known that Matilda had been sceptical about the
few tentative offers of rescue she had received from Copenhagen, and
had ignored them. He therefore outlined her supporters' conditions
in a concise and business-like manner, as follows:

1. She must assure them of her willingness to return to Denmark
to take over the Government.

2. She must co-operate with her adherents in every possible
way.

3. She must try to persuade the King of England to extend his
protection and assistance to the enterprise.

This last clause, Wraxall warned the Queen, was the most important, adding that Woodford had announced, 'His Majesty is too offended ever to permit his royal sister to return to Copenhagen.' [10]

Before leaving for the castle, Wraxall wrapped this document in a personal letter, in which he asked Matilda not to read the enclosure till she was alone, boldly adding, 'It is particularly incumbent to conceal it from Her Royal Highness the Princess of Brunswick.' When Matilda entered the gallery, where her Court and the Princess were assembled, she came up to Wraxall and said, 'I understand that you have a letter from Mr Mathias.' 'I have, Madame,' Wraxall replied. 'It regards the company of comedians who are preparing to arrive here.' The Queen took the letter to the window and began to read it, while Wraxall engaged her sister in conversation; she put it in her pocket; when she rejoined Wraxall and Augusta, her face was flushed, and she appeared extremely agitated. The whole company then went in to dinner. 'The Queen and the Princess', Wraxall says, 'were always seated ... in two splendid armchairs towards the middle of one of the long sides of the table, separated by a space of nearly two feet ... I was placed opposite them. During the repast Her Majesty soon recovered her gaiety and presence of mind, keeping me in continual conversation, as did the Princess. But no sooner was the dessert served, than the former, pushing back her chair, drew out my letter and, holding it in her lap, read it from beginning to end, raising her head from time to time, uttering a few words, and then resuming her occupation. This act of imprudent curiosity and impatience naturally alarmed me. However, we soon repaired to the drawing-room ... I returned to the inn, and waited till I should hear from the Queen.' That same evening, Wraxall was visited by Baron von Seckendorf, who told him that Matilda had agreed to all the conditions. Next morning, he brought the young man her seal, and a message desiring him to convey her co-operation to the Hamburg group. [11]

On arrival in that city, Wraxall met Baron de Bulow, to whom he gave the seal and the good news. De Bulow said that he and his comrades must have a definite promise of help from George III before they began to effect their revolution. 'We trust', he went on, 'that the Queen will dispatch you as her agent to England.' He gave Wraxall the names of their principal supporters in the Danish provinces, and concluded, 'We want only the name and protection of George III to secure us from every possible reaction.' It was then agreed that de Bulow should follow Wraxall to Celle, and meet him in a post-house at Zahrendorf, a village halfway between that city and Hamburg, to make the final arrangements.[12]

On arrival at Celle, Wraxall heard, 'with no small satisfaction', that Augusta's visit had come to an end. He at once called on von Seckendorf, who told him to wait for the Queen in a pavilion in the French Garden, where she would meet him, accompanied by a single lady. She arrived, and they walked about, talking, 'most unreservedly', says Wraxall, 'for more than an hour', while the lady waited in the pavilion. 'She described, as to an equal,' he goes on, 'the King and her sister ... Her dress was very simple and plain.' They then entered the pavilion, where a dessert of fruit was laid, and Matilda told Wraxall that he could speak freely, as her attendant did not understand English, and proceeded to outline her plans. She intended to write 'in the most pressing terms' about her restoration to her brother, through Lord Suffolk, and also through Baron von Lichtenstein, at that time a visitor to the Court of St James's, asking them to arrange a private interview between Wraxall and George III.[13]

Wraxall then set off for Zahrendorf, where he 'patiently waited' for de Bulow, 'who arrived wrapped in a cloak which concealed his person'. After conferring for several hours, they parted, de Bulow to Altona and Wraxall to London, which he reached on November 15th. His approach to Suffolk was barred by the excuse of a fit of the gout, and he proceeded to von Lichtenstein's residence in Pall Mall. The Baron received him warmly, and promised to arrange a meeting with the King.[14]

After several days of suspense, von Lichtenstein sent for Wraxall and told him, 'His Majesty enjoins you not to return to Lord Suffolk. The business must be managed ... through me. Nor will the King admit you to any personal audience, because, though all cordiality has ceased between him and the Danish Court ... ever since his sister's arrest, yet, as the relations of peace and amity still exist between the two crowns, he wishes to retain the power of denying, in case of unforeseen accident, that he has seen or received an agent sent for the purpose of [the Queen's] restoration.' Von Lichtenstein then asked for 'a minute account on paper' of Wraxall's plans. 'His Majesty', he went on, ' ... will then be better able to form a judgment ... Time must be allowed for deliberation.'[15]

In some disappointment, Wraxall was kept kicking his heels in London till January 15th, 1775, when he received the King's reply. It consisted of four articles. He read them in great anxiety.

NOTES

1. N. Wraxall, *Memoirs*, vol. IV, p. 178.
2. C. F. L. Wraxall, *Life and Times*, vol. III, p. 173.
3. Op. cit., vol. III, p. 174.
4. N. Wraxall, op. cit., vol. III, pp. 174–6.
5. Ibid.
6. Op. cit., vol. IV, pp. 180–84.
7. Ibid.
8. Ibid.
9. Ibid.
10. Wilkins, *A Queen of Tears*, vol. II, p. 274.
11. N. Wraxall, op. cit., vol. IV, pp. 185–6.
12. Op. cit., vol. IV, p. 189.
13. Op. cit., vol. IV, p. 191.
14. Op. cit., vol. IV, p. 193.
15. Op. cit., vol. IV, p. 194.

IV

Difficulty and Danger

MATILDA HAD been less optimistic than Wraxall about the success of his approach to George III. 'You must go very quietly with my brother,' she said. 'If we manage with address, he will favour the attempt—but it will be tacitly, not openly'—adding that she herself could not help him financially, for she owed money to friends in Holland and elsewhere, and had no jewels to sell. She then warned him not to tell the King that she knew Augusta to be a spy. George III's reply to her supporters bore out her view of his attitude, and ran as follows:

1. He gave his approval to her restoration.

2. He desired that no reprisals should be used on Queen Juliana's party.

3. He guaranteed repayment of all moneys spent in the revolution.

4. He would authorize his representative in Copenhagen to announce his approval of the Queen's restoration—*after it had been accomplished*.[1]

This last phrase embodied all that Matilda's supporters had most dreaded; for the King of England's public approval before they began to move was essential to their cause. His lying low until they succeeded would make their task so difficult as to be very nearly impossible. But Wraxall was convinced that they would not be daunted by the King's caution—and so was von Lichtenstein, who told him to return at once to Celle. Having shown Matilda her brother's conditions, he must then convey them to de Bulow, who was waiting impatiently in Hamburg.

Wraxall arrived in Holland on February 6th, reaching the German frontier on the 12th, to find that the River Dinckel was in flood. His landlord assured him that, although the four horses drawing his carriage would have to swim, the crossing could be safely effected. All went well; but at Münster the carriage overturned, and at Osnabrück Wraxall found the Weser 'swelled to a prodigious size'. His equipage was repaired, to be placed on a barge, and he reached Celle on the evening of February 17th.[2]

Next morning, he called on von Seckendorf, and an appointment was made with the Queen for four o'clock that afternoon. Her page, Mantel, was to escort him. They entered the castle by a private way, and Wraxall was left in 'a spacious apartment'. A few minutes later, the Queen came in, alone, in a state of great agitation. She spoke fast and rather indistinctly, as her brother sometimes did, but, says Wraxall, 'her manners were very ingratiating.' He goes on, 'We conversed ... in the most unreservedly undisguised manner. Her Majesty made me the recital of her reign—of the revolution—of her own conduct on that fatal night ... Her words are engraven on my heart ... More than once, I forgot I was talking to a Queen. She was dressed in a brown silk polonaise, trimmed with green silk, her hair powdered, a locket on her bosom. Her underlip is too large ... but that violence in speaking becomes her; she is thinner in the face.'³

Matilda then gave a very amusing imitation of Prince Frederick's mannerisms, breaking off to lament her brother's refusal to see Wraxall. She pointed out that his conditions—which had been conveyed to her by von Seckendorf—amounted to a withdrawal from her cause. She also described the results of the *coup d'état* of 1772. 'I would have avoided such a topic,' says Wraxall, 'for obvious reasons. But she entered on it with so much determination that I could only listen, while she recounted to me ... names and particulars ... of the most private nature. I am, however, far from meaning that she made any disclosure unbecoming a woman of honour and delicacy.' (In other words, Struensee was not mentioned.) Suddenly, Matilda exclaimed, 'It is past six, my absence will be noticed,' and sent for Mantel to take Wraxall to another part of the castle, where he waited till it was dark before returning to his lodging.⁴

Next day, he set off for Hamburg with the packet containing George III's conditions. By this time he had become aware that he was being shadowed by Juliana's spies, and that his life was in hazard whenever he moved. When he visited de Bulow, the Baron seized the dispatches and read through them several times; he found them most discouraging. 'They must, however,' he said, 'be transmitted to our friends in Copenhagen with as little delay as possible, and we must await their reply.' It was decided that Wraxall's offer of taking them there would arouse suspicion, and an 'unknown gentleman' was entrusted with the packet. This person returned to Hamburg with the Danish conspirators' answer on March 13th.

They had been deeply chagrined by George III's neutral attitude.

'We want his decision to be made ... when we arrest the Queen-Dowager, her son and the principal members of the Government,' they wrote, and insisted on the simultaneous support of the British Minister in Copenhagen, adding, 'It is therefore indispensable to make new exertions in London.' They concluded by asking Matilda to appear in Copenhagen within an hour or so of the arrests.

It was agreed that Wraxall should return to Celle to arrange Matilda's co-operation in this scheme and then go on to London to plead for more effective support from her brother. He reached Celle on March 21st—to find that Princess Augusta was again in residence. 'Her Majesty therefore', he says, 'laid her injunctions on me to keep myself concealed, adding that as soon as the Princess should quit Zell, she would immediately admit me to her presence.'[5]

As Augusta showed no inclination to leave, Matilda decided to risk seeing Wraxall that same night, at eight o'clock. In pouring rain, and wrapped up to the eyes, he waited by the drawbridge, dodging the movements of the sentries. Mantel then appeared—with an umbrella—and a huge cloak, which he threw over Wraxall, covering him completely. He guided him to the Queen's little library, and told him to be patient. 'For it is uncertain', he explained, 'at what hour Her Majesty will quit her company.'[6] He then gave his charge a note from von Seckendorf, in which the Baron had written that the Queen would be able to stay with Wraxall till eleven o'clock. As he himself did not care to venture out in the storm now raging, he would expect to see Wraxall at eight the next morning. He concluded, 'Order your horses for nine o'clock, and leave under God's protection.'[7]

In the event of Wraxall's being kept waiting for some time, Mantel had lit two candles and opened the bookcases: but the young man was too agitated to read. His thoughts dwelt less on what he was about to do than on the dangers he had already undergone. Halted by the flooding of the Weser, he had 'lost all patience and shed tears of anger and sorrow', exclaiming (so he afterwards believed) 'In the name of Heaven, am I to perish in one of these confounded ditches? Is this message ... the last I shall ever carry?' His repaired coach seemed to him like his coffin; and at Osnabrück he had told the postilion that he would 'put him to death on the spot', if it was again overset.[8] Later, on terrible roads, he had felt himself 'past the worst and hastening to a queen', in spite of the fact that he was prepared for 'instant death'. He neared Celle in conditions that 'might have inspired terror in the boldest heart; but the approach to my destination gave me courage.'[9] (It seems that he had been more afraid of drowning than of the assassin's knife.) Describing these dangers to his father, he had declared his belief in the help of 'that Being who protects the race of man', supplemented by his own 'presentiment ... of future elevation', adding, 'Some protecting genius ... averts every fatal accident from me ... If ever virtuous glory had power to animate a young man's bosom, it ought to do so in mine! ... *She* has laid her commands on me to be careful for *Her* sake.' He then remembered that his divinity had failed to repay the hundred pounds he had spent in her service. However — 'My expectations are neither languid nor sanguine. If they succeed, *She* neither can nor will forget me.'[10]

At this point, Matilda came in, 'charmingly dressed', Wraxall records, 'though without diamonds'. She was wearing a gown of crimson satin, and her hair had been powdered and piled high, giving her an air of majesty he had not before observed. Wraxall set a chair for her, which she refused, and they remained standing during a talk of some two hours.[11]

Matilda began by saying that she was eager to start for Copenhagen whenever her presence was required — but that an escape from Celle was out of the question. Her guards and sentries were gaolers; she was watched night and day. She might drive as far as Hanover; but any attempt to approach the frontier would result in an imprisonment which must confine her within the walls of the castle for the rest of her life. She therefore proposed to write asking her brother's permission to leave. Without it, she could not move, although her most ardent wish was to 'share every hazard with my friends and to quit this place at the shortest possible notice'.[12]

Wraxall saw the sense of this reasoning; but he was greatly cast down by the Queen's next speech. She now knew, she said, that the Baron von Lichtenstein was about to leave England, and would probably be gone before he arrived there. It occurred to neither of them that the King might have ordered him to do so. 'I shall nevertheless write to him,' she went on, 'and he has promised me that in case of his departure before you reach London, he will take care to leave instructions for regulating your conduct.' Wraxall thanked her, and she told him that as soon as George III's consent to her leaving Celle arrived, she would put on male dress and ride with him to the frontier. She then spoke of the money she owed him; she could not repay it now, but she was sure that her brother would. 'You have run every hazard in order to serve me,' she said. 'Meanwhile, write to me freely and unreservedly from

England on every point, and rely on my recollection of your services.'[13]

As she reverted to their plans, Wraxall became afraid of her being missed; at last he said, 'Is it Your Majesty's pleasure that I should retire?' Matilda consented, adding, 'I hope you will not be long gone,' and gave him her hand to kiss.

She turned and walked to the door. Afterwards, Wraxall dwelt on that moment of farewell. It seemed to him that she had regained much of the beauty he had once dreamed of; she appeared well and happy. Smiling, and as if about to say something more, 'She had never', he says, 'looked more engaging than on that night, in that attitude.' He waited. She paused by the half-open door—surely she wished to stay a little? Then she went out.

A moment later, Mantel came in, wrapped him up as before, and they returned through the storm to the inn. Next day, Wraxall started for England, reaching London on April 5th. He found that von Lichtenstein had been replaced by Hinüber, the Hanoverian Chargé d'Affaires, to whom he had to entrust all his papers—de Bulow's, Matilda's and Seckendorf's letters, supplemented by one from himself to the King, begging for a private audience.

He waited in an agony of suspense for sixteen days. Then he approached Hinüber, who said, 'I have received no orders from His Majesty respecting you.' In despair, Wraxall wrote to Matilda, de Bulow and von Seckendorf, asking for instructions. Should he remain in London, and continue to try for an audience, or return to Celle?

De Bulow replied, 'Every preparation for the projected enterprise is advancing. I lament the silence hitherto observed towards you, but I beseech you to … remain where you are, and to wait for my next despatch.'[14]

Wraxall did as he was told. He heard nothing from Matilda or from von Seckendorf. Meanwhile, he was informed by de Bulow that affairs in Denmark were in a critical state. Still he waited—and received no news of any kind.

NOTES

1. Wilkins, *A Queen of Tears*, vol. II, p. 283.
2. N. Wraxall, *Memoirs*, vol. III, pp. 194–6.
3. Wilkins, op. cit., vol. II, p. 285.
4. N. Wraxall, op. cit., vol. III, p. 198.
5. Op. cit., vol. III, pp. 200–202.
6. Ibid., p. 203.

7. C. F. L. Wraxall, *Life and Times*, vol. II, p. 231.

8. Op. cit., vol. II, p. 217.

9. Op. cit., vol. II, p. 219.

10. Op. cit., vol. II, pp. 297–8.

11. N. Wraxall, op. cit., vol. III, p. 203.

12. Ibid.

13. Op. cit., vol. III, p. 204.

14. Op. cit., vol. III, pp. 204–6.

V

Escape

MATILDA HAD a more realistic approach than Wraxall to her restoration; but her refusal to try crossing the frontier without George III's leave did convince him that they must proceed openly and with the King's approval. Furthermore, she realized that her changed appearance would disappoint those of her former subjects who had been entranced by her beauty, for she had again put on weight. In her last interview with Wraxall she said sadly, 'Could I come, or did I come, no one would recognize me, as I am much altered since I was in Denmark.'¹

And now three weeks had gone by without any exchange of letters. Although chagrined by the King's refusal to see him, Wraxall was still confident of success. Matilda's silence may have been caused by her giving up hope; on the other hand, she might have written letters which Augusta seized and held on their brother's behalf.

On April 21st, 1775, Wraxall wrote again to Seckendorf, de Bulow and Matilda, asking whether he should return to Germany. He heard from de Bulow desiring him, as before, to remain where he was. No word came from Matilda.²

Just before Wraxall left Celle an epidemic which came under the vaguely generic heading of 'fever' had broken out in that city. This type was known as 'the purples' by Matilda's contemporaries; one nineteenth-century biographer has described it as typhus and another as scarlet fever. Soon after Wraxall's departure for England it reached the castle, and one of the first victims was a page, who died on May 5th. In the evening of that day Matilda, who had been very fond of the boy, was sitting with her ladies; suddenly, she announced her intention of going to see the body. They protested, and she seemed to yield. Then she sprang up, and before they could stop her, ran upstairs into the room where he was lying.

On the way back someone told her that little Sophie von Benningsen had just been put to bed with the same infection. Matilda, much distressed, went out to walk in the French Garden, where she remained longer than usual, with the result that she felt very tired, and went to bed. Three days later, she was still exhausted; going upstairs to change her dress for dinner, she had to be supported by one of her ladies, to whom she said, 'I must force myself to seem less tired than I really am, so that my good Ompteda, who did not like my driving out, will not scold me.'

When she came in to dinner, her throat had become sore and she was shivering. She got through the meal somehow; but when they left the table and the cards were set out, she felt too ill to play. Her ladies put her on the sofa and suggested that she should look on while they had a game; but Mantel intervened. 'Her Majesty should go to bed immediately,' he said, and Matilda was thankful to obey. That night she was much worse; and in the morning Baroness d'Ompteda sent for her physician in ordinary, Dr Leyser. Matilda told him that she had woken from a nightmare about her dead servant. By this time, she had yielded to a premonition of death; it was as if the page had summoned her to join him. 'You have twice saved me from illness since last October,' she told Leyser, 'this is beyond your skill. I know I cannot be helped by medicine.'

Leyser assured her that she was wrong; but he took the precaution of sending for the more expert Dr Zimmerman from Hanover. Matilda then desired Pastor Lehzen to attend her; he was warned by Zimmerman that she was very ill indeed. As he entered the bedchamber Matilda said faintly, 'You did not imagine me as ill as you find me.'

Lehzen fell to prayer and then left her. He returned in the afternoon and again in the evening, to find her less feverish and quite composed. Both physicians thought that she was beginning to recover. The Queen asked Lehzen to write, at her dictation, to George III. She began to speak, but found herself too weak to continue. 'Write what you think proper,' she told the pastor. When he had done so, she read the letter (it has not survived) and desired him to send it to England.

Five days passed without much change in her condition. She asked about Sophie von Benningsen, and hearing that she was out of danger, murmured, 'Then I can die happy,' and shut her eyes. Just before midnight, on May 11th, 1775, she died in her sleep, aged twenty-three years and nine months. 'I never remember', Pastor Lehzen wrote to a friend, 'so easy a dissolution, or one in which death lost all its terrors ... She fell asleep like a tired traveller.'

On May 19th Wraxall's valet stopped him as he was leaving his lodgings and said abruptly, 'Have you heard that the Queen is dead?'

The young man thought he was speaking of Queen Charlotte, who had been ailing, and replied, unmoved, in the negative. 'I mean', his servant went on, 'the Queen of Denmark.' A few hours later, Wraxall was told that the news had been brought to George III as he was riding out from Richmond.

Stricken and appalled, Wraxall found himself unable to communicate with anyone in Celle. On May 25th he heard from von Seckendorf, who gave him the details of Matilda's last hours. He said that she had repeated one of Gellert's hymns, forgiven all her enemies, desired her ladies not to visit her and 'suffered as a Christian, with remarkable patience and complete awareness of her condition'. She had said nothing about her children; nor did she send any message to the Princess Augusta.

Wraxall then applied himself to writing an obituary, which may have helped to inspire the bogus *Memoirs of an Unfortunate Queen*; that work appeared in the following year. Very much impoverished, he saw no prospect of George III's promise to refund him being fulfilled. Having carefully filed all his correspondence with de Bulow and von Seckendorf, he added to this collection the latter's missive of May 25th, which concluded, 'It has been necessary, after no more than forty-eight hours [for the lying-in-state] to deposit Her Majesty's body in the vault of the Dukes of Zell, until such time as we receive directions from the King of England regarding the funeral. [The Queen's removal] was accomplished reverently and decently by the Baron von Lichtenstein.' (This functionary was now resident in Hanover, and had been corresponding with George III as to his plans for Matilda; these letters are no longer extant.) Von Seckendorf did not add that Matilda had asked to be buried beside her brothers and sisters in Westminster Abbey.

Wraxall's thoughts ('I am wrapt', he told his father, 'in horror, sorrow and consternation') then turned to another aspect of the tragedy—had Matilda been poisoned by one of Queen Juliana's spies? He wrote to Mantel asking for his opinion, and was reassured. 'I remember', Wraxall continued, 'her parting words, her look ... I did not know, I did not see, that Death followed her step and shut the door for ever between her and me.'

It did not occur to the poor young man that at some point after that last meeting Matilda might have given up all hope of returning to Denmark, or that she might have hung over the body of the page with intent to catch the infection—which in any case, was rampant in the castle. Whether or not she had what is now called a death-wish, will never be known. Dying more peacefully than she had been able to live, she kept her secret, passionately mourned by all who had followed her fortunes. The castle became an abode of grief. The townsfolk shut their shops, draped themselves in black and wept for their 'beloved and good Queen'. George III sent no directions for the funeral, which took place in the little church of Celle on May 13th. He paid for it, however; the bill came to three thousand pounds.[3]

The mahogany coffin, placed on a hearse which was drawn by six horses, had an escort of soldiers, marching with arms reversed; others lined the route; behind them crowded the citizens of Celle. The household, led by Baroness d'Ompteda and Baron von Seckendorf, followed on foot. Pastor Lehzen received the cortège and preached the funeral sermon; then the coffin was lowered into the family vault. It lies between those of Duke George William and Sophia-Dorothea.

The news of Matilda's death reached Copenhagen on May 19th, and was at once broken to the King, who succumbed to an agony of grief. Although Queen Juliana was unable to conceal her joy, she gave orders that the Crown Prince and Princess Louise should be fitted out with mourning garments. On the following night she and her son accompanied Christian to the play; the night after that, a Court ball took place, at which Christian was forced to dance; as he had not done so for several years, his performance was a poor one. Next day, he held a reception, during which, according to Mr Woodford, 'his countenance and manner were such as startled the Foreign Ministers.' In that same week, he was helped — for he was nearing collapse — to launch two frigates, after which his attendants removed him to the country.[4]

Some months later, the principal citizens of Lüneburg and Celle got leave from George III to put up the monument to his sister in the French Garden. Professor Oeser of Leipzig was commissioned, and carried out the work in pale grey marble. There, where Matilda had walked and chatted and lingered over picnic meals in the little summer-house, it stands in the centre.

The sculptor confined his presentation of the Queen to a profile, thus emphasizing through the overwhelming figures of Mercy, Benevolence and Truth, the Lady Bountiful aspect of her character. He had never seen her in her days of beauty, and the medallion shows neither majesty, nor charm nor personality. But the Lüneburg-Celle Committee were well pleased with this tribute. Suitably backed by limes and sycamores, it was grand, elaborate and, quite obviously, expensive. There is no doubt that Matilda, a young woman of un-sophisticated taste, would have admired it as much as they did.

That those half-dozen sprawling, allegorical images almost obliterate her likeness is symbolic; for her tragedy was partially caused by an instinctive shrinking from the duties, as from the publicity, of her position. The gracious stateliness she eventually succeeded in assuming was neither endemic nor sustained. Loving and beloved, passionate and impetuous, stretched on the rack of marriage with a lunatic, it was inevitable that she should have failed in her profession. And for those of her rank the punishment of failure was merciless and perdurable.

NOTES

1. Wilkins, *A Queen of Tears*, vol. II, p. 280.
2. N. Wraxall, *Memoirs*, vol. IV, p. 206.
3. C. F. L. Wraxall, *Life and Times*, pp. 244–7; N. Wraxall, op. cit., vol. IV, pp. 206–7, vol. V, pp. 420–7; Wilkins, op. cit., vol. II, p. 297–9.
4. Wilkins, op. cit., vol. II, p. 306.

Conclusion

SOME TWELVE years after the death of Caroline Matilda, the Crown Prince of Denmark and Princess Louise came to Celle and called on Madame de Plessen, who told them about their mother's last days and described her death. They were then received by the pastor of the church of that city, who conducted them to the ducal vault. Both visits were private and soon concluded; but those few who saw them were struck by the contrasting looks of the brother and sister. He was short, slight and fair; she was rather tall; her aquiline profile, set off by a mass of light-brown hair, enhanced the liveliness and intelligence of her expression. She was now about to be married to the Duke of Augustenberg. She and the Crown Prince were visiting Celle for the first time, their former efforts to do so having been frustrated by Queen Juliana.

That lady's attempts to substitute her son for the rightful heir had resulted in the Crown Prince's majority being delayed for two years, and in her refusal to establish a regency; officially, Christian VII, now hopelessly insane, was still in power. But his son, although only sixteen, was not so easily put down; and the country was behind him. At a meeting which took place in April 1784, and was presided over by the King and Prince Frederick, he got up and read out a memorandum requesting Christian to dismiss Queen Juliana's Cabinet. He then laid the paper before his father and asked him to sign it, which he did. Prince Frederick, taken by surprise, tried in vain to intervene. Christian, pursued by both Princes, ran out of the room. In the struggle to get hold of him Prince Frederick was defeated by the heir, who clutched his father with one hand and forced away his rival with the other. He then retreated, with Christian, to the latter's apartments, where they remained, protected by the royal guard. A few hours later, the Crown Prince was proclaimed Regent by the group with which Mr Wraxall had been associated, and wildly cheered by the people.[1] That gentleman, who had received a thousand pounds from George III and had begun to write his memoirs, allowed himself a single comment on the less seemly aspect of his heroine's career. 'I pretend', he says, 'not to justify her conduct with respect to Struensee, either in a prudential or a moral point of view. For although I honour the Queen, I honour truth above all queens.'[2] Wraxall was further consoled by the relegation of Queen Juliana and her son. Dying in 1796, she was buried in the cathedral of Roskilde. For many years the local peasants visited her tomb in order to spit on it.

The Crown Prince did not succeed his father till 1808; he was then forty. One of his first actions was to destroy the palace of Hirschholm, of which only the gardens now remain. He had loved his mother; but he shrank from any reminder of her relations with Struensee; and in his mind Hirschholm was inextricably associated with that tragic idyll.

When the young Prince and his sister approached their mother's coffin—when the Latin inscription made it clear that she was lying before them—the Princess fainted. The Queen's body had so swollen after death that the coffin was enormous: almost as broad as it was long.[3] The brother and sister then left the church of Celle. They never visited it again.

NOTES

1. Wilkins, *A Queen of Tears*, vol. II, p. 310.
2. Op. cit., vol. IV, p. 208.
3. Nors, *Court of Christian VII*, p. 282; Wilkins, op. cit., vol. II, p. 313.

Bibliography

Andersen, Hans	*Fairy-Tales and Other Stories*, London, 1930.
Calendar of Home Office Papers	London, 1881.
Carter, N.	*Letters*, n.d.
Chapman, H. W.	*Privileged Persons*, London, 1966.
Chesterfield, Lord	*Letters*, London, 1969.
Curtis, E. R.	*Lady Sarah Lennox*, London, 1932.
Doddington, Bubb	*Diary*, Oxford, 1965.
Edwards, P.	*Frederick Louis, Prince of Wales*, London, 1929.
Falkensjold, Count	*Mémoires des Comtes de Struensee et Brandt*, Paris, 1789.
Hervey, Lord	*Memoirs*, London, 1931.
Hesse, Prince Charles of	*Mémoires*, Copenhagen, 1816.
Jesse, J. H.	*Memoirs of the Court of England*, London, 1843.
Jesse, J. H.	*Memoirs of the Reign of George III*, London, 1841.
Lecky, W.	*England in the Eighteenth Century*, London, 1890.
Letters of King George III	edited by Bonamy Dobrée, London, 1935.
Moore, J.	*View of Society and Manners in France, Switzerland and Germany*, London, 1781.
Münter, B.	*A Faithful Narrative of the Conversion and Death of Count Struensee ... to which is added the History of Count Enevold Brandt*, London, 1774.
Murray Keith, R.	*Memoirs*, London, 1849.
Nors, P.	*The Court of Christian VII*, London, 1928.
Northcote, R.	*Memoirs of Sir Joshua Reynolds*, London, 1790.

Plumb, J. F. — *England in the Eighteenth Century*, Harmondsworth, 1950.

Plumb, J. F. — *The First Four Georges*, London, 1956.

Procès de Caroline Mathilde — Paris, 1829.

Public Advertiser — London, 1766.

Reverdil, P. — *Mémoires de la Cour de Copenhagen*, Paris, 1858.

Walpole, Horace — *Letters*, London, 1905.

Walpole, Horace — *Memoirs and Portraits*, London, 1963.

Wilkins, W. H. — *A Queen of Tears*, London, 1904.

Wittich, C. — *Struensee*, n.d.

Wortley Montagu, Lady Mary — *Letters*, London, 1906.

Wraxall, C. F. L. — *Life and Times of Caroline Matilda*, London, 1864.

Wraxall, Nathaniel — *Memoirs*, London, 1884.

Index